THE
MONEY
MACHINE

THE
MONEY
MACHINE

HOW THE MUTUAL FUND INDUSTRY WORKS –
AND HOW TO MAKE IT WORK FOR YOU

DANIEL STOFFMAN

Macfarlane Walter & Ross
Toronto

Macfarlane Walter & Ross
An Affiliate of McClelland & Stewart Ltd.
37A Hazelton Avenue
Toronto, Canada M5R 2E3

Canadian Cataloguing in Publication Data

Stoffman, Daniel
The money machine: how the mutual fund industry works – and
how to make it work for you

Includes index.
ISBN 1-55199-052-0

1. Mutual funds – Canada. I. Title.

HG5154.5.S76 2000   332.63'27   C00-931930-1

Macfarlane Walter & Ross gratefully acknowledges support for
its publishing program from the Canada Council for the Arts,
the Ontario Arts Council, and the Government of Canada through
the Book Publishing Industry Development Program.

Printed and bound in Canada

This book is for Dr. Isaac Stoffman,
good father, wise investor.

CONTENTS

Mutual funds converted the savings of millions of Canadians from safe GICs and savings bonds to risky stocks. In the process, they propelled the greatest bull market of all time.

The founders of the mutual fund industry became multimillionaires by being in the right place at the right time – just when millions of boomers were looking for an easy way to make their money grow.

For most of the mutual fund industry, selling "products" is more important than managing money.

Two big fund companies have the same investment philosophy – and very different results.

PREFACE

In 1995, I wrote a book called *Boom Bust & Echo* in collaboration with David K. Foot, an economist with a special interest in the impact of population aging on Canada's economic and social life. Much of the book was about the adventures of the baby boom, the most powerful population cohort because it is the biggest, comprising a third of the entire population. In researching the book, one of the questions we asked was: How will the maturing of the boomers affect investing?

As soon as the question was asked the answer was obvious. The boomers were paying off their mortgages and their kids were growing up. Millions of them were entering their 40s and 50s, the stage of life when people begin to get serious about saving for the future. But these middle-aged boomers were busier than ever, in both their professional and social lives. Few of them had time to educate themselves about investment and to manage their own portfolios. This hadn't been a problem for members of previous generations, who had tended to save through interest-bearing investments such as Canada Savings Bonds and guaranteed investment certificates. These investments required little knowledge or supervision; they were simple to understand and absolutely safe, with no chance of loss of capital.

Things were different for the boomers. Interest rates had declined precipitously, so they were looking for other ways to invest, ways that could provide the growth they would need to support them in retirement. The stock markets were the obvious place to look because they offered growth. But they also offered risk. And stocks are complicated. How to choose which ones to buy, when to buy, and when to sell? And what if you were just starting out and didn't have enough money to assemble a diversified portfolio of stocks? Mutual funds were the answer. They offered professional management, growth, and diversification in one convenient package.

When the boomers as a group turn their attention to some product or service, the result is always an explosive rise in demand. It happened to baby food in the 1950s, rock music in the 1960s, rental accommodation in the 1970s, residential real estate in the 1980s. But by the end of the 1980s, most of the boomers were housed, and so the real estate boom had run its course. What was next? "Equity mutual funds," we wrote in *Boom Bust & Echo*, "are Canada's next investment boom." Those words have been proven accurate. As recently as the early 1980s, mutual funds had been a minor part of the Canadian financial services industry. By the end of the 1990s, they had become the investment vehicle of choice for the middle class.

For many Canadians, the switch to mutual funds has worked out well. As the bull market roared upward through much of the 1990s, funds were able to deliver high returns, just as they had promised. But the double-digit returns masked an important problem, namely that mutual funds are an expensive way to invest. It is not surprising that this would be the case: convenience is always expensive. But was there any good reason for Canadian funds to be twice as expensive as American ones? None was apparent, and critics of the industry seemed justified when they said that fund companies and fund sellers were exploiting the ignorance of the Canadian investor.

Ignorant many of them undoubtedly were. Surveys showed that a surprising number had invested in equity funds under the illusion that they were protected by deposit insurance; in fact, of course, it is the nature of investing in equities that you could lose every penny.

Most knew better than that, but even the relatively well-informed had little idea how much it was costing them to invest through mutual funds. And those who did know about management fees assumed they were negligible. If one is investing for the long term, they are anything but.

This book was written not to condemn mutual funds but rather to help investors understand them so that they can use them to their own advantage. Mutual funds, wisely selected, do exactly what they claim to: they offer the small or average investor professional management of a diversified portfolio that few individuals would be able to assemble on their own. But if Canadians are going to entrust their financial futures to the fund industry, they had better know something about how that industry operates.

I wanted to find out where the mutual fund industry came from, how it works, why it works the way it does, and where it is headed. And I wanted to show readers that there are other, more cost-efficient investment vehicles that deserve a place, alongside mutual funds, in their investment portfolios. Once Canadian investors know these things, they will be in a much stronger position to make the mutual fund industry work for them.

This book is based on dozens of interviews with people who work in the industry or observe it from outside. The business is full of remarkable people, and I am grateful to those who were so generous with their time and knowledge. Many of these sources are acknowledged in the text. Among those who aren't, Ellen Roseman and Heather Whyte were especially generous in providing background information and suggesting sources. I would also like to thank David Cork for sharing his insights and David Foot, whose analysis of Canadian demographics helped me understand what was happening in this fascinating industry.

In addition to interviews, I pored over a massive pile of printed matter, from official reports to mutual fund prospectuses to yellowing old newspaper clippings. I am indebted, especially for the early history of the industry, to the following books: *Fidelity's World*, by Diana Henriques; *Building Futures*, by Robert Jones; *The Reckoning*, by David Halberstam; and *The Money Game*, by George Goodman, who writes under the name Adam Smith. The section on Bernie Cornfeld relies heavily on *The Bernie Cornfeld Story*, by Bert Cantor, who was a Cornfeld associate.

Readers wishing to keep up with developments in the mutual fund industry would be well advised to consult their local daily newspaper. Coverage of personal finance is an area in which Canadian papers have dramatically improved their performance in recent years. I have found the following columnists especially informative: Ellen Roseman in the *Toronto Star*, Jonathan Chevreau in the *National Post*, Michael Kane in the *Vancouver Sun*, and Rob Carrick and Duff Young in the *Globe and Mail*.

Gary Ross, who is one-third of Macfarlane Walter & Ross, was a source of encouragement, from before the project began until it was finished, and the result owes much to his editorial wisdom, as it does to that of Barbara Czarnecki, who edited the final manuscript in meticulous fashion. As always, I am indebted to my wife and inhouse editor, Judy Stoffman, who is a constant source of support and inspiration.

Daniel Stoffman
May 2000

CHAPTER ONE

THE ULTIMATE BUSINESS

In 1965, when most Canadians had never heard of mutual funds and most of those who had heard of them thought they were some sort of scam, Russell Isaac, from Campbell River, British Columbia, travelled to New York City to track down a man named John Templeton.

Isaac had worked for Sears Roebuck in British Columbia, Saskatchewan, Oregon, and Washington state, rising to the position of store manager before switching to the investment business. Earlier that year he and his partner, Jack Cox, had established Great Pacific Management in Vancouver to sell mutual funds. In 1964, Isaac himself had not known what a mutual fund was, although he had studied finance at the University of British Columbia. When Cox explained the concept, Isaac decided mutual funds had a great future; thus the grandiose name Great Pacific, an amalgam of Canadian Pacific, then the biggest company in Canada, and Great West Life, the financial company with the biggest sales force.

Isaac went to New York and Montreal to meet some money managers. "While you're in New York," Cox suggested, "go and see this guy Templeton. He's in Rockefeller Center. He's got an interesting little fund that's going nowhere." The fund, Templeton Growth, had exceptional performance but only $4.8 million in assets, most of which belonged to friends and associates of Templeton. It had been incorporated in Canada to take advantage of American tax laws that encouraged Americans to invest in foreign-based mutual funds. The fund was not for sale in Canada and was available only to American investors. Templeton was unknown outside the financial industry. The Manhattan phone book listed the Rockefeller Center office, but the woman who answered Isaac's call said Templeton didn't work there.

"Where would I find Mr. Templeton?" Isaac asked.

"He's in Inglewood, New Jersey."

"Where's that?"

"Across the Hudson."

"Where's the Hudson?" Isaac almost said before catching himself. He didn't want her to think he was a hayseed.

"John always takes the bus," the woman told Isaac. He followed her directions and got on a bus.

Still chairman of Great Pacific at age 70, bursting with energy, Isaac enters a room like a bantamweight climbing into the ring. He remembers that sunny day in New York vividly because it was one of the most important in his life. The bus driver knew where Templeton's office was – an old three-storey house with a big lawn in front and a gold-lettered sign bearing the investment firm's name.

Isaac went in and a receptionist offered him some fudge. Templeton hadn't arrived yet, so Isaac asked where he could get lunch. He was directed to the cafeteria in a hospital across the street where Templeton himself lunched most days. By the time Isaac returned from lunch, Templeton had shown up; he ushered the visitor into a library with a gilt ceiling and walls lined with shelves of leather-bound books. They talked until 6 p.m. about mutual funds.

Templeton asked, "What would you do with Templeton Growth Fund?"

Isaac said, "We'd sell it. It's a great fund."

So the one-time logger and fishing guide from Vancouver Island became the first broker anywhere licensed to sell Templeton Growth. It was an even better catch than the 40-pound salmon he once reeled in. Thirty-five years later, Templeton, like Warren Buffett, is a legendary investor idolized around the world for his money-making skills. Templeton Growth has evolved from a Canadian stock fund for American investors to a global stock fund for Canadian investors. It contains $10.9 billion in assets, which makes it the largest mutual fund in Canada and proves that Isaac was right about mutual funds being a good business. They are such a good business that by the fall of 1999, Great Pacific was managing $2.9 billion for 100,000 clients and Russ Isaac's own net worth was $10 million. Investors who picked the right fund at the right time have done pretty well too; Isaac knows of one Templeton associate who invested $100,000 in the fund's early days, a stake that has grown to $400 million.

Some inventions continue to amaze us long after they've been invented: nuclear reactors, for example, or spaceships, or e-mail. Others seem so obvious we think the only reason we didn't invent them ourselves is that someone else just happened to invent them first. The ice cream cone is that kind of invention; so is the mutual fund. Yet if some genius hadn't come up with the notion of shaping a wafer into a triangle, joining two of its edges, and putting a scoop of ice cream on top, we might still be eating ice cream only out of bowls. Some other genius had to dream up the idea of pooling a lot of small amounts of money into a large amount and using that large amount to buy a diversified portfolio of investments, thereby giving the small investor the kind of access to stock markets previously reserved for the rich. The mutual fund was incredibly obvious – after someone thought of it.

The person credited with this stroke of genius is a Scot named Robert Fleming, who created the Scottish American Investment Trust in Dundee in 1873. The first Canadian mutual funds were launched in the early 1930s, but it wasn't until the 1980s, when the huge post-war baby boom generation started saving for retirement, that millions of Canadians began funnelling billions of dollars into funds. In 1982, Canadian mutual fund companies had $4 billion under administration. By 2000, mutual funds were propelling the greatest bull market of all time, and that $4 billion had multiplied 100 times, to $400 billion. The consulting firm Ernst & Young, assuming the bull will keep charging ahead with the fund industry firmly in the saddle, projects that by 2008 Canadian fund companies will be managing $1.5 trillion worth of Canadians' savings.

Steve Wynn, a Las Vegas hotel and casino developer, once offered this excellent advice: "If you want to make money in a casino, own one." Think of a mutual fund as a casino. Rule one at a casino is that the house always wins: players win or lose, depending on their luck, but the casino always takes its percentage. In the same way, whether investors win or lose, the fund company takes a piece of every dollar invested. That's why Richard Charlton, who sells funds out of Oakville, Ontario, and is a principal in a company that manages them, calls mutual funds "the ultimate business. We don't have any factories, there's no warehouses, no accounts receivable to try and collect. There's no labour fighting with management over who should get paid what. It's all about the mutual fund telling a story to a broker who can tell that story to his client. Then the mutual fund collects management fees."

That's as concise and as accurate a description of the mutual fund industry as you are likely to find. And what's the story that the mutual fund tells the broker, who tells it to the client? That mutual funds allow Canadians to share in the growth of the domestic and global economies, thereby ensuring that when retirement rolls around they will be able to continue living in the affluent style to which, as baby boomers, they have become accustomed. The best thing about funds, so the story goes, is that they give the average person access to the kind of professional money management that, in the days before Russ Isaac set out to find New Jersey, was available only to the rich. Funds, in short, are what Bernie Cornfeld, an early titan of the fund industry (before he wound up in a Swiss jail), called "people's capitalism."

That's the official line and it's true as far as it goes, which isn't far enough. When you scratch the surface to determine how the mutual fund industry works, you discover surprises. The first is that, while most people think of a mutual fund as an investment, the people who work in the industry don't. They think of it as a "product." When I started researching the subject, it took me a while to figure out what they were talking about, although I had owned mutual funds for 15 years. I couldn't quite get my head around the idea that a mutual fund is a consumer product, like a bottle of cola or a pair of shoes. And that a company that manages a mutual fund and selects the stocks and other investments that go into it is a "manufacturer" of the product. And that a person or company that sells mutual funds to consumers – investors – is a "retailer" of the product. Not that it's unreasonable for mutual fund people to think this way. Why else would they be in business if not to make money? And what better way to make money than by selling a product you can persuade the public it needs?

For the consumer, though, there are problems with the notion of mutual funds as products. We can try Coke, Pepsi, and the store brand and make an informed decision based on taste and price, both of which are transparent. Not so mutual funds. We are in no position to compare funds because the only data we have is past performance. And while Pepsi tastes the same this year as last, we don't know that a fund will perform the same this year as last. The fund manager's investment style may no longer be effective because of changes in the economic climate. The fund may have attracted so much money that the manager can't manage the way she used to. Or the manager might have been lured away to run someone else's mutual fund and been replaced by someone with a different taste in stocks. So the product we're getting might be a different product than the one we think we are getting. The manufacturer may have filled the Coke bottles with Pepsi.

Then there's the matter of price. The prices of Coke and Pepsi and the store brand are there to see on the supermarket shelf. Most mutual fund investors don't know how much they're paying to have their money managed, because the industry doesn't want them to know and has artfully hidden the price. That's one reason Canadians pay more than Americans for funds, and the reason fees charged to Canadian investors have been rising while those charged to Americans have been falling. The extravagant fees Canadians have been willing to pay to invest in mutual funds probably explain why Canada has more than twice as many funds, on a per capita basis, as the United States.

If you own units in a fund, you can find out how much your company is raking off the top by looking under "expense ratio" or "MER" (for management expense ratio) in the monthly mutual fund tables published in many Canadian newspapers. The MER, also called the management fee, comprises most of the costs of operating a fund, including payments to investment managers and salespersons. If a fund shows a one-year return of 8% and an MER of 2%, your money actually earned 10% but the fund company kept 2%. At first glance, the differences in MERs among funds seem minor: for example, if Russ Isaac had sold you Templeton Growth you would be paying an MER of 2% while a competing fund, Equitable Life Global Growth, was charging 3%, and another competing fund, Cambridge Growth, had an MER of 4.95%. These seemingly small differences turn out to be huge if you are doing what the industry says you should be doing – investing for the long haul. Assume three investors each plunked down $10,000 and kept it invested for 30 years. One had Templeton Growth, one had Equitable Life Global Growth, and the third had Cambridge Growth. Assume that each fund grew by 10% a year before MER and that the MERs remained constant during that time. At the end of 30 years, the Templeton investor would have $100,626, the Equitable Life investor would have $76,123, and the Cambridge investor would have $43,481. In this example, the Cambridge fund would have reported an annual return to the investor of 5.05% (10% minus the MER), little more than the 4.95% the fund managers kept.

Investors take risks, which means that some of them don't do very well. The manufacturers and retailers of the "products" don't take risks, they take a cut, which is why Russ Isaac drives a Jaguar and Richard Charlton drives a Bentley and John Templeton has forsaken New Jersey for Nassau. The investment industry loves mutual funds because they allow the people in the industry to take a chunk of whatever money you have in a fund every single year that you own it. That's why a broker would rather sell you a fund than a stock or a bond. He gets a commission when you buy or sell those other types of investments but in between he doesn't get anything. Mutual funds provide a constant stream of income to both the retailers and the manufacturers.

That's why the mutual fund industry is a money machine – highly efficient, remarkably resilient, and poorly understood.

Running a mutual fund is such a good way to make a pile of money that a lot of people start funds. There are twice as many mutual funds as stocks listed on the Toronto Stock Exchange. "There are 2,000 mutual funds and 1,800 of them are crap," says Joe Canavan, whose company, Synergy, operates mutual funds that Canavan classes among the 200 non-crappy ones. Actually, if you count every fund in all 33 categories devised by the Investment Funds Standards Committee, there were 3,219 as of May 2000. Most of the stock funds were indeed crappy, inasmuch as they weren't performing as well as their benchmark indexes, such as the Toronto Stock Exchange's 300 (TSE 300), which represents about 85% of the total value of all Canadian stocks, and the Standard and Poor's 500 (S&P 500), which represents about 75% of the value of all American stocks, as selected by an American financial information and research company.

Which brings up another problem with mutual funds that quickly becomes apparent when you probe beneath the surface. The major benefit of funds, or so we are told, is that they provide the small investor with access to the skills of professional money managers. But if professional money managers are so skilled, how come funds that dispense with the brains of managers and just buy all the stocks in, say, the TSE 300 index have been posting better returns than managed funds?

The view of portfolio managers towards those who doubt the value of active investment management is like the view of doctors towards those who doubt the value of medical science. Brokers and financial advisers don't like index funds either because they don't get paid much for selling them. But growing numbers of investors like them and are buying them. Should they? What happens if the stock market goes into a prolonged slump? In that case, wouldn't investors be better off in a managed fund that can sell stocks before their prices disintegrate rather than an index fund that has no option but to stay invested?

Of course we all know what's going to happen to the stock market. It is going to fluctuate, as an American billionaire named J. Pierpont Morgan once predicted. But will it fluctuate up more than down? A lot of knowledgeable people these days think not. They think share valuations are too high, especially those of high-tech and Internet companies that have never earned a dime, and they're fond of comparing the recent stock market euphoria to such historical events as the tulip mania that seized Holland in 1634, when people borrowed all the guilders they could get their hands on to buy one tulip bulb. The bulb market crashed, of course, but at least they could grow a tulip with their investment. Today's speculative stock market investors will have only worthless paper if the doom school is correct.

For those who prefer positive predictions, there are plenty of them as well. One of the most optimistic is that of James Glassman and Kevin Hassett, who in 1999 published a book called *Dow 36,000* to advance their belief that the Dow Jones Industrial Average (based on 30 American blue-chip stocks) will rise to 36,000 by 2005. The Dow was 13 times as high in 1999 as it was in the 1980s, having risen from 800 to more than 11,000. A level of 36,000 is not much more than three times 11,000, so maybe it's not as far-fetched as it sounds. Hassett and Glassman, both of whom work at the American Enterprise Institute, give every appearance of being sane. Hassett taught economics at Columbia University and was a senior economist for the Board of Governors of the Federal Reserve System, the U.S. version of the Bank of Canada. Why, in their opinion, is the market going up, and why will it go up a lot more? Because traditional methods of appraisal have not captured the true value of stocks, they argue, and only now are investors finally figuring out what stocks are really worth.

If the doomsayers are right, it is dangerous to have your money in stocks. If the cheerleaders are right, it's dangerous not to. And there are dozens of permutations of both scenarios. The one that makes the most sense to me is that the peculiar demographics of North America, in particular the predominance of the post-war baby boom, is driving economic growth and the advance of stock markets. An eloquent proponent of this view is Martin Braun, president of a

Toronto investment counselling firm, who points out that the start of the new millennium finds the huge boomer generation in its most productive years during a period of low labour force growth, rapid technological advance, and low inflation. Because of the impact of the boom and of new technology, the economy has been growing at three times the rate of the labour force. That is a recipe for higher productivity and a good reason for stocks to go up. As for the lofty valuations that worry the doomsayers, Braun argues, they apply only to about 10% of stocks.

While we can bank on J.P. Morgan's prediction, we can't be certain of much else where the stock market is concerned. We do know that we're living through an era of phenomenal change and that the explosive growth of mutual funds both reflects and is a big part of that change. Millions of people depend on mutual funds invested in stocks to finance their retirements. They have every reason to be nervous because stocks are inherently risky, meaning that they can go down in value. This is new. Previous generations, as they approached retirement, had their savings in Canada Savings Bonds and term deposits. They knew exactly what they were going to earn from those investments and they knew that, barring economic calamity, they weren't going to lose a penny of the principal.

As if the uncertainty of relying on stocks weren't enough to rattle the ordinary investor, the fund industry grows more complex by the day. There are health funds and leisure funds and entertainment funds. There are "ethical funds," which suggests there must be unethical ones as well. There is a "bull-bear" fund and a "long-short" fund. There are dividend funds that don't earn dividends, and global equity funds, which are not the same as international equity funds. The best-selling funds in 1999 were "RRSP-eligible clone funds." These are funds that allow the investor to circumvent the Canadian government's rule that only 25% of a Registered Retirement Savings Plan (RRSP) can be invested outside Canada. Clone funds are considered Canadian content because they invest mainly in Canadian treasury bills (short-term government debt). A small portion of the money in the fund is used to buy forward contracts created by people called "financial engineers." These contracts are "derivatives" because their value is *derived* from the actual foreign equity fund of which they are a clone. Get it? If you do, you may be one up on the broker who sold you the clone fund.

It would be the rare investor who is not confused by all this. It does seem that mutual funds have certain minor flaws, such as underperforming the stock market and being overpriced. Yet leaving our money in cash earning low interest seems like a strategy for an impoverished retirement. We need to have at least part of our wealth in stocks, but even if we know enough to pick them ourselves, most of us can't afford to buy more than a few. We need diversification to cushion the risk of exposure to stocks. How do we get diversification? One way, the most popular way, is to buy mutual funds.

There are other ways as well. You can buy a whole bunch of individual stocks. Dale Domian, a finance professor at the University of Saskatchewan, owns 120 different Canadian stocks, three times as many as some mutual funds own. Or you can buy index participation units, such as i60s and Spiders and WEBS, which are like index funds but are listed on stock exchanges with all the other stocks and have lower fees than index funds. The i60s are favoured by those who think mutual funds are a bad way to invest, including Mark Heinzl, who espouses his views in a 1999 book unambiguously titled *Stop Buying Mutual Funds*.

A few blocks north of Russ Isaac's office in downtown Vancouver is the local branch of Merrill Lynch, where a financial adviser named John Caspar works. I thought I'd ask Caspar if people should stop buying mutual funds, although I knew his answer, given that Caspar sells mutual funds. But he is no ordinary fund and stock pusher. Caspar writes one of the smartest financial advice columns in the country in a weekly paper called *Business in Vancouver*. He likes to give contrarian advice with references to economic history. He often points out that the best investment anyone can make is to pay off a mortgage, advice that is not going to make a stockbroker any money. Some brokers suggest that, on the contrary, you should increase your mortgage and use the money to buy mutual funds.

Caspar is a 40-year-old with a wry sense of humour and strong opinions, based on erudition and experience, about investment matters. I asked him if millions of Canadians who have invested hundreds of billions of dollars in mutual funds should be nervous. He said yes, they should, because a fisherman neighbour of one of his colleagues has hung up his net and become a day trader. History tells us this is a bad sign. In 1987, Caspar had a ground-floor office in North Vancouver overlooking a main street. "We had floor-to-ceiling windows and I could see what was happening on the street, which was on a mail route and a major bus route. I remember one day when a bus and a Canada Post truck were double-parked outside our office. The bus driver and the postal truck driver were inside, checking on their stock portfolios, thinking that any minute they'd be able to retire. I thought, 'When bus drivers are planning on giving up driving the bus to be economically independent because of their fabulous picks on the stock market, it must be time to sell.'"

Two weeks later the markets crashed.

Not that Caspar's got anything against fishermen. It's just that his colleague's neighbour is not an investment professional, he's part of the crowd, and the crowd, as a famous book called *Extraordinary Popular Delusions and the Madness of Crowds* points out, is inherently irrational. When the crowd thinks the price of tulip bulbs has nowhere to go but up, you can be sure the price of tulip bulbs will go down. Caspar believes in the "history will repeat itself" school of thought as opposed to the "new paradigm" school of thought, which says technology and globalization have brought fundamental changes to the world, that the future will not look like the present, and that skepticism is misplaced if it undervalues companies that have no earnings but spectacular futures.

Paradigm shmaradigm, says Caspar. In the 1920s, the market soared, partly on the strength of a communications medium that everyone was excited about because all they had to do was buy a new piece of technology and, presto, they had access to a whole new world of information and entertainment, all for free. Sounds like a description of the Internet, but Caspar is talking about radio. The radio was, and still is, an excellent invention, and a lot of people made a lot of money buying radio stocks during the 1920s. A lot of them lost it all in 1929 when the stock market collapsed. Caspar thinks globalization and the advance of technology are hugely important. But he doesn't see why they should cause us to abandon normal standards for evaluating the worth of businesses.

And there is certainly no new paradigm to be found in the behaviour of investors. Amateur investors know that an important principle of investing is to buy low and sell high. But as any broker will tell you, few of them have the nerve to put that principle into practice. "At the grocery store, we embrace the concept that a lower price for a commodity is a good thing," says Caspar. "We want to buy tuna when it goes down in price, not when it goes up. In the stock market people would prefer to pay a higher price. Suppose I talk to you about a stock that I think we should add to your portfolio, and it's $80. You look at the research, you call me back next week and say, 'Let's buy it.' And I say, 'That's great because it's gone down to $70.' You hesitate. You would be more comfortable if it had gone up to $85."

You bet I would, for the same reason I'd rather put my money on a horse that had improved in its last outing instead of one whose performance had deteriorated. But investment professionals say that is bad thinking. They want you to view investing not as gambling but as owning a piece of a business. Amateurs like me need help from professionals who not only know that it's better to pay $70 than $85 for a piece of a good business but are actually capable of doing it. Having an expert manage your money minimizes the risk that bad things will happen to your money. In fact, the management of risk lies at the heart of what mutual funds are all about.

"How familiar are you with the work of Carl Friedrich Gauss, who was writing on probability theory around the middle of the 19th century?" Caspar asks.

"Not too familiar."

"I mention it only to show that there is nothing new about this. Probability and risk are one and the same thing, and probability theorists knew hundreds of years ago that people are more loss-averse than they are risk-seeking. The extent to which you are interested in the utility of an additional gain is inversely proportional to how much you have already. If I have this big nest egg, increasing it by a little bit is not really as meaningful to me as losing some of it. So risk is a crucial issue when you're managing money.

"Mutual funds handily address two of the biggest issues, egg risk and basket risk – that is, specific risk and market risk. Specific risk is the risk that I have very few eggs. If all I have is General Motors, Coke, and Microsoft, say, I have a very high level of specific risk because if one of those eggs drops and breaks I'm really hurting. You want to have a bunch of eggs, not just one. And you want multiple baskets.

"Specific risk is easy to manage because we know that once we have 20 stocks in a portfolio we have mitigated a lot of risk, and once we have about 40 we are not getting any additional utility by diversifying any further. That's egg risk.

"The second risk is basket risk, the risk that no matter how well diversified I am in that basket, if I drop the basket all the eggs are going to break and that's the end of the story. Resources fall in value, the Canadian market falls out of bed, all my money is in France because I think France is hot and France does badly. So now we need to make sure that we have different asset classes. Herein lies the problem for the average investor. For me to have 100 shares of Merrill Lynch is going to cost me $15,000. So for me to be well diversified, just in the U.S. equity basket, I need a lot of money. And to have multiple baskets, I have to have a great deal of money.

"So mutual funds handily answer the question 'How can I manage specific risk – that is, have multiple eggs – and how can I have multiple baskets?' I can select one mutual fund that gives me a great level of diversification and virtually no specific risk. And I can put together a portfolio with different baskets in it that gives me diversification from any one market. Market risk can't be diversified away, it can only be managed through diversification. I can select the different asset classes in the proportion that I'd like to build a portfolio that has a risk profile suitable for me. Mutual funds do a really good job of that."

I left Caspar thinking that *Stop Buying Mutual Funds* was not good advice unless you have enough money to buy several baskets, each holding a couple of dozen eggs. That way you get risk protection without paying those little management fees that, when you do the math, turn out to be big. But if you're able to buy that many individual stocks, you're rich, or close to it, and rich people have never needed mutual funds.

I decided to go and see Vancouver's most famous mutual fund manager, Wayne Deans. For a portfolio manager, being named Fund Manager of the Year is comparable to an athlete getting on the cover of *Sports Illustrated*. It's an honour but it's also a jinx. A baseball player who gets on the cover of *Sports Illustrated* because he's leading the league in home runs will probably be hitting a lot of pop flies shortly afterwards.

That's sort of what happened to Deans, a freelance fund manager as opposed to one who is an employee of a fund company. The fund that made him famous was the Marathon Equity Fund, which had a return of 49.9% in 1996. Every mutual fund investor dreams of earning 50% on her money so she can tell her friends and acquaintances whose money earned 2% in the bank what a smart investor she is. So many people wanted to own Marathon Equity that more money was flowing in than Deans could handle, and the fund had to be closed to new investors.

The Fund Manager of the Year is selected by a panel of experts, and the award is given out each year at a gala dinner organized by Vorg Inc., a Toronto speakers' bureau specializing in business and finance. Deans got the award for 1996; his exploits were celebrated in magazine articles, and he found himself in great demand as a public speaker. In 1997, Marathon Equity returned −9.4%. In 1998 it returned −33.3% and Deans was not named Fund Manager of the Year. The weird thing is that he wasn't doing anything different. He's a specialist in buying small, undervalued companies, and that style of investing stopped working in 1997. Telling a guy like Deans he should have changed his style because it wasn't working would be like telling the slugger who went into a slump that he should stop swinging and bunt instead.

Deans, an ex-Montrealer, dresses with flair, favouring expensive striped shirts and suspenders. He drives sports cars and goes skiing in Colorado with race-car drivers. And he's blessed with a sense of humour. These attributes give him more charisma than the typical fund manager. Combine them with that 50% return and it's not surprising he became a celebrity. It was the last thing he wanted. Here's how it happened: "You would go and give a presentation and some reporter would write some crazy stuff about you as if you were some kind of wizard." And here's how it stopped: "We got lousy returns because the market's gone down and small caps [stocks of smaller companies] have gone down the most, so now we're real dummies. But we weren't that smart before and we're not that stupid now."

Investors kept pouring money into Deans's funds because they knew a fund managed by Deans was sure to keep going up, even though Deans himself told them it wouldn't. He went out and made speeches to investors in the funds he was managing and took flak because the fund had too much cash in it and not enough stocks. This is odd, since one of the justifications for hiring a pro like Deans to manage your money is that he won't invest it unwisely, which might mean he keeps it in cash until he can find stocks worth buying. But that conflicts with the prevalent view, among both investors and people in the industry, that an equity fund "product" should have only equities in it. If you want someone to manage cash or bonds for you, buy a balanced fund or a bond fund or a money market fund, not an equity fund.

Deans was managing equity funds specializing in small-cap stocks, and there weren't any small-cap stocks that he wanted to buy. Investors would ask, "How much cash have you got?"

"Forty per cent," Deans would say.

"Well, what are you doing raising cash?"

"I'm not raising cash. You're putting cash into my mutual fund."

"What are you doing with it?"

"Nothing. I can't find anything to buy because the prices of the companies all went up too high. And then you gave me the money after the prices went up. Why didn't you give me the money last year when we had a lousy performance so I could buy my companies at a cheap price?"

The investors would go home unhappy and Deans would get up at 6 the next morning and drive across the Lions Gate Bridge to sit in his office all day talking on the phone and watching the stock prices and not buying because the prices were too high. Then prices started going down and Deans thought, "Great, I'm going to have an opportunity to buy these businesses at a better price a year from now."

No such luck. "What does the public do? They redeem all the cash because the performance was lousy. And they take the cash and give it to AIC [another mutual fund company], which had a hot year but which is going to go into the tank this year because it owns all those bank stocks." (He said this about six months before the AIC Advantage funds went into the tank in 1999 because they had too many bank stocks.)

This is the same problem identified by Caspar: investors, fickle as they are, wait for the price of a stock or fund to go up and then they buy it. When it goes down they sell it. "They get it backwards. They see AIC had a 40% return and they want some of that 40% return. Well, this is not a savings plan. Where did that 40% return come from? The prices of the stocks in that portfolio on average went up 40% last year. So in effect they were buying businesses that were overpriced. And of course the market takes the prices down to normal, and people point their finger at the money manager and say, 'He fucked up this year.' Well, he didn't do anything. The rate of return looks normal now."

This raises an important issue. Will mutual fund investors who think they deserve 40% rates of return learn to be satisfied with normal returns, normal being closer to 10%? Deans worries that they won't be. Even those who are smart enough to look at a decline as a buying opportunity are often wrong, he says, because a hot fund may still be overpriced even if its price has slipped a bit. "The public has this stupid view that you can't lose money on stocks. They have the idea that you buy on 'dips.' Where did that ever come from, that you buy on dips? It's just plain dumb. If the bloody thing is overpriced, why buy it on a dip? It is still overpriced, just a little less overpriced. They are just going to blow their brains out. But mutual fund marketers go out there and sell all this crap to build assets."

Which raises another important issue, one that only a freelance portfolio manager would care to mention. A manager who's an employee of a fund company would not be likely to point out that the goals of fund companies and the interests of investors may not always be in sync. Funds are products, and manufacturers and retailers are never going to discourage you from buying their products. How many Coke ads say you'd be better off drinking water? Except for rare cases when a fund is closed to new money, the fund company is not going to advise against buying into a fund just because the fund manager thinks there are no stocks worth buying. Fund companies live off their management fees, which are a percentage of the total amount of money in the fund. The more money investors put into the fund, the bigger the management fee. Fund companies didn't appreciate it when Deans told investors they shouldn't be putting money into the funds he was managing, which may be why he isn't managing as many funds these days.

Not that Deans is against mutual funds. On the contrary, he's all in favour as long as investors have realistic expectations. In 1996, Deans would give presentations in which he would ask, "How many people think 20% returns on common stocks are normal?"

Out of 400 people, 399 would put their hands up.

Then he would say, "You are going to be very disappointed. There may be a new paradigm and there may be an age wave. Those things influence our behaviour and the things we buy, but they don't take away certain realities that never change. No matter how much you shift the paradigm or change the demographics, we are buying businesses and you are living off the cash flow."

Eventually, the market manages to figure out what the businesses that are trading on it are actually worth, but sometimes it takes years for that to happen. Deans says, "When I talk to people about stocks I always talk about at least 10-year periods, and if they are realistic they should think in terms of 10% to 12% returns." And he would argue that his small-cap portfolios will probably do better than that if your stomach is strong enough to hold them for 10 years. During that time there will be some years when you gain 50% and others when you lose a big chunk of that, and at the end of the 10 years you will have made 15% per year, which is more than you would have made if you had kept the money in a sock or a bank or a money market fund.

What happened to Deans in 1997 has also happened to other celebrity managers, most notably Frank Mersch of Altamira. These managers were heroes when their funds excelled and bums when their funds faltered. Yet performance wasn't always the be-all and end-all of mutual funds. There was a time when the prime virtue of a fund manager was not performance but prudence. If you were a mutual fund investor 40 years ago, and not many were, you had decided to entrust some of your money to a solid fund company in the expectation that, through diversification and professional management, you would share in the growth of the economy. You didn't invest in a mutual fund for the short term, so the fund's short-term performance wasn't of great interest to you. Even if you had wanted to check the fund's performance from one day to the next, you couldn't because results weren't published daily. You certainly didn't think of switching your money to the latest hot fund because there was no latest hot fund, just as there were no celebrity managers. As the 1960s progressed, all that began to change.

CHAPTER TWO

THE INVENTION OF AN INDUSTRY

One spring day in 1961, Ron Meade, a newly minted graduate of McGill University, was walking down St. James Street in Montreal looking for a job. St. James was the financial hub of Montreal, lined with the offices of banks and brokerages, and Meade assumed one of them would have a job for him, though he had no experience in banking or finance and freely admitted he knew little about either.

Meade's experience was that things usually worked out in his favour, and he had no reason to believe his stroll down St. James wouldn't result in a job. The people in the employment offices on St. James probably wondered why he wasn't in Ottawa, applying to work for External Affairs, or perhaps looking for a teaching position at a ritzy private school. Either would have fit his qualifications better, since he was the son of a British diplomat, spoke four languages, and had just acquired an arts degree. Meade had been born in Switzerland; grown up in Peru and Argentina, speaking mostly Spanish; attended a private school in England; and summered on his French grandmother's Normandy estate. Then he went to Heidelberg University (because his father was stationed near there) before deciding to complete his university education in North America. He chose

Princeton but his father chose McGill because it was cheaper, which is how Meade wound up in Montreal.

Meade is related to André Gide on his mother's side and Ford Madox Ford on his father's. These were big names in the literature departments at McGill but they carried no weight on St. James Street. Still, something about Meade obviously intrigued the employment officers: he got three job offers that day. One was from a company called Greenshields, in its underwriting department. Meade had never heard of underwriting and for a moment he thought they were talking about undertaking, definitely not something he wanted to do. He bluffed his way through the interview, figured out the job had to do with raising money for large companies, and decided it would be a good way to learn about the investment business.

He was right. The job was like a post-graduate degree in business. Before the decade was out, he and two partners, Eric Baker and Christopher Winn, had set up a money management company called Altamira. It would be nice to report that Meade named the company after the Altamira Caves in northern Spain, site of one of the most important discoveries of paleolithic art, but it was named after a watering hole in Sausalito, California, watering holes being more to Meade's taste than cave paintings. By the 1980s, he was in Toronto and Altamira was growing and hiring such people as a talented equity manager named Frank Mersch. But there was a problem. Altamira was managing pension funds for large companies and most of the money was invested in fixed-income securities such as bonds, so there wasn't much in the way of equities for Mersch to manage.

A solution soon offered itself in the form of the Hume Funds, which Ron Hume, of the Hume Group Ltd., was eager to unload. Hume had built a successful company selling home-study investment courses and publishing a financial newsletter called the *Money Letter*, which featured advice from the likes of Morton Shulman and Andy Sarlos. On the theory that such brilliant advice should be put into practice, the Hume Funds, managed by Shulman, Sarlos, and the other advisers, were launched in 1985. They turned out to be some of the worst funds in the country, and before long Hume wanted out. In 1988 the Hume Funds became Altamira funds. Altamira went on to become one of the biggest and best-known mutual fund companies in Canada, and Meade and many others associated with the company in those early days became multimillionaires.

A similar tale of big things from small beginnings, though with a less cosmopolitan flavour, could be told about Warren Goldring, Jim O'Donnell, Arthur Labatt, or Bob Hager, all of whom were pioneers of the modern mutual fund industry in Canada. Most of them started out in the 1950s or 1960s managing pension funds or the holdings of wealthy individuals and then gravitated towards mutual funds for the public. They struggled at the beginning and through much of the 1970s, a bad decade for stocks; but by the 1980s billions of dollars were streaming into their funds, throwing off millions of dollars in management fees. The pioneers found themselves richer than they ever expected to be.

They succeeded in part because they were smart and capable and had the nerve to take a chance on an investment vehicle that, for most Canadians, was an untested novelty. But they succeeded mainly because they were in the right place at the right time. When Meade graduated from McGill, the Canadian economy was in the midst of a period of sustained and powerful expansion. As a by-product of that expansion, vast wealth was accumulating, much of it in the pension funds of companies and unions. These expanding pools of cash caught the attention of the entrepreneurs who would go on to build the mutual fund industry well before any of them had figured out that there would be such an industry.

Demographics hugely favoured Meade and the other mutual fund pioneers. While they were launching their careers, the Canadian baby boom was at its peak, pumping out newborns at a rate of 475,000 per year, 100,000 more than today's much larger Canadian population is producing. Canada was one of the youngest countries in the world, and it had a shortage of well-educated workers to perform such tasks as managing money. The people best placed to exploit these favourable circumstances were those who, like Meade, were born in the 1930s. Too young to fight during World War II, they were just the right age to participate in the booming post-war economy. Whether they started car dealerships or real estate companies, the hordes of boomers who streamed into the marketplace during the 1970s and 1980s fuelled explosive demand for the goods and services the 1930s generation had to offer. And when the boomers, in their 40s and 50s, began saving for their retirement, they needed professional money management and were drawn, like birds to a feeder, to the industry created by the founders of such companies as Altamira, Mackenzie, and AGF. In retrospect, it was predictable that Canadian mutual fund companies would enjoy great success in the 1980s and 1990s, but in the 1960s none of the founders could have forecast the extent of that success, least of all Ron Meade. He was just looking for a job.

The groundwork for the mutual fund industry had been laid between the world wars. Until then, the only fund-like vehicles were the investment trusts in Britain and the United States patterned after the Scottish American Investment Trust created by Robert Fleming in Dundee in 1873. These were like the mutual funds of today in that managers pooled money from a lot of people to buy stocks and other investments. But they were unlike today's funds in an important way. The shares of the trust were traded just like the shares of any other company and, because of the capriciousness of the market, their value on a given day didn't necessarily reflect the actual value of the trust's investment portfolio. So while ownership of shares in a trust did provide the small investor with a diversified portfolio, he couldn't count on being able to sell that portfolio for what it was really worth when he needed to cash in.

Edward Leffler, son of a Milwaukee railroad worker, who became a stockbroker in Boston, thought the small investor deserved better – a fund that would redeem its shares on demand at a price deter-mined by the value of its portfolio. Such a fund would issue new shares whenever anyone wanted them, and thus be "open-end" in contrast to the old-style "closed-end" investment trust, which required the investor to buy existing shares on the market. And so, in March 1924, Leffler and some associates launched the first modern mutual fund, Massachusetts Investors Trust. It had a portfolio of 46 stocks including 5 shares of General Electric, 10 shares of the Nash Motor

Co., and 10 shares of Naumkeag Steam Cotton Co. This fund survived the crash of 1929 and is still going strong. By 1999 it had US$12 billion in assets and had increased its stake in General Electric from 5 shares to 1.9 million.

Three open-end mutual funds opened for business in Canada in the 1930s and for almost two decades had the field to themselves. Two of the original funds – Corporate Investors Ltd., launched in 1931, and Commonwealth Investment Corporation, started in 1933 – were balanced funds holding bonds and other debt instruments as well as stocks. The third, the Canadian Investment Fund, was Canada's first equity fund. Opened in Montreal in 1932 by Calvin Bullock Ltd., a New York investment firm, it is still in business as the Spectrum United Canadian Investment Fund. Alan Chippendale, the young American broker sent to Montreal to manage it, established a conservative investment style emphasizing blue-chip companies. The same style was favoured by Investors Syndicate Inc. of Winnipeg, which established Canada's fourth mutual fund in 1948. By 1959, Canada had 30 mutual funds with a total of $557 million in assets.

Students of the psychology of investing long ago concluded that investors are motivated by two primal emotions, fear and greed. Until they discovered mutual funds, most people were excluded from the stock market by fear. They knew that stocks could deliver better returns than the bank, but they also knew they would have to pay for those returns by taking on risk – they might lose their money. The problem for a non-wealthy person was that his savings were small and he couldn't afford to put them at risk. This was why, except for the speculative fever of the 1920s, share ownership had been mostly the preserve of a sophisticated and moneyed minority. For them, investing was a conservative activity, something you did not to become wealthy but to stay wealthy. Such people were able to afford a diversified portfolio of blue-chip stocks. Often they employed professional investment counsellors to supervise their holdings. They took risks but the risks were mitigated. Mutual funds offered the same mitigation of risk to the masses.

Perhaps the single most important reason why mutual funds, which made no great impact for several decades, are now so wildly popular is that they allow the risk-averse small investor to overcome fear sufficiently to indulge in a bit of greed. It happened gradually. Investors Syndicate – now Investors Group, Canada's largest mutual fund company – had a large sales force that introduced thousands of middle-income Canadians to mutual funds over their kitchen tables. Articles appeared in newspapers and magazines about how some people were getting rich, even doubling their money in a year or less, by buying shares of mutual funds.

In the early 1960s, the industry was staid by today's standards. It didn't know about marketing. Mutual funds had not yet become products, fund companies had not yet become brands, and fund managers were as unlikely to become celebrities as bank officials. Although he remained at the helm of the Canadian Investment Fund from 1932 until 1968, Alan Chippendale was unknown except to his family, friends, employers, and colleagues. If the industry was going to take off, it needed some pizzazz, some excitement. Two Americans delivered those things in ways that would permanently change the mutual fund business, indeed the entire investment industry.

It's no accident that both Gerald Tsai and Bernie Cornfeld were outsiders with no allegiance to the tradition-bound WASP estab- lishment that dominated Wall Street (and Bay Street as well). Tsai, a native of Shanghai who became known on Wall Street in those less sensitive days as "the Chinaman," created a new style of port- folio management. The son of a Ford Motor Company manager in pre-Communist China, Tsai was a brilliant student who got a job in 1951 as a securities analyst for a Wall Street brokerage house. A year later, he joined Fidelity, today a global mutual fund super- power, then a fledgling outfit with a staff of about 20 people. For six years, he worked as an analyst for Ed Johnson, who owned the company and was also its best portfolio manager. Johnson and Tsai were among the first to understand that the changing economy called for a new investment style.

The old style was to buy large, conservatively managed compa- nies – utilities, steelmakers, railroads, the telephone monopoly – and hold on to them. In his years as an analyst, Tsai became convinced that this strategy's best days were over. Stocks of the big companies with old technologies were not growing as fast as the stocks of small companies with new technologies, companies like Xerox, Polaroid, and IBM. Tsai wanted to put this thesis to the test, and he persuaded Johnson to let him manage a new fund, Fidelity Capital, whose mandate would be to outperform competing mutual funds by trading aggressively in the hottest stocks he could find.

Incredible as it may seem today, when performance is the standard by which all mutual funds are judged, this was a new approach. Previously, preserving the unitholder's capital while attaining steady but modest profits without undue risk was the goal of the fund manager. Tsai and Jack Dreyfus, a New York fund operator, were the first to aim openly and unabashedly for spectacular gains. Tsai was different in other ways as well. He believed in market timing (trying to predict the ups and downs of share prices) rather than conventional long-term investing; in the course of executing this strategy, he would buy or dump huge blocks of shares all at once, thereby influencing the price of the shares by his own trades, something most fund managers had always tried to avoid, and still do.

Fidelity Capital started slowly in 1958, weathered a rocky period in the stock market, and by 1964 had grown to $223 million. In 1965, a laudatory *Business Week* profile, with a photo of Tsai wielding a slide rule in front of a wall of stock charts, launched him as the first mutual fund superstar. Shortly afterwards, Tsai left Fidelity, and in 1966 he formed his own fund, the Manhattan Fund, hoping to attract about $25 million from investors. He had underestimated the power of celebrity. The public poured $274 million into the Manhattan Fund on its first day of operation, and Tsai was managing more than $400 million by the end of the fund's first year.

The example of Tsai and Dreyfus inspired many others, and the numbers of aggressively managed "growth funds" multiplied. It also spread to Canada, where the *Financial Post* had to establish a new category, "Speculative Funds," in its mutual fund survey in order to list such performance or "go-go" funds as AGF Special and United Venture. It had taken only half a decade for Mr. and Mrs. Average Investor to embrace the cult of performance.

If investors were now ready to be greedy, an American in Paris named Bernie Cornfeld was ready to help them. Cornfeld, the most flamboyant character the mutual fund industry has ever produced, is all but forgotten today, which suits the industry just fine. But in his heyday he achieved what would have seemed all but impossible before he came along: he made mutual funds glamorous. He did this by making an awesome amount of money very quickly and spending it with wild abandon. A Jewish former cab driver and social worker from Brooklyn, he brought high-pressure sales and marketing methods as well as massive publicity, much of it unwelcome, to mutual funds.

Starting from nothing in the late 1950s, Cornfeld founded Investors Overseas Services (IOS) in Paris to sell mutual funds to U.S. military personnel and other expatriate Americans. By 1970, he had $100 million (a huge personal fortune now, a fabulous one then) and headed a company with one million customers and 20,000 employees. He travelled the globe in a couple of private jets. After the company's headquarters were moved to Switzerland, Cornfeld's main residence was a lakeside townhouse in Geneva that Napoleon had built for Josephine. Other nights, he slept in his permanent five-room suite at New York's Carlyle Hotel, or in one of the homes he kept in Europe's major capitals, or in his 40-room, 12th-century castle in France, which was protected by a moat with an operating drawbridge. At the castle, he was able to indulge his passion of riding on one of his eight horses or pampering his pack of Great Danes. He had a fleet of Rolls-Royces, Cadillacs, and sports cars. He owned half of Guy Laroche, a Parisian fashion house, ordered 20 new suits a year, and employed a full-time party organizer. He enjoyed the company of dozens of beautiful women, including Audrey Hepburn and Julie Christie.

Cornfeld led the sort of bachelor lifestyle idealized by Hugh Hefner's *Playboy* magazine. Bert Cantor, an associate who wrote a book called *The Bernie Cornfeld Story*, describes a typical evening in the Geneva house in 1969. Arriving for dinner at 8:30, he found that Cornfeld wasn't home yet but several others were waiting for him – a Geneva tax lawyer, someone from *Time* wanting to do a deal, a young American woman wanting to sell him an interest in a music group, two former *Playboy* bunnies, a French actress, a French model, Cornfeld's personal photographer, and his personal assistant. Everybody sat in the living room in silence waiting for Cornfeld, who still hadn't shown up by 9:30. "An ocelot came in and peed in a silver bowl full of salted almonds on the coffee table," recounts Cantor. "No one noticed. The ocelot clawed playfully at a bowl of long-stemmed roses on an end table and knocked them over, denting the silver vase and spilling water on the floor." Finally, Cornfeld appeared and they all sat down to a late dinner in a room with a marble floor decorated with marble busts of Greek gods and French kings. Dinner, prepared by Cornfeld's Italian chef, was southern-fried chicken with chocolate sundaes for dessert. The guests drank an expensive Bordeaux, Cornfeld's house wine, while Cornfeld, a teetotaller, indulged in his favourite beverage: "Coca-Cola in the family-sized bottle, served to him by one of his footmen with all the aplomb of a wine waiter in a top restaurant decanting a fine vintage."

How could he afford all this? Like Steve Wynn, he understood that it is better to own a casino than to be a patron. And he understood that the salesmen – the dealers and croupiers in the mutual fund casino – make the business tick. In the early 1950s, Cornfeld had taken a part-time job selling mutual funds in New York to supplement what he was making as a social worker. The company he worked for, Investors Planning Corporation, specialized in contractual plans, instalment buying schemes that were frowned on by the U.S. regulators and illegal in some states because they were considered unfair to customers. But they were very profitable to the seller, and after he moved to Paris in 1955, Cornfeld persuaded Jack Dreyfus to let him sell the Dreyfus Fund in Europe on a 10-year instalment plan with a high commission payable at the time of purchase. "If your management is aggressive, you need aggressive salesmen," Cornfeld explained at the time. "The way to get aggressive salesmen is to show them how they can make a lot of money."

When he was starting out, Cornfeld had to knock on prospects' doors himself. When recruiting Cantor to IOS, he described with pride how he persuaded a woman to sign a contract to contribute $50 a month for 10 years to buy mutual funds from IOS. At first the woman refused, not because she couldn't afford $600 a year but because she always bought new clothes in the spring and fall, so the only time she had money to put aside was in the winter and summer. "I told her that we had a special program for people like her. It was called the 'Summer-Winter Savings Program.' All she had to do was spend like a maniac during the new clothes season and put away $100 a month the rest of the time. That added up to $600 a year – $6,000 in ten years – right where we started, and I made the sale."

As IOS grew, Cornfeld concentrated on building and training a large sales force, and he became famous for the question he asked prospective salespersons: "Do you sincerely want to be rich?" It was essentially a pyramid selling scheme in which sales reps shared the commissions of other sales reps they recruited. Head office kept 20% of the money invested and out of that paid the sales reps 8.5%, so there was plenty of booty to go around; by the mid-1960s, more than 100 IOS salesmen had become millionaires. Like the Canadians who became wealthy by getting into the mutual fund business at just the right time, Cornfeld had perfect timing. The American stock market was booming and the hot new performance funds were attracting millions in new money. Cornfeld's pitch was that just because you didn't live in the United States didn't mean you couldn't take part in the bonanza. And even if you knew nothing about investing, you could own stocks with little or no risk by owning funds such as those of Dreyfus and Fidelity.

When the French government became suspicious of his activities, Cornfeld moved IOS to Geneva. Based outside the United States, IOS was beyond the reach of the U.S. regulatory authorities. Cornfeld's sales army was thus able to make its pitch in more extravagant terms than the Securities and Exchange Commission (SEC) would have allowed in the States. It didn't take long for Cornfeld to figure out that management fees would be even more lucrative than sales commissions, so IOS created its own funds as well. Exactly the same thing is happening in Canada now as companies such as Assante and Investment Planning Counsel, originally formed to distribute other companies' funds, are launching their own.

IOS expanded at a tremendous clip through the 1960s, reaching $3 billion in assets by the end of the decade. In addition to mutual funds, it sold insurance and speculative resource plays in Canada and Africa. There weren't enough stocks to absorb all the money IOS had to invest, so Cornfeld plowed millions into junk bonds (those issued by companies with poor credit ratings). Besides Cornfeld, the other key player in the company was a Harvard-trained lawyer named Edward Cowett, whose great talent was situating different parts of the IOS empire in various tax and regulation havens around the world. IOS expanded its sales campaign from expatriate Americans to local residents and eventually had sales operations in the Middle East, Asia, and Latin America as well as Europe. IOS didn't operate in Canada, but it did take advantage of favourable Canadian tax laws to set up a Canadian subsidiary to run its Fund of Funds, which invested in other mutual funds.

The need to finance huge sales commissions and outlandish expenses forced IOS to put its clients' money into increasingly speculative ventures. Many of them, predictably, went bad, and in 1970 the whole house of cards came tumbling down. At an annual meeting of IOS Ltd. in Toronto's Royal York Hotel, shareholders booted Cornfeld out of the company. He was prosecuted for fraud and spent 11 months in a Swiss jail before being acquitted. By then, Robert Vesco had taken control of IOS, which he and others looted of more than $200 million that belonged to the company's clients. Vesco became a fugitive and IOS went bankrupt in 1973. Cornfeld, who was left with about $15 million, resurfaced briefly in the 1980s with a scheme to set up an IOS-type sales force to sell health aids aimed at improving sexual performance. An acquaintance told *Forbes* magazine that the master salesman had modified his famous pitch – "Do you sincerely want to be rich?" – to "Do you sincerely want to get laid?" Cornfeld died in London in 1995 after suffering a stroke.

This sordid saga was not the mutual fund industry's finest hour. But the rest of the industry couldn't claim that it shared none of the blame for IOS's misdeeds, because major American fund companies had profited greatly from Cornfeld's success in selling their funds overseas. In Canada, mutual funds were a harder sell after the collapse of IOS. Ironically, it was the rock-solid Investors Group that had the most grief because its name was so similar to that of Cornfeld's company. But while the industry would like to forget Cornfeld, it can't deny that he was a path-breaking figure. IOS was the first to have mutual funds with a chequing account attached, and it started the first fund specialized in stocks of a single foreign country. It was also an innovator in offering insurance and other financial services to fund customers. Above all, Cornfeld, with a sales force composed mostly of investment illiterates, showed that it was possible to sell vast quantities of something as intangible as mutual funds by using the same techniques already perfected for selling encyclopedias and vacuum cleaners. He turned mutual funds into mass-market consumer products.

In the long run, Cornfeld probably helped the industry more than he hurt it, and not just because by the time he was finished, millions of people knew what mutual funds were. In Canada, the powerful insurance companies, which could have sold mutual funds had they wished, were leery of the stock market and became even more disdainful following the IOS debacle. As for the banks, until the 1980s they were excluded from getting into the fund business and had little interest in it anyway. So the independent mutual fund companies had the field to themselves, which is why small companies like Trimark, AGF, and Mackenzie soon grew into big companies.

Even the large brokerage firms wanted nothing to do with mutual funds, recalls Warren Goldring, founder of AGF Management Ltd. AGF stands for American Growth Fund, which started in 1957 as the first American equity fund open to Canadian investors. "A.E. Ames [a major Toronto brokerage] would not allow one of our representatives in the door. They said, 'We can do everything you can do. We sell stocks and bonds, and our clients are clients of Ames, and we don't want them to be clients of AGF or anyone else.'"

That left two distribution routes – a company could set up its own sales force, or it could sell funds through independent financial planners or small investment companies like Russ Isaac's Great Pacific. AGF and several others had their own sales force during the 1960s, and they prospered for the same reason IOS was prospering on the other side of the Atlantic. "We grew fast in the '60s because the U.S. market seemed to be going ever onwards and upwards," says Goldring. "Exciting things were happening – jet planes, colour TV, the birth control pill. Our funds grew and grew. And by 1969 we had about $300 million [in assets under management]."

Goldring, a straight arrow, has little in common with a reckless spendthrift like Cornfeld. But in one way he is similar. Cornfeld had been a socialist before he discovered that capitalism was more profitable; perhaps influenced by that background, he captured the essence of the industry's mass appeal when he coined the phrase "people's capitalism" to describe the way mutual funds made it possible for the average wage-earner to get in on the stock market. Goldring, like many others in the business, echoes that idea to this day. A soft-spoken man with a gentle manner, his office is on the 31st floor of the TD Bank Tower in Toronto – the capitalist heart of Canada. "Mutual funds is a people's business," he enthuses. "It's very broadly based. You can invest as little as $20 a month."

Put aside small amounts and watch your money grow. Be an owner, not just a wage slave. That's also the message Russell Isaac used to build up Great Pacific in Vancouver. Today, slick television and print ads sell mutual funds, and the industry collects most of its assets over the phone or, increasingly, via computer. In the 1960s and 1970s, funds were sold by salesmen who called on the prospects in their homes. Isaac's background was a big advantage. He had logged for five years, loading timber onto rail cars. And there is a picture of him on the wall of his office in his fishing guide days; wearing an old-fashioned cap, he resembles Jimmy Cagney in one of his early tough-guy roles. So this was someone who could relate to the longshoremen and other hourly workers who made up an important part of his client base. He knew enough, for example, not to carry a briefcase because it distanced him from his customers.

"Most people didn't know what a mutual fund was, so you had to educate them. You would never close a sale without a minimum of three separate meetings. The longshoremen were making $15,000 to $20,000 a year. They lived in east Vancouver in good homes.

They could afford to invest." Isaac would get these people to sign contracts similar to the one Cornfeld clinched with the woman who had no money to spare in spring and fall because that was when she bought clothes. These contractual plans were common-place until the mid-1970s. They were not a good deal for clients because sales commissions ate up a huge chunk of their initial investments. In the plans Isaac sold, 50% of the first year's contri-bution went to commission and the rest of the commission was taken off gradually over the next nine years. Isaac says he was always frank with his customers about the implications of these plans. "I used to give clients a guarantee. I would say, 'If you redeem this before 10 years are out, I guarantee you a loss.'"

The contractual plans had disappeared by the 1980s but the high front-end loads payable at the time of purchase, typically 9%, were increasingly a barrier to growth because customers hated them. The customers didn't want to pay high commissions but the sales force had to get paid, or they wouldn't be motivated to sell the funds. How to satisfy both customers and sales reps? That was the dilemma facing the industry in the 1980s, one that Jim O'Donnell solved by inventing the back-end load, also known as the deferred sales charge (DSC), by which the customer didn't pay any sales commission as such unless she sold the fund within seven years.

"Deferred sales charge" is the sort of jargon that makes eyes glaze over, but in the world of mutual funds it's an emotional issue. The DSC made mutual funds more attractive to millions of people and is a big reason why the industry has attracted so much money over the past decade. But critics are now saying the DSC is bad because it hides the sales commission in the management fee, thereby making these annual fees higher than they should be and returns to investors lower.

I went to see Jim O'Donnell in his Toronto office to ask about this. He started talking and half an hour later still hadn't got around to answering my question about the DSC. In this way, O'Donnell, a much-admired legend in the industry, is like another legend, Henry Kissinger, who used to open his press conferences by asking, "Who has questions for my answers?" As in a Kissinger press conference, it doesn't matter what the question is. O'Donnell knows exactly what he wants to say and says it when he wants to.

O'Donnell is a legend because he was the first in Canada to grasp that the mutual fund business was less about managing investments than about selling investment products. That's why he invented the DSC – not because it was better but because it made funds easier to sell. Unlike most of the other leaders in the industry, O'Donnell was more of a marketer than a money manager. Along with Alex Christ, he built Mackenzie Financial Corp. into a mutual fund giant in the 1970s and 1980s. He did it by making Mackenzie into a brand name. One tactic was to pour millions of Mackenzie's money into Scott Goodyear's car racing team which, when you think about it, is an amazing thing for an investment management company to do. What has investment management got to do with car racing? The answer is that it has as much to do as cigarettes or beer or any other product whose logo is sewn onto a race-car driver's uniform. If a mutual fund is just another consumer product, not much different from its competitors, the marketer has to find a way to get the public to notice it. Would a rational person invest his savings with Mackenzie just because a guy zooming around a track at an insane speed has the Mackenzie logo on his outfit? Of course not, but O'Donnell knew that many mutual fund consumers are not rational. They chase last year's winner for no good reason. They buy high and sell low. Brand recognition is important to them, so they are more likely to invest with a company they have heard of than one they haven't. Sponsoring car racing was simply a way O'Donnell could make more consumers aware of Mackenzie. Moreover, car racing was an excellent symbol for an industry in which performance, rather than prudence, had become the highest priority.

Much of O'Donnell's marketing effort was aimed at the financial planners and brokers who were Mackenzie's link to the investing public. He had a reputation for staging lavish sales conferences but also, more important, for establishing warm personal relationships. If a small-town planner wanted him to speak to a handful of prospective clients on a miserable January night, O'Donnell would come. He had a gift for making friends on the retail side of the industry and genuinely cared about these friends. After the death of Russ Isaac's wife of 32 years, Dorothy, Isaac got a call in his Vancouver office from O'Donnell wondering if he was free for lunch the next day. They had a two-hour lunch in which they talked not about investment but about grief and mourning and death and life, matters which O'Donnell, a staunch Roman Catholic who once considered the priesthood, has thought long and hard about. When they had finished, Isaac asked O'Donnell if he could drop him off anywhere. O'Donnell said, "If you have time, you could drop me at the airport."

Isaac asked in amazement, "Did you fly all the way out here from Toronto just to have lunch with me?"

O'Donnell said, "Russ, you needed someone."

O'Donnell is a soft-spoken, unpretentious man who would never tell a story like that about himself. But he will tell of the time he was in a small town being introduced as the guest speaker at a service club meeting. The chairman said, "Before we hear our speaker, I want to give you the dope on the picnic," which he did. Then he said, "Let me give you the dope on the raffle," and he did. Then he said, "And now here's the dope from Bay Street."

Instead of answering my question about the DSC, O'Donnell goes to a board in the conference room in the office of the O'Donnell Group of Funds, the company he started after he left Mackenzie in 1993, and draws diagrams to demonstrate the history of the stock market. Pretty soon there are lines all over the board showing the different phases the market has gone through since the 1920s. In some of the phases, stocks are undervalued; in other phases, they're overvalued. In the 1950s, for example, stocks were a good deal and a few smart people were buying them. By the 1960s they were overvalued again so, naturally, a lot more people were buying. The 1960s, says O'Donnell, were an example of a "distribution stage, a period of high expectations. That's when you gather the masses, because everyone wants to associate with success."

The distribution stage is so called by students of the stock market because it's when the smart people who accumulated shares when they were cheap distribute them to the not-so-smart people at a higher price. Mutual funds became important during the 1960s because the masses wanted to invest and funds were a system of mass distribution. In 1967, Rick Mauran, a friend of O'Donnell's who owned a couple of restaurant chains, Swiss Chalet and Harvey's, bought a company called Mackenzie Fund Sales. He changed the name to Mackenzie Financial Corp. and started the Industrial Growth Fund. He hired Christ and O'Donnell, who had previously worked together at Dominion Securities, to manage the fund.

Not long afterwards, the market went into one of its bad phases. AGF and all the other companies that had their own sales forces disbanded them, Investors Group being the only exception. Mackenzie was selling Industrial Growth through brokers and independent planners, so O'Donnell saw this as an opportunity. "The people who had been in the captive sales forces were disillusioned. I phoned up these guys, dragged them into the office, and said, 'The problem is that you had only one product. You have to be able to sell a variety of products.' Then I helped them get licensed as independent people." Naturally, the formerly captive salespeople, now independent mutual fund dealers, were more inclined to sell Industrial Growth than the funds of the companies that had just fired them. By 1982 Mackenzie had $1.3 billion under administration.

So the money was flowing, but it wasn't flowing fast enough. Here O'Donnell gets around to explaining the origins of the DSC. "What was obvious was that we had a large investing public that wanted to give us more money. The barrier to getting that money was this." He points to his board, where he has scrawled a big ugly "9%" on top of all the squiggly lines, representing the front-end commission that the salespeople were taking out of mutual fund contributions at the time of purchase. "Who in their right mind would pay 9% to somebody to put their money into a managed product [mutual fund]?"

If Mackenzie had already been able to collect $1.3 billion from people not in their right minds, imagine how much it might collect if it could tap the wallets of the sane ones as well. O'Donnell came up with this revolutionary insight: "In marketing, if you want somebody to use your product, you give it away free. If you're Gillette and you want people to use your razor blades, you give them a free razor."

That was it. The mutual fund was a free razor. The management of the fund was a year's supply of blades. The razor's free, the customer pays the company for the blades, and the company pays the salesperson for putting the razor in the customer's hands. The customer is still paying a sales commission, of course, but it comes out of the management fee extracted from the client's money invested in the fund. The customer doesn't really know she paid a sales commission, since there's no mention of it on the statements she gets from the seller and the fund company. This simple but brilliant sleight of hand was implemented in 1987. The effect was almost magical. All of a sudden the sane people started buying Mackenzie funds. "It doubled our business in one year," says O'Donnell.

Under this system, the dealers got only 5% up front instead of 9%, which made some of them angry, but O'Donnell worked his persuasive powers on them. "I said, 'I'm going to increase your business tenfold. You're going to get 5% instead of 9%, but if I can increase your business tenfold obviously the volume is going to be greater at the bottom line than it was when you were getting 9%.'"

O'Donnell hadn't finished inventing. To cement his relationship with the all-important middlemen, he invented the "trailer fee." The seller, in addition to the 5% he gets from the fund company upon selling units of the fund, also gets half of 1% of the amount his client has invested every year the money stays in the fund. This is supposed to cover advisory services that the retailer provides to the client, although the retailer gets the money even if he provides no service other than sending out quarterly statements. Most mutual fund investors don't know they're paying an annual fee for advice because, like the sales commission, this fee is part of the MER, which is not shown on their statements.

The DSC and the trailer fee were soon adopted by all mutual fund companies that distribute primarily through intermediaries. Whether this was a beneficial development for the consumer is highly questionable, but it is definitely a good arrangement for manufacturers and retailers. Imagine how happy a car dealer would be if she could get you to pay her for the car she sold you not just at the time of purchase but every year you owned it.

Because of trailer fees, brokers and financial planners have a steady stream of income and are therefore enthusiastic sellers of mutual funds as the best of all possible investments. In fact, they have become so dependent on mutual funds that without trailer fees from mutual fund companies, many of them would go out of business. Because of the DSC, meanwhile, their customers are reluctant to cash in their fund investments; if they do, they will have to pay the deferred sales charge. So the DSC and the trailer fee were crucial developments – "the two things," says O'Donnell, "that kick-started the industry."

Once the mutual fund industry had been kick-started, the key was to keep it running at top speed. The way to do that was through ever more aggressive marketing. There were many ways to market mutual funds, as an immigrant from the United States named Paul Starita would demonstrate. Starita, who talks in a sort of De Niro accent, is an aggressive businessman with a knack for attracting attention to what he's selling. One of his more notable attention-getters was his promise, as chairman of CIBC Securities Inc., that if CIBC funds weren't among the top 50% in performance, CIBC Securities would pay a rebate to investors. The funds didn't live up to Starita's promise and CIBC had to shell out $1 million.

The son of a Brooklyn pastry chef, Starita studied engineering and then wound up on Wall Street, where he became an expert in information systems. He took a job with the Bank of Montreal and then moved to Royal Trust (which has since become a subsidiary of the Royal Bank). Royal Trust was where he first got involved in mutual funds in the early 1990s and where his natural gift for marketing found expression. He urgently needed to succeed because he and two partners had bought 20% of Royal Trust Investment Services and were $4 million in debt as a result.

Starita considers his first major marketing coup the introduction of a Royal Trust money market fund. As marketing coups go, a money market fund is less sexy than auto racing, but it worked wonders for Royal Trust. Money market funds invest in treasury bills and other government and corporate debt instruments. They pay interest several percentage points higher than a bank deposit. They're just as safe and almost as convenient because you can cash in your units at any time. Consumers, including some very wealthy ones, surprised the industry by investing huge sums in money market funds even though the returns are about a percentage point less than if they'd bought treasury bills directly, the difference being the management fee the fund company takes out of the fund's returns.

When Starita was getting Royal Trust mutual funds under way, money market funds were uncommon. He saw them as a way to get attention because he could advertise higher interest rates than the banks. The independent mutual fund companies hadn't started money market funds, because the low management fees such funds had to have to compete with comparable investments such as treasury bills or guaranteed investment certificates (GICs) left no room for fat sales commissions. This attitude, says Starita, was "sheer ignorance. They didn't understand that the name of the game was to get the assets on your books and then begin to convince people that it makes sense to move into something else. It's as simple as the annual switch from cash or money market into the RRSP. We would do a mass mailing in November. If you had a money market account, check the box and we will immediately stick the money into an RRSP – even if it was just moving it into a money market fund within the RRSP."

Starita gets excited when he talks about this stuff. He's waving his arms about like a conductor making beautiful music. "Once I've done that, now I have both, I've got your deposits and I've got your RRSP. I'm not going to be competing for the bloody RRSP. Then it's a question of moving [the client] up the food chain to something more interesting." (Something higher up the food chain would be an equity fund with a more profitable management fee.) Once Royal Trust had $1 billion in its money market fund, the banks took notice and started money market funds of their own. The independent fund companies followed suit.

Starita's next triumph was to acquire a massive amount of newspaper advertising for a laughably low price. They were the first-ever full-page ads for a mutual fund company, and they shook up the competition even more than the money market fund. Starita wanted to promote Royal Trust mutual funds in "Canada's national newspaper." The economy was in recession and advertising lineage was down, so he figured he should get a really good deal. The *Globe and Mail* said its policy was not to budge from its rate sheet. Starita said his policy was that he wanted competitive bids from the *Globe*, the *Financial Post* (which had just gone daily), and the *Financial Times*, a now-defunct weekly that was being distributed with the Saturday *Globe*.

The *Globe* may have been nervous about losing a big ad campaign to the upstart *Post*. Whatever the reason, its bid was so low that at first Starita couldn't believe it. He and Simon Lewis, one of his co-investors and vice-president of marketing, decided to take two years of full-page ads in the *Globe* instead of just one. At that point, the *Post*, not wanting to be left out, also offered a ridiculously low rate. And the *Financial Times*, which hardly had any ads at all, offered the back page of the paper for a year for just the cost of printing. Suddenly the fledgling mutual fund subsidiary of a trust company with a measly 100 branches had huge ads in three newspapers every week. "Our competition thought we were crazy," says Starita. "They thought we were spending $7 million a year on advertising. We weren't even spending $700,000 and we were getting unbelievable exposure. We were the fastest-growing mutual fund company for those two years. We grew from $600,000 to $5.4 billion."

For his next number, Starita took his act on the road. The road show, in which mutual fund companies promote their wares from coast to coast, has since become a basic part of the industry's promotional machinery. Mutual fund and financial planning companies stage meetings so their customers can hear about the benefits of funds from the people who run them or from those who promote them. Starita didn't invent the road show but he took it more seriously than anyone had before, prompting competitors to do the same. While he was running Royal Trust mutual funds, he went to 32 cities twice a year, speaking to about 20,000 people in total.

It was a gruelling business but the loquacious Starita loved it. Just as he had found that he could exploit rivalries among newspapers to get cheap advertising, he also discovered that local media in Canada's small and medium-sized cities were hungry for consumer-oriented news, especially when it was spoon-fed by a colourful guy with a De Niro accent. "I would get up in the morning, do morning radio in the next town on the phone, then fly to the next town. On arrival I would do a call-in show. For lunch, the branch would invite 40 people with larger accounts. Then I would try to do the local newspaper and the local TV station. At 5 p.m., I would meet with the local branch personnel. At 7, I'd speak for an hour. I'd never push my product. I'd say the educated client is the better client because it reduces misunderstanding. I'd go through the historical relationship of fixed income to equity and why a mix is important. And then I'd talk about the current world economic situation. I would talk about whatever Canadian economic topic was happening at the time – declining dollar, deficit. Then I'd give my recommended portfolio and say we happen to have some of those. Not like some of the road shows: 'You're a fool if you don't buy mutual funds, you're stupid, you're an idiot.' I never did that. And we had question periods that sometimes lasted two hours."

Under Starita's leadership, Royal Trust was the first to put a "brand name" money manager, Marty Zweig, on a Canadian mutual fund. Zweig was well known to the sophisticated minority of investors who had seen his appearances on *Wall Street Week*, an investment program on American public television. There were evidently quite a few sophisticated investors, because when Starita brought the host of *Wall Street Week*, Louis Rukeyser, to Toronto, he filled Roy Thomson Hall twice in one day.

Recently Starita has been splitting his time between Toronto, where he runs a company that manages real estate investments for pension funds, and the University of Victoria, where he directs a program of short courses on North American business practices for foreign executives. He is also working in an advisory capacity for Veronika Hirsch, a fund manager formerly with AGF and Fidelity who now runs a fund family under the Hirsch brand. Meanwhile, the mutual fund marketers have marched on, though they have not strayed from the path broken by O'Donnell and Starita, a path whose destination has always been to turn mutual fund companies into brands.

"Branding" is one of the buzzwords of our day, but what does it mean? What exactly is a brand? "Manufacturers make products but consumers buy brands," says Randy Van Der Starren, senior vice-president of marketing for AGF. I called Van Der Starren because I had seen him on *Undercurrents*, a CBC television program, talking about mutual fund advertising on television. The fact that mutual funds advertise on television, and that they do enough of it for *Undercurrents* to do an item about it, is proof of how the industry had been transformed by the end of the 1990s from a branch of the investment management business into a manufacturer of what Van Der Starren calls "a commoditized category." The transformation is also evidenced by the fact that a mutual fund company would hire somebody like Van Der Starren, who has no training in finance; he came to AGF after working at several advertising houses, including Ogilvy & Mather and Young & Rubicam.

If you can get the customer to develop an "emotional relationship" with your product, Van Der Starren explains, you have successfully created a brand. To develop such a relationship, AGF ran television ads showing Santa Claus and Spiderman enjoying retirement. These ads said nothing about the performance of AGF's funds. Van Der Starren says they were intended not to sell funds but rather to give the viewer enough "trust and confidence" in AGF that he would remember the company the next time he met with his financial adviser.

Getting the consumer to have trust and confidence in a mutual fund company is easier said than done. Think of the top brands in the world, names like Sony and IBM and Mercedes. The value of such brands is the reputation they carry for quality and value, especially important for busy people who can't afford the time and frustration of dealing with products that don't work well. A great brand, in other words, is a warranty. The owner of a Sony TV chooses Sony when she is looking for a CD player because, on the basis of her experience with her Sony TV and Sony Walkman and the company's reputation, she's confident the CD player will perform as promised. Brands such as Marlboro or Coke promise that what's in the package will taste the same wherever in the world the product is purchased. But a mutual fund company can't make credible promises of performance or consistency because those are influenced by fluctuations in securities markets and changes in the economic environment, factors over which the company has no control.

So what is AGF selling when it buys time on television to show Santa Claus at his retirement party? Well, it's selling a comfortable retirement. But then so is everybody else, and everybody else is a lot of mutual fund companies. In 1998 the industry spent $125 million on television, which is more than the beer industry spent. That fact is astonishing when you consider that at the beginning of the decade there was no mutual fund advertising at all on television.

Most mutual fund advertising on TV is pretty sober stuff – Gord Cheesborough of Altamira talking about his terrific bond fund, somebody from a bank urging investors not to dump their mutual funds just because the stock market is misbehaving. AGF decided upon a whimsical approach to help it stand out in a crowded field. Its ads showed Gumby flaked out on a beach and Spiderman trying to get out of a sand trap. The idea was to link characters associated with childhood to the concept of retirement. Somehow that would make consumers feel warmly towards AGF and have trust and confidence in the company. It evidently worked: AGF's name recognition and, more important, its sales have gone way up because of these ads. "It's much more emotional than it is rational," Van Der Starren points out.

Fidelity, the world's biggest fund company and the fastest-growing one in Canada, also sells retirement. It doesn't show retired people in its ads, however, because it doesn't think young and middle-aged buyers of mutual funds want to imagine themselves at 75. "You want to see yourself, tops, at 55," says Brian Henderson, vice-president of marketing for Fidelity's Canadian operation, who, at 34, is about seven years older than the average Fidelity employee. Henderson grapples every day with the problem of how to market a mutual fund. "It's very difficult. There are two problems with it: it's intangible, and the benefit is arguably 25 or 30 years away, outside of the benefit of having a sense of security as you are getting towards your goal. It's not like you can take a bite and say it tastes good or it is whiter and brighter. That's why advertising generally in the category is mediocre to bad, and why people are floundering about how to promote their products. You get blank stares from marketers who are used to dealing with 'fizzier' and 'breathtaking.'"

Any marketing that's effective in the long run has to have some connection with reality. Since a fund company can't credibly promise consistent performance, what can it say about itself that's true and therefore believable? It can say it has the resources to manage money well and the size and stability to stay in business and keep your money safe. So a giant like Fidelity has a major advantage over its smaller competitors when it can say, as Henderson puts it, that "15 million investors can't be wrong, and we got to be the biggest by doing a good job." Saying such things in a credible way is the only way fund companies will be able to create enduring brands. Only the largest companies will be able to do it, which is a major reason why, in the first decade of this new century, the industry will consolidate into fewer and larger companies.

The process of consolidation was well under way as the 1990s faded into history. It began in 1996 when first a bank, then an insurance company, tried to take control of Altamira Management Ltd., the company Ron Meade helped to found a decade after he went job hunting on St. James Street. The result was one of the nastiest takeover battles in Canadian corporate history. It was a painful experience for Meade, Frank Mersch, and the others involved, but they had only themselves to blame for building a company worth fighting over. With Meade at the helm, Altamira had grown into the 10th-largest mutual fund company in Canada, with $14 billion in mutual funds and pension money under management. More than a dozen executives and fund managers had become millionaires because of the company's success.

The Altamira people had been fortunate that the giants of the Canadian financial services industry, the banks and insurance companies, had not been interested in mutual funds and had left the field wide open to independent companies. By the 1990s, however, the success of the industry had captured the attention of the behemoths. The big fear in the corridors of financial power was "disintermediation," a mouthful of a word that essentially means somebody else is managing money you used to manage. Canadians weren't putting money into the banks' GICs and the insurance companies' whole-life policies the way they used to. They were buying mutual funds instead, and the banks and insurance companies didn't like that at all.

The big boys could, and did, start their own mutual funds. Buying an existing fund company was the quickest way to build assets, though, and Altamira was an inviting target. For one thing, its funds were generally better performers than those the banks and insurance companies had started. Its flagship, Altamira Equity, had one of the best records of all the Canadian stock funds while under the management of Frank Mersch, an aggressive trader whose success had inspired business writers to anoint him as "the Wayne Gretzky of Canadian fund managers." Largely because of him, the Altamira name had strong brand recognition. Best of all, it was one of the most profitable mutual fund companies in the country because almost all its sales were direct to the public.

Any manufacturer that can cut out the retailers (brokers and financial planners) will save what amounts to about 1% of mutual fund assets under management every year. Unlike other large direct sellers, such as MD Management Ltd. (whose funds are available only to doctors and their families) and Phillips, Hager & North Investment Management Ltd. (which sells to the public but requires a high minimum investment), Altamira did not pass these savings on to its customers in the form of lower MERs. Instead, it kept its fees at about the same level as companies that sold through intermediaries and retained the millions it wasn't paying out in commissions and trailer fees.

Adding to Altamira's appeal as a takeover target was the split in its ownership among four different groups: Meade and his co-founders

(11%); a group of 40 employees led by Mersch (28%); Almiria Capital Corp., a Montreal-based venture capital company owned by Altamira's founders and about 30 large institutional investors (30.5%); and Manufacturers Life Insurance Co. Ltd. (30.5%). Because these various owners did not always see things the same way, potential suitors could, if necessary, use divide-and-conquer tactics.

All the shareholders agreed it was the time to sell. Competition was heating up in the industry and everybody knew Mersch's fund couldn't be a top performer forever. They also knew the stock market would not keep up its winning ways indefinitely and that when it tumbled, so would the value of the mutual fund companies. Mersch and the other portfolio managers were particularly eager. Most of them were people of modest backgrounds who had risked a lot to help make Altamira a success. Some, including Mersch, had borrowed money to invest in the company in the early days. Mersch had taken out a $70,000 loan to buy 5% of the fledgling company. "We were very poor," chief financial officer Stuart McKenzie said later in a court hearing.

By 1996 they had become very rich, but they still felt vulnerable. What if the value of Altamira fell before they had a chance to cash in? It was time to be wealthy not just on paper but in their bank accounts as well. And something else was exacerbating their nervousness about Altamira's future: the Ontario Securities Commission (OSC) was investigating some peculiar trading activity by Altamira in a junior oil stock called Dorset Exploration Ltd. as well as Mersch's role in a private investment in Diamond Fields Resources Inc.

Offering the company to the public in a share offering was considered and rejected, in part because of the OSC investigation and in part because the employees didn't want the world to know how much money they were making. "Frank [Mersch] had this fear that people would see his net worth and he would have cranks on his doorstep harassing his family," recalls Meade. "These guys were making millions of dollars that they would never have made in the real world because of the generous profit-sharing that we had. Even the CFO of the Royal Bank didn't make as much as Stuart McKenzie." (Altamira employees were getting 25% of operating income as profit-sharing, well above the norm for a public company.) There was another important reason for not taking the company public as well. The managers feared a negative reaction when unitholders discovered how profitable Altamira was.

So a share offering was out. That meant they needed someone to buy the whole thing. Meade went fishing for a buyer among the large financial institutions that wanted to build their fund businesses. One offer emerged, from the Toronto-Dominion Bank, which indicated informally that it would pay $765 million in cash and shares, or $41.50 per Altamira share. That's about what Meade had hoped to get. He and his founding group were happy, the employee group was happy, and Almiria Capital was happy. Manulife, however, was not. In return for agreeing to the sale, it wanted the other owners to pay it $45 million out of their share of proceeds on the grounds that its interest in Altamira had been diluted a year earlier when employees had received shares in return for a reduction in profit-sharing. Manulife also wanted the $45 million as an inducement to leave $3 billion worth of its clients' money in Altamira once it was owned by TD. Some of the Altamira shareholders denounced this demand as "greenmail." After much bickering and the intervention of a mediator, Manulife agreed to accept a premium of $15 million.

While this was going on, word of the negotiations leaked into the press. TD started to have second thoughts. Meade thinks that Frank Mersch himself helped scare off the bank by telling Richard Thomson, TD chairman at the time, that buying Altamira would knock $2 off the value of TD's shares. Informed of Meade's interpretation, Mersch asks, "Why would I try to scuttle a deal where I am going to end up with 2.1 million shares of TD? That's the last thing I wanted. It'd be very nice to be clipping TD dividends for the rest of my life." Mersch did meet with Thomson and relayed the Bay Street consensus that buying Altamira would initially push TD's share price down. "It wasn't Frank Mersch," says Mersch, "it was Hugh Brown [an influential bank analyst] who was saying that if they bought Altamira he would downgrade TD. So when Dick Thomson asked me, I just told him what the street was saying."

Brown wasn't the only one. Morgan Stanley, a major American investment company, suggested at the time that TD could better enhance shareholder value by buying back its own undervalued shares than by making acquisitions. Ultimately the bank agreed. "We looked at that [Altamira] deal and a stock buyback, and we went with the stock buyback," a TD executive later told the *Financial Post*.

TD's decision ignited a war among Altamira's shareholders. The founders and some of the institutional shareholders of Almiria Capital furiously accused Dominic D'Alessandro, CEO of Manulife, of deliberately sabotaging the deal. D'Alessandro proclaimed his innocence and quickly made an offer of his own: $30 for all the Altamira shares Manulife didn't already own, later upped to $32, or $660 million in total. The founders and institutional shareholders of Almiria Capital were beside themselves. In their opinion, D'Alessandro was lowballing them, offering almost $10 a share less than they would have got if he had played ball with TD. Some of the institutional shareholders of Almiria Capital even threatened to stop doing business with Manulife. "Why the hell would you want to do business with somebody like that?" asked an anonymous executive at a company whose health benefits were managed by Manulife, quoted in the *Globe and Mail*. But the employee shareholders didn't feel that way – to the indignation of Meade and his friends, they accepted Manulife's offer. Meade and the venture capitalists were now, so it seemed, out in the cold. D'Alessandro would not need them to exercise control of the company once this deal was done. He had divided and conquered.

Manulife had bought its original stake in Altamira in 1991, before Mersch's spectacular performance had turned the company into a powerhouse. Manulife's purchase was, according to John Richardson, who was running Manulife's Canadian operations at the time, "a strategic investment" because Manulife knew it had to be in the mutual fund business. That was why it had created its own Cabot series of funds and Vista segregated funds. (A segregated fund carries an insurance policy that protects the investor's principal.) And although it was never written down explicitly, it was understood at the time of the deal that eventually Manulife would buy out Altamira; otherwise, said Richardson, it would have set up a separate mutual fund company of its own.

It was Meade who had brought Manulife in, and by doing so, says Mersch, he put Altamira on the map. "It was a very, very good deal for Altamira. We took a billion dollars of their assets into our fold. Subsequently we took more and more assets from them. Before, we only had $200 million under administration. Our performance was extraordinary but the pension consultants [who advise companies on managing their pension funds] wouldn't sell us because we didn't have over $1 billion in assets. So strategically we had to make that move just to vault the asset value up."

Manulife had been a passive investor in Altamira until D'Alessandro arrived as CEO in 1994 and started, as he did wherever he went, to shake things up. D'Alessandro had emigrated with his family to Canada from Italy as a child, grown up in a working-class Montreal neighbourhood, and graduated from high school at 14. After becoming a chartered accountant, he rose through the executive ranks at the Royal Bank before getting the top job at Laurentian Bank, which, after a series of takeovers, he built into the sixth largest in Canada. By the time he got to Manulife, he was used to being in control. The Altamira situation bothered him. Here was a successful company in the fastest-growing part of the financial services business. Manulife owned a significant chunk but didn't control it, didn't even have a seat on the board, even though it had billions under Altamira's management. D'Alessandro was used to giving orders; Altamira was being run by Meade, who wasn't used to taking them. What's more, Meade was just as tough as D'Alessandro and proud of having helped build Altamira from nothing into a major player in the fund business.

John Vivash, who worked for Manulife after playing key roles in launching the fund businesses of Fidelity Canada and CIBC, recalls D'Alessandro asking him, "What would you do? We own 30%, and my people are telling me they aren't doing the job of managing money for us."

Vivash replied, "I would never be in a strategic relationship with a company where I owned less than 50% or more than 1%. You can't fire them because you shoot yourself in the foot by harming your own investment, and you can't tell them what to do. I'd raise my stake to 50% or sell the 30% I've got."

D'Alessandro agreed and, the TD deal having fallen through, was now trying to buy Altamira. Matters were complicated by his relationship with Meade. Simply put, the two men detested each other. Meade is a big, soft-spoken man with a gentle manner that can give way to a fiery temper. D'Alessandro, small and combative, is known for bringing the pungent language of the street into the boardroom. Meade had grown up in sophisticated international circles, far from the modest working-class Montreal neighbourhood that had nurtured D'Alessandro. But the most important difference was neither background nor personality. Meade was an entrepreneur who had built a business; D'Alessandro was an organization man who had climbed corporate ladders. Meade was one of the risk-takers who had created the mutual fund business. D'Alessandro was the agent of one of the financial Goliaths that wanted to snatch it away. Meade was the industry's past; D'Alessandro, so it seemed, was its future.

Meade thought D'Alessandro was jealous of Altamira's success. A senior executive at Manulife told him that when D'Alessandro first arrived he wanted to know who owned the expensive cars in the parking lot. At that time, Altamira's office was next door to Manulife's on Bloor Street in Toronto. The two companies shared the same parking structure, and the Altamira cars were said to have attracted D'Alessandro's attention. "I have a 600S Mercedes, so he was particularly jealous of me," Meade said. "I said to him, 'If you want to be rich, then become an entrepreneur and take risks.' His office was as big as my house, so if status was what he wanted, he had it. But for real money, for capital, you have to take some risks. Once an entrepreneur becomes successful, people think, 'I am as smart as he is, why is he richer?' That is what Dominic felt. But he never took any risks."

The atmosphere at Altamira resembled that of a dog park where two unneutered males, each convinced of his supremacy, have been let off the leash. One player in the events later said Meade and D'Alessandro had a "bigger dick syndrome" that prevented them from agreeing on anything. Meade was not about to let D'Alessandro grab Altamira for less than it was worth. So strongly did he feel that he told D'Alessandro in a private meeting he would "lay waste" to Altamira before seeing it fall into Manulife's hands. He regretted the remark the instant it was out of his mouth. Of course he would not lay waste to a company whose economic well-being was so important to his own. In fact, he would not even know how to go about laying waste to the company, nor would the other executives at Altamira have let him. But the remark showed the extent to which D'Alessandro had got under Meade's skin. Not long after the Manulife offer was made, the Altamira founders and Almiria Capital sued Manulife and the Altamira employees who had accepted it.

The position of the employee-shareholders was critical. Not only did they own enough shares to provide Manulife with control of the company but, as Meade acknowledged, they were Altamira's chief assets. Without the team of portfolio managers who had made Altamira's funds successful, the company wasn't worth much. The fact that the employees had accepted his offer proved it was fair, said D'Alessandro, because they were shrewd investors who spent their days evaluating the worth of businesses. Even if a better offer might be out there somewhere, the managers were keen to link up with Manulife because they were planning to stay at Altamira as both employees and owners. As such they would be competing not only with the big Canadian banks and insurance companies but with Fidelity, the fearsome invader from the south, and perhaps with Vanguard, another American giant rumoured to be considering a Canadian foray. All of these companies dwarfed Altamira. Linking up with a strong multinational like Manulife offered the employees some protection and also the possibility of lucrative expansion using Manulife's marketing infrastructure both in Canada and abroad.

There was also the nagging problem of the investigation into Altamira's trading practices. The securities commission was looking at a 19-month period in 1993 and 1994 during which Altamira funds had owned as much as 29% of Dorset Exploration and accounted for more than half the trading in the stock. On almost half the days on which it traded Dorset stock, Altamira had made the last trade of the day, at a price higher than the previous trade, thereby setting the closing price that appeared in the paper the next morning. Part of the problem was that many of these trades were from one Altamira fund to another at prices set internally rather than on the open market. Was this a variation on an old practice called "painting the tape," in which crooked speculators traded shares in a company among themselves, creating a false impression of momentum, and then cashed in when the suckers started to buy?

Then there was the Diamond Fields affair. In 1993, Dass 25 Holdings Ltd., a B.C. company, had bought shares of Diamond Fields Resources Inc. well before Diamond Fields became famous for finding nickel at Voisey's Bay in Labrador. Six weeks later, Diamond Fields zoomed from 15 cents to $2.65 when large investors, including Altamira, started loading up on shares. The OSC alleged that Mersch was the owner of Dass, which appeared to put him in a conflict of interest between his personal investing and his management of the mutual fund. Mersch's position was that the real owner was a friend of his, Peter Cunti, and that he had only arranged the deal on Cunti's behalf.

According to Mersch, both TD and Manulife knew about both cases, had discussed them with the OSC, and had satisfied themselves there was no reason not to go ahead with the deal. But would other potential suitors feel the same way? If the OSC found Altamira guilty of wrongdoing and came down hard, that might diminish the value of Altamira. That was just one more reason to consider D'Alessandro's offer favourably.

Meade admitted later that he had underestimated the extent to which the employees felt vulnerable financially. After the TD deal fell through, he left for a week in Nassau. "While I was gone, a lot of the people here were sitting back stunned. They had been counting their nickels before it happened. I hadn't got my expectation level up that high. Other people had. The difference was that I had other resources. Altamira was not my only nest egg. For them it was."

Another important factor was that Mersch, the biggest employee shareholder and the leader of the portfolio managers, was convinced that the fund industry was heading for a fall. Several months before, according to Meade, Mersch had said to him, "Find a buyer right away. This thing can't last, the market's going to crater. We have to realize now before it all disappears on us."

Meade says he replied, "Why do you feel this uneasiness, Frank? I think we've got a good solid business, and even if the market tanks, we'll live through it and come out the other side stronger and better."

The court battle got started in November 1996. The founders and Almiria Capital argued that Manulife's deal with the employee-shareholders was illegal because it violated a shareholder's agreement giving all shareholders a right of first refusal on the sale of shares by another shareholder. Manulife and the employees, naturally, offered a different interpretation of this agreement. The case dragged on for months.

I first met Meade in June 1997 while the case was still under way and he was spending much of his time with lawyers. We had lunch at Prego Della Piazza, a fashionable restaurant in the Yorkville district whose owner, Michael Carlevale, greeted Meade warmly. Meade enjoys the good things in life and the success of Altamira means he can afford them. He is a habitué of the best restaurants, has played golf with Michael Jordan and Ivan Lendl (Lendl, he says, is the better golfer), skis in Colorado, and takes the sun in the South Pacific. He has an 85-foot boat. He has grown children and a wife, Simone, who is half his age and looks even younger. A few days before our lunch, Meade tells me, he and his wife were on a plane and the flight attendant, assuming Simone was his daughter, asked him if she was allowed to have the Bloody Caesar she'd ordered.

The story shows Meade can laugh at himself, but it's obvious he's hurt and angered by the stance of Altamira's employee-shareholders. "Most of these guys weren't worth $2.50 when I hired them," he says. It's understandable he would feel that way. But one thing bothers me, and that's when he says he probably won't go back to the office this afternoon because, although he's still chairman and CEO of Altamira, he doesn't have much to do, since he is not on speaking terms with the rest of management. My wife, it occurs to me, has an

RRSP account with Altamira. And the CEO isn't on speaking terms with the rest of management? Maybe that RRSP account should be transferred somewhere else.

It turned out I wasn't the only one worried about the effect of Altamira's civil war on its ability to manage the assets it had been entrusted with. Altamira's funds were hemorrhaging money, especially the flagship Equity Fund, whose performance had faltered badly. Altamira was now the 17th-largest fund company, down from 10th when the ownership dispute had started. On the institutional side, clients such as Abitibi Consolidated Inc., the City of Saskatoon, and York University had pulled their pension funds out.

Altamira executives were assuring everybody that it was business as usual, but the customers weren't buying it. The financial press had carried too many stories quoting different factions of ownership and management insulting one another. Towers Perrin, a Toronto pension consultant, said the following in a mailing to its clients: "Certain of Altamira's senior portfolio managers have maintained a high profile and active role in the ongoing dispute. In addition, the portfolio managers have considerable personal wealth at stake in this process. Given the high stakes and time demands, this situation has the potential to be and, we believe has been, extremely distracting to the portfolio managers and their primary focus – that of managing client investment assets." In January 1997, Wendy Brodkin, a principal in Towers Perrin, wrote to Philip Evans, Altamira's chief operating officer, saying Towers Perrin was recommending to clients that they pull their funds out of Altamira.

Damaging as this sort of thing was, it wasn't enough to frighten the parties into resolving the dispute. For all the wrangling over the shareholders' agreement and ancillary matters, the basic issue was simple: How much was the company worth? D'Alessandro's position was that Manulife would be a buyer at a cheap price and a seller at an expensive price. Meade's position was that the price should be neither cheap nor expensive but fair. But it was fair, countered D'Alessandro, proof being that it was the only formal offer on the table and the wise Altamira fund managers had agreed to it.

Meade thought he had definitive proof that D'Alessandro and the Altamira employees were wrong, but he'd made a mistake that prevented him from making the proof public. Before launching the suit, his side's law firm had asked RBC Dominion, a large investment dealer, to do an independent evaluation of Altamira. Because they couldn't be sure the evaluation wouldn't back up Manulife's position, however, they didn't mention it in their affidavits and therefore couldn't introduce it as evidence at trial. When the report came in, it said Altamira was worth $40 to $42 a share, $10 more than Manulife's offer. More frustrating still, during the court case Canada Trust had made an offer of $38 a share, subject to being able to talk to Mersch and the other employee-shareholders. But Manulife had an agreement preventing the employee-shareholders from talking to other bidders. Nor would Manulife respond to an offer from Meade and his side, offering the insurance company $38 a share for its piece of Altamira.

In September 1997, a way was found out of the impasse. A Boston-based venture capital company, TA Associates Inc., having sniffed around Altamira for more than a year, finally made an offer of $38 a share, $6 more than Manulife's offer. The deal was worth $784 million. That was fine with both founders, the Almiria venture capital group, and the employee-shareholders. Manulife was tired of fighting over Altamira and it too accepted TA's offer. The court battle, now redundant, was dropped. Meade got $30.6 million and stayed on as a director but would no longer play a part in management. The employee-shareholders cleaned up, especially Mersch, who got $45.6 million in cash and shares.

As for the OSC's interest in the Dorset case, just before the TA deal was done the commission made its decision. It reprimanded Altamira for its trading practices but accepted the company's position that it had not tried to manipulate the market or mislead the public. Altamira promised to reform its trading practices and paid $75,000 as part of the settlement. This was little more than a rap on the knuckles, and it seemed that Altamira's nightmare was over. It was time for a fresh start, so TA hired a much-admired executive,

Gordon Cheesborough, from Scotia McLeod to be president and CEO. Altamira now had a new boss untainted by the rancour of the takeover battle or the Dorset incident.

But there was more bad news to come. Back in 1994, Mersch had suffered the misfortune of being named Fund Manager of the Year, and now he was going to have to pay for it. His fund, Altamira Equity, a shining star for several years, had become a dog, largely because Mersch had bought resource stocks when he should have bought bank stocks. Then, in May 1998, his career with Altamira came to a sudden end when the OSC accused him of lying in the Diamond Fields affair. A month later, the securities commission banned Mersch from trading for six months. As if that weren't bad enough, Mersch had to relinquish most of his $45.6-million share of the TA deal because the deal required the fund managers to stay at Altamira for at least a year. (Altamira, of its own accord, now has a rule that personal investments by its fund managers can be only in Altamira mutual funds.)

The six-month layoff was tough for someone who loves the action as much as Mersch does. I spoke to him about the battle for Altamira almost a year and a half after he left. We talked on the phone, which is the proper way to interview him since he spends most of his time with a phone on his ear. In his heyday at Altamira, his desk was action central, the place where Mersch sucked up information from all over and deluged Altamira's trading desk with buy and sell slips. Now he's back in action in an investment company called Casurina Ltd. Partnership, a hedge fund named after a pine tree. "You know me," he says, laughing. "I have to do something."

A hedge fund is a mutual fund for the rich and sophisticated. It has a high minimum investment (in this case, $150,000) and can do things to enhance returns that a mutual fund isn't allowed to, namely borrow money to invest and sell short (selling a stock you don't own in anticipation of buying it later at a lower price). Mersch had wanted to launch a hedge fund in the last couple of years he was at Altamira but was turned down. "I was getting tired of running the Equity Fund and I was looking for new challenges. And they said,

'We can't afford you away from the Equity Fund because you are synonymous with the Equity Fund, it's a risk to our business.' I said, 'Look, I'm tired of it,' but they wouldn't let me."

What happened to Mersch is similar to what happened to Wayne Deans on the Marathon Equity Fund. Both are brilliant at spotting small companies on the way up. But when you've got hundreds of millions in your fund, even a big win on a small-cap stock isn't going to make much difference to your performance because your holding in the stock will be only a minuscule part of your total portfolio. It was frustrating for Mersch. "I couldn't buy small caps any more, I couldn't do this, I couldn't do that, there was too much money. Now I don't run a lot of money [$50 million as of November 1999], so I've got to think, I've got to focus, and I'm having fun again. I've always liked stocks, I like making money for people, and I like helping businesses. I've invested in every small company, and that's probably why the people that have given me money to manage are the ones whose companies I invested in years ago – because I helped them build their businesses, from Gerry Schwartz to half the oil patch. They've all got long memories."

Actually, Schwartz, president of Onex Corp., didn't invest any money with Mersch, but he did offer to buy Casurina. "I went to him and said, 'Gerry, I'm trying to raise some money,' and he said, 'Well, I'll buy your company.' Gerry always wants to own everything. But I didn't want that, I just finished a process where I was owned."

Mersch is still devastated by what happened at Altamira. "To this day I wish we had taken the Manulife bid instead of the TA bid. I'd still be in Altamira probably. I wouldn't have been pushed out. I learned a long time ago that you don't always take the highest bid. Sure the TA bid was $38 instead of $32, but there were other issues." One of those issues was that Manulife removed $3 billion in pension assets from Altamira once the TA deal closed. "With Manulife, we would have had more money to run, we would have been their pre-eminent money management shop. You see what Manulife is today, their U.S. operations, their Asian operations, you know we would have been the engine to that. We would have been able to build our organization more fully, hire more people, get more managers and provide a bigger array of products. Also we would have got shares in Manulife, and today it's a publicly traded company [it was not at the time of the proposed purchase], which would have been more tax-effective in the long run for all the managers. So accepting $38 – on an after-tax basis it's not great; whereas the $32 bid with shares in a company that eventually goes public and you have the upside of those shares, being in a bigger entity and diversifying your risk, seemed to be better. And also we cared about the business. Ronnie didn't care – he just wanted the best price."

That's unfair to Meade, who cared deeply about the company he had co-founded, built, and managed. But it is true he had come into it originally as a venture capitalist and had always intended to sell at a profit when the time was right. "Venture capitalists are greedy," said Mersch. "That's their mandate. That was clearly defined from day one. The whole thing was structured to be fast-tracked and to be sold. And it's amazing that we were able to execute as well as we did. We were all focused and we just worked our tails off."

Their timing was perfect. The early 1990s, when Altamira was growing rapidly, was when interest rates had declined so much that investors were frightened out of cash. Bank deposits and other income investments would not be able to return enough to finance their retirements, and mutual funds seemed to offer enough mitigation of risk to allow risk-averse investors to venture into stocks for the first time. Recalls Mersch: "We were at the very cusp of declining interest rates where we took all those people who were in GICs and converted them into mutual fund disciples. My role was very simple: deliver numbers and convince people to come out of a GIC or Canada Savings Bond because rates were going down to 4% and buy a vehicle that could give them the opportunity to make 15% to 20%. The mutual fund industry converted billions and billions of dollars in GICs into mutual funds."

It was a great time to be managing a fund. "The more people put money into the funds, the more money goes in to buy stocks, and because there is a limited supply of stocks you drive the value of the stocks up. So you are basically taking that money out of one area and putting it into another, to the point where the money itself generates performance. It's a never-ending double-, triple-leveraged type of business until sales start to slow. When that happens, all of a sudden you don't have the leverage, you don't have the growth from the sales. Then if the performance slips you get negative leverage."

That's what happened to Altamira Equity and other formerly high-flying funds that struggled as the 1990s came to a close. The sale of Altamira happened just as mutual funds were entering a period of slower growth. So Mersch, who owned resources when he should have owned banks, turned out to be right in the case of his own industry; since the sale of Altamira, the stocks of publicly traded mutual fund companies have declined. "We sold at the top," Mersch says. Apart from that, though, it didn't work out the way he had hoped. "In many respects I feel like I got my heart ripped out. The whole ownership struggle is a very interesting lesson in greed. We had a great business and we fucked it up."

Although Altamira remains an independent company, it may not stay that way for long. Two of its three ownership groups, Almiria Capital and TA, are venture capitalists who eventually will want to take their profits. That Altamira nearly became the property first of a bank, then of an insurance company, foreshadowed the consolidation of the industry now under way.

And the fall of Mersch marked the beginning of the end of the celebrity manager. Another celebrity manager, Veronika Hirsch, also had an embarrassing fall from star status. Like Mersch's, her funds were top performers. She figured prominently in ads, first for AGF, then for Fidelity. Then it came out that, while at AGF, she had bought special warrants in a Vancouver company, Oliver Gold Corp., for her private account before buying the same securities at a higher price for a fund she was managing. (A warrant allows the owner to purchase securities at a set price within a specified time.) This could be interpreted as using the buying power of the fund to propel the stock price higher. Hirsch denied it, saying she bought for herself when the stock was speculative and for the fund only when it looked more solid. Complicating the affair was that Hirsch, who lives in Toronto, had used a B.C. address to buy the shares, which were intended only for B.C. residents. Fidelity gave her the boot and in 1997 she had to pay $140,000 to securities regulators, her $100,000 profit on the shares plus a penalty.

Not surprisingly, Fidelity has no intention of promoting a celebrity manager again, nor has AGF repeated the gamble it took on Hirsch. Both Mersch and Hirsch had been household names, albeit briefly. Now one room would hold all the Canadians not employed in the fund industry who could name a single AGF or Fidelity fund manager. With Mersch gone, Altamira is also a celebrity-free zone.

The growth and consolidation of the industry and the demise of the celebrity manager are linked. "When you reach a certain critical mass, the star system increases the risk to the franchise," explains Cheesborough, Altamira's boss. "Your risk becomes greater and greater, because if the person gets sick or is killed and everyone thinks that's what the business is, then by definition the business will become sick or killed." Instead of building stars, Cheesborough sought to build performance. A new team was appointed to run the Equity Fund, which by 1999 had re-established itself as a top performer. A new offering called the e-business fund, the first in Canada to be focused on Internet stocks, had sensational results, and some new index funds boasted below-average MERs. But it would take a long time to undo the damage that the ownership battle had done to the company. Long after it had been resolved, money continued to flee Altamira. Its chances of regaining the rank it once had are slim, given the intensified competition it now faces.

The sad saga of Altamira demonstrates the vulnerability of the brand. No matter how good a mutual fund company's investment management, it can't deliver performance the way Coke and Toyota can deliver performance. The customer understands that but, at the very least, expects stability, expects the managers to be focused on managing his money. He does not expect them to be fighting among themselves in public. If you can't deliver stability, you're going to lose your customers, and once you've lost them it will be hard to get them back.

Why did Altamira destabilize? Ironically, because it was so successful. "There are two points of stress in a company," says Ron Meade. "Failure, when people leave the sinking ship, and great success, when people can act in a very independent fashion. The latter is what happened here. There was simply too much money."

CHAPTER THREE

THE DISTRIBUTION DILEMMA

Should there ever be a Mutual Fund Hall of Fame, Ed Johnson, owner of Fidelity Investments – Mr. Johnson, as everyone called him – will be the first inductee. Fidelity, which he founded in 1946 and which his son, Ned, now owns and runs, is the largest mutual fund company in the world, managing US$1 trillion and accounting for 10% of the trading volume on the New York Stock Exchange.

Back in the 1950s, when Fidelity was still small, Mr. Johnson already had a reputation as an unconventional thinker. He was interested in such non-financial subjects as psychoanalysis and Zen Buddhism, and he tried to relate what he learned to the behaviour of the stock market. "The market," he once said, "is like a beautiful woman – endlessly fascinating, endlessly complex, always changing, always mystifying."

It was for such pearls of wisdom that a young Canadian named Bob Jones travelled to Boston in the 1950s. To Jones, a Winnipegger in his 20s, Mr. Johnson was not a competitor but a guru, one of the smartest investors in the United States. What's more, he always had time for a chat when the polite young man from the prairies dropped by to see him.

Jones never dreamed his company would one day be competing against Mr. Johnson's company. At the time he was one of two managers of Investors Mutual of Canada, a mutual fund started in Winnipeg in 1949 and owned by Investors Syndicate. He'd been a bond analyst for two years, but he didn't know much about stocks and took every opportunity to educate himself. His visits to Mr. Johnson, and to other money managers in Boston and New York, were part of that education. Back then, the parent company of Investors Syndicate, Investors Diversified Services of Minneapolis, was the largest mutual fund company in the United States. As the years went by, Fidelity would surpass it. In Canada, meanwhile, Jones would become president of Investors Group, the fully Canadian successor to Investors Syndicate, which is now the largest mutual fund company in this country. At the end of 1999 it had almost $41 billion in assets under management, an impressive $9 billion more than the number two company, Royal Mutual Funds Inc., a Royal Bank subsidiary.

In 1987, Fidelity under Ned Johnson came north to start up a mutual fund operation in Canada. Despite Fidelity's size, it was a risky proposition. Although Americans dominate much of the Canadian economy, the financial services industry has remained a Canadian preserve. In the 1980s American banks and brokerage houses tried to gain a foothold in Canada but failed because the entrenched Canadian banks and brokerages were too dominant.

At first, Fidelity seemed headed for the same fate. Celebrated at home, it was almost unknown in Canada. It was weak in Canadian equities and few Canadians were interested in the foreign funds that were its strength. But it persisted and by the late 1990s was rapidly gaining ground. When the *Globe and Mail* illustrated a story in December 1998 with a drawing that portrayed the mutual fund companies as horses in a race, Investors Group was solidly in the lead, but coming up fast, in sixth place, was Fidelity. The drawing was already out of date a year later; Fidelity by then was in fourth place with $28 billion in assets and still gaining.

Randy Van Der Starren, AGF's advertising genius, refers to mutual funds as "a commoditized category," a fancy way of saying that there isn't much to choose among them. If that's true, if one fund is pretty much the same as another, the key to success is not how good you are at picking stocks but how good you are at selling funds. And that's exactly what the horse race pitting Investors Group against Fidelity and the other contenders is all about. The winner won't be the best investment manager but rather the best distributor.

Of course, there are important differences in mutual funds, especially funds in different categories. But a comparison of two large funds in the same category usually reveals that they have more in common than their managers might care to admit. Take, for example, diversified Canadian equity funds, the core investment of most RRSPs. In the 15 years to the end of 1998, these funds had an average compounded return of 8.9%. Fidelity hadn't been operating in Canada long enough to have a 15-year record, but if it had, its diversified Canadian fund's record would have been about the same as Investors Canadian (8.3%) or Trimark Canadian (10.9%) or AGF Canadian Growth (9.2%).

Distribution is so important to fund companies that they take their portfolio managers away from their work to travel the country meeting the all-important intermediaries. David Picton, who runs the Synergy Momentum Class fund, is one of the brainiest and most successful portfolio managers in Canada. Yet even he told me, as he was about to leave on a cross-country tour, "This business is all about selling." Ron Meade echoes that sentiment. Now that he no longer plays a management role at Altamira, Meade keeps busy as chairman of Investment Planning Counsel (IPC), a financial planning company that sells mutual funds under the Counsel brand. IPC has been growing by buying up small investment dealers around the country. "If financial planners can get together," he says, "the next big money will be made on the distribution side of the business rather than the money management side where the big money has been made in the past. The power will now shift over to the owner of the client."

"Owning" the client is the ambition of every broker and fund-retailing financial planner. What makes client ownership possible is the apparent complexity of mutual funds and of investing in general. High schools should teach the basics of investment but don't; the industry itself has made it seem complicated and forbidding. The ignorance of the average customer gives the middleman great power, comparable to the power wielded by anyone selling a technical product to someone who doesn't understand what she's buying but is convinced she needs it. Many people, for example, feel they need a sound system at home, but hardly anyone knows much about the technical aspects of audio, things like harmonic distortion, impedance, or frequency response. That's why almost every buyer walks out of the store with the equipment the salesperson wanted to sell him.

Same with mutual funds. The power of the salesperson is as old as the industry itself. In 1962, a study by the Wharton School of Finance, commissioned by the U.S. Securities and Exchange Commission (SEC), found that the most important factor affecting sales was not a fund's past performance but how much it paid its salespeople. Human nature being what it is, most salespeople, the Wharton scholars discovered, preferred to sell the fund that paid them the highest commission, regardless of whether that fund was well managed or suitable for the particular client. Bernie Cornfeld became rich because he understood this long before the professors at Wharton ever started their research.

Investors Group and Fidelity are both sold by salespeople who are paid commissions and trailer fees. But there is an important difference. Investors has its own dedicated sales force, 3,800 strong, coast to coast. Until recently, these people sold only Investors Group mutual funds. Fidelity, on the other hand, distributes its funds only through intermediaries, including brokers for large investment firms such as Nesbitt Burns and financial planners, who can sell funds from a variety of companies. There is a third method of distribution, direct to the consumer, for those who prefer not to be "owned" by commissioned salespersons. Direct selling is used by the banks and by a handful of independent companies such as Altamira and Phillips, Hager & North (PH&N). Buying a fund from PH&N is like buying a coat at the manufacturer's warehouse rather than at a retail store: the product is just as good and you get it cheaper because there's no middleman to pay.

The most pressing issue in the industry today is which distribution system will dominate in years to come. Logic would suggest that the times are right for the direct method. The Internet makes it easier than ever to research stocks and funds, and to trade them. Moreover, cutting out the middleman makes the product cheaper. Household names like Dell Computer and L.L. Bean are among the dozens of companies that have prospered by exploiting the consumer's willingness to get good products cheap by cutting out the retailer. Mutual funds are even better suited than computers and clothing for this kind of distribution because they're intangible; nobody has to be home to take delivery. Paul Starita, who thinks direct selling via computer is the wave of the future, points to the rapid growth of on-line investment services and to the fact that the huge baby boom generation is on the verge of retirement, which means they'll have more time to take personal charge of their investments.

Despite these trends, however, what the industry calls the "advice channel" has been growing faster in recent years than the direct channel. The reason is that, while the boomers may be close to retirement, they haven't retired yet. Not only haven't they retired, most of them are in the busiest stage of their lives and don't have time to do their own investment research. And the convenience of using the Internet may have been oversold. Sure, I can switch on my computer and find out which airline is flying when from Toronto to Paris and make my own booking, but it's time-consuming work. Why do it when I can simply place a call to my travel agent, who has all my data and preferences on file, and have her do the work? Doing investment research and decision-making is also hard work, no matter how skilled one is at surfing the Web. Besides, a good financial adviser does more than just sell mutual funds. People need advice on estate planning, on saving for their kids' education, on their taxes. If the adviser can do all that and do it well, maybe he'll earn the fees he's collecting.

A few years ago, it seemed the Investors Group model of the dedicated sales force would disappear. Every company but Investors had disbanded its sales force, and Investors, although it had retained its top position, had been going through some rough years. Recently, though, Investors has rebounded, and one reason is that it finally realized Jim O'Donnell had been right all along: a financial planner has to offer more than one line of funds. So Investors' sales reps can now offer the funds of several other companies as well as those managed by Investors. At the same time, mutual fund dealers such as Ron Meade's IPC and Assante Corp. are starting their own funds. They're becoming manufacturers as well as distributors and, in the process, turning themselves into organizations that look a lot like Investors Group. Jones estimates that 90% of these mutual fund dealerships are run by people who started out at Investors. The insurance companies, which always had their own sales forces, are also now pushing their own brands of mutual funds. So Investors, a company that for the last 15 years has looked like an anachronism, is starting to look like the wave of the future.

Investors Group's 18-storey headquarters on Portage Avenue is the tallest building visible from my Winnipeg hotel. The company owes its prominence in the mutual fund industry to a young American law student, John Tappan, who in 1894 decided that working people needed a way to save money without having to use the banks, which they distrusted and found intimidating. This was an early version of "people's capitalism," and it was a novel idea at a time when it was self-evident that capitalists should own capital and workers should work. What ordinary people needed, Tappan decided, was advice and a systematic way to save. So he invented a financial instrument he called the savings certificate: you commit to invest, say, $15 a month for 15 years and are guaranteed a certain amount at the end of that period.

That was the beginning of the instalment savings contract sold through a sales force. Tappan's company, Investors Syndicate, thrived. Thirty years later it expanded to Canada, which was fertile ground because Canadians, especially western Canadians, were just as distrustful of banks as Americans. A Canadian head office was eventually established in Winnipeg mainly because of its proximity to Minneapolis, where the American parent company was based.

Bob Jones, now enjoying retirement at age 75, led me to an unoccupied corner office on the top floor with a view of the splendid Legislative Building, whose Golden Boy bearing a sheaf of wheat symbolizes the prosperity of the West. Jones is an unassuming man with wavy grey hair and a winning smile, but you can sense the steel under-neath. Anyone who has run Investors Group is battle-hardened, having done combat not only with competitors but also with the members of his own sales force, who are hard people to satisfy.

In the late 1960s, during the heyday of Gerald Tsai, it seemed everybody but Investors Group had a speculative "go-go fund" to sell. The Investors Group reps wanted one too and most of them signed a petition demanding it. "This is the jet age and we're still flying with propellers," one of them told a sales conference. Jones and the other investment managers refused to dabble in high-risk stocks. They were eventually proven right when the go-go funds plunged in 1969, the start of a long bear market. Still, the sales force never stops demanding an expanded range of products to sell. Jones recalls a sales meeting in 1978 at which one salesman took the podium and gave the company six months to get its act together "or else." Jones proceeded to the podium and invited the disgrun-tled fellow to his office, where he said he'd be happy to receive his written resignation.

Jones fondly recalls his monthly overnight trips to Minneapolis on the Great Northern Railway as a young Investors employee. The highlight was the opening of the bar as soon as the train reached the U.S. border. The trips were necessary because Jones, who had a uni-versity degree in commerce, had been hired to manage mutual funds, something he knew little about. To educate him and other members of its staff, the company brought in an economist from Chicago, John Langum, for monthly briefings. It was the early 1950s and "it was pretty easy to make money in equities because everything was booming, especially resources," recalls Jones. "There was very little securities analysis. It was pretty rudimentary."

Today, for example, someone doing Jones's job would have a "target price" for a stock he owned, a price that his analysis showed the stock should reach within, say, one year. Jones had never heard of that concept until, on one of his visits to Minneapolis, an American counterpart asked him his target price for a stock he was planning to buy. "I had no idea of a target price," he recalls. "I just thought it was going to go up." But he was a shrewd investor nonetheless. Jones was so good at extracting every last ounce of information from a balance sheet in an annual report that sometimes the managers he was visiting thought he had gained access to their private books.

The buyers of Jones's mutual funds were the same people who had bought Investors savings certificates, including farmers all over the prairies. "When we went into mutual funds," he says, "the farmers understood, because they were in the risk business themselves." The nature of risk, of course, is that sometimes you lose. During the losing times the people who bear the brunt of customer disillusion are the sales representatives. In those days, the reps had to talk customers into accepting a front-end commission of 8.5% (of which they kept over half). That made the customers all the more dissatisfied when the market failed to perform.

When that happened, the reps felt like going into hiding, as a lot of them did during the dark days (for the stock market) of the 1970s. Interest rates were sky-high, the market was in the doldrums, and nobody wanted to buy mutual funds, so two-thirds of Investors' sales force decided they were in the wrong business and quit. The ones who remained must often have regretted their decision. Jones recalls: "Some of our salesmen, walking down the street, would see a client coming and cross the street because they couldn't take the punishment."

The real story of Investors Group isn't at the Winnipeg head office. It's in Moncton and Nanaimo and Kingston and hundreds of other cities and towns where the ubiquitous Investors salespeople work. Pat Lumbers plies his trade in Toronto. He looks like a linebacker, which is fitting since an uncle, Leonard Lumbers, once owned the Toronto Argonauts. Lumbers worked for a major accounting firm before joining Investors Group in 1988. He's what the industry calls a "big producer," with almost 600 clients who have entrusted him with nearly $50 million. In 1999, Lumbers's commissions and trailer fees brought in gross income of $320,000. That was shared with a part-time associate and two assistants, but there's enough left over, he says, "to keep the wolves at bay."

A friend of mine put me in touch with Lumbers. "You must talk to Patrick," she said one evening after perhaps one martini too many. "I had $35,000 and I gave it to Patrick and now it's $500,000. He's a wonderful man." She had been put in touch with Lumbers by a psychologist friend who credits Lumbers with making it possible for her to finance the education of her three children in American universities.

It's people like Lumbers – the middlemen – who have made Investors the industry leader. Lumbers gives an impression of solidity, wearing a dark suit and a white shirt on his financial house calls and carrying a serious black briefcase bulging with documents. One of the lessons Investors learned during the terrible 1970s is that if your sales representative only sells mutual funds, you're in trouble, because there are going to be periods when hardly anyone wants to invest in mutual funds. The modern sales representative, to succeed over time, has to be a professional financial adviser, able to offer advice on everything to do with money. That means getting involved in some sensitive issues.

"Money is the most personal thing," says Lumbers. "When someone wants to get divorced, I always say, 'Don't do it, it's too expensive, you can't afford it.' They come back and say they have to get divorced, the marriage is untenable. And they usually want to change their job and sell their house too. That's too much all at once. So you get them focused back in. 'If you're going to do this, maybe you should sell the house first, then get a separation agreement. Don't move cities, because your friends are here. You're going to have a lot of stress.' Yesterday I spent two hours dealing with that sort of thing."

Starting an account with Lumbers is a more time-consuming affair than signing on with a new family doctor. Usually, there are at least two meetings before a new client agrees to set up an account or the two of them decide they weren't meant for each other. The first thing Lumbers wants to see is your tax return. If you won't show it to him, you can get your mutual funds someplace else. "There is so much information on a tax return, it's almost as good as a financial review," he says. "For example, if someone has Canada Savings Bonds, you know either this person is poorly invested or they are very, very conservative." He'll ask you how much your house is insured for. If the premium is $1,500 and a glance around tells him the premium should be only $800, he knows you've got valuable stuff in the house. All this is part of his "personal financial review." Do you have a will? Dependants? What estate planning have you done? Have you set up testamentary trusts? Maybe you're looking after a 95-year-old grandmother or you've got two kids in private school. It's all grist for Lumbers's mill. "Some people say, 'I'm only investing $10,000,' but you still need to know everything. If you don't do a comprehensive job, it will come back to haunt you later. There's no quick answer."

If you do sign on with Lumbers and you prosper together, he'll treat you well. My friend (we'll call her Sarah – she doesn't want the world to know how wealthy Patrick has made her) was one of 80 people Lumbers and his associate treated to dinner at North 44°, one of Toronto's best restaurants (whose owner and chef, Mark MacEwan, is an Investors client). The dinner, with seven wines, cost $100 a person. "My clients are worth that," says Lumbers. "They're more than worth it." The company thinks its sales reps deserve first-class treatment as well. The biggest producers were chauffeured to the 1999 annual meeting in Winnipeg in white stretch limousines.

I looked at Sarah's statements to see for myself how well she's done. In fact, she had come to Lumbers in 1994 with $75,000 in an RRSP and $59,000 in unregistered savings, a total of $134,000. Since then she has been depositing about $16,000 a year, or $80,000, for a total amount placed under Patrick's management of $214,000. The bottom line on Sarah's Investors Group statement as of June 30, 1999, was $500,874, more than twice what she put in, which explains why she is a satisfied customer. Of course, it helped that she put her trust in Patrick during the greatest bull market in history. He put her money in stock funds, and stocks have been going up. One of the funds, Investors Science and Technology, went up more than 100% in 1999.

Still, Sarah's success shouldn't be minimized. Other people have lost money or made much less during the same period. They might have had too much in a fund that was going through a bad patch or been stuck in one of the oversized Canadian equity funds (including some run by Investors) that are chronic underperformers. Or they might have been overexposed to Asia when the Asian markets tanked. Or they might have fallen into the hands of a dishonest adviser like Linden Dornford, a Toronto mutual fund dealer who, in 1995 and 1996, took $365,000 that clients had entrusted to him for investments and used it for other purposes. Or perhaps they fell prey to an adviser who likes to churn her accounts – unnecessarily selling one fund and then buying another, to the detriment of the client, who gets hit with sales charges, and to the benefit of the salesperson, who earns extra commissions through this otherwise useless activity.

Lumbers is the opposite of a churner. He preaches patience. If Latin American stocks plunge, his clients can be relied upon to call him and say, "Sell." To which Lumbers will reply, "No. Latin America has dropped by 50%, so now it's time to invest more to bring it up to the 1% we had decided it would be."

Some clients just don't get it; they want to revamp their portfolios every three months. Sometimes Lumbers tells them to get lost. Not that he's eager to get rid of clients. In 1996, he was distressed to lose an 88-year-old man who had been with Investors since 1957 and had $500,000 in three funds. He had made capital gains of $150,000 on each of the funds which would be taxed if he sold them, which was exactly what the man's accountant persuaded him to do. "I don't know if his accountant was on the take. He had made 14.8% [annual compound interest] over his life with Investors Group. I wish all my clients made that. I felt badly that the person was getting bad advice."

Lumbers has owned stocks since he was four. As a boy, he used the money he earned caddying to buy shares of Spar Aerospace and Velcro. He is a believer that investing in stocks is the best way to build wealth, but of course he can't guarantee that it will always work, especially in the short term. One recent client is a 54-year-old woman with very little in the way of assets. She doesn't own a house and earns $43,000 a year. She had only $25,000 in her RRSP and said to Lumbers, "I'm going to retire in 10 years – what do I need to do?"

What she needs to do is invest $500 a month and hope like hell the stock market goes up. Although conventional wisdom says you reduce reliance on equities as you approach retirement, she doesn't have time to take a balanced approach. "I'm going to put her in equities because I don't have a choice," says Lumbers. "But if the market is in a downturn for 10 years, she's going to be in trouble."

Lumbers sells annuities, insurance, and GICs as well as mutual funds. He also offers advice. When Sarah's employer, as part of a cost-cutting campaign, offered senior employees a buyout, Lumbers urged her to take it even though she would have less money to invest. He helped find summer jobs for her kids. When she was going on a long trip, he gave her no peace until she had updated her will. He recommended a lawyer and also got her an accountant. When she receives a cheque in U.S. dollars, he drops by to pick it up and deposits it directly into a U.S. dollar fund so she doesn't have to pay exchange. The standard trailer fee in the industry is 0.5%, but because Investors covers its reps' office expenses it pays less, 0.33%. So Lumbers's trailer fee (Investors calls it a "retention bonus") on her account for 1999 worked out to around $1,600. "It's not enough," says Sarah, who has such faith in him that she's given him authority to make changes in her portfolio. Her knowledge of investing is limited, but she does examine her statement four times a year. "I just look at the bottom line and it's such a nice round number."

Lumbers wouldn't want Sarah to become one of those people who love having that "nice round number" so much that they're loath to spend it. He has clients, older people who lived through the Great Depression, who have accumulated a lot of money but refuse to use it for their own enjoyment. Lumbers thinks there's too much emphasis in our society on money as an end in itself. "Listen to the ads on TV – everybody's talking about money. My kids talk about money. I'm a little sick and tired of money. Money is only something that's there. Your most important thing is your health. Second is your family. Third, in order to have the things you want, is money."

Sick as he might be of money, Lumbers is well qualified to manage it (in addition to the accounting, he's a certified financial planner). He also has experience, which he thinks is most important of all. "The first five years are just learning. When you're looking for a financial adviser, you want someone with 10 years' experience." Buyer beware is an important philosophy no matter what one is shopping for, of course, but nowhere more important than in the field of financial advice. It's not legal to set up in business as a doctor, lawyer, or accountant unless you have legitimate training and credentials in those fields. Anyone can rent an office and put out a sign proclaiming himself a financial planner, even if he doesn't know how many cents there are in a dollar. A broker has to pass the Canadian securities course; a financial planner doesn't. That will start to change in 2001. The Canadian Securities Administrators, which groups together provincial securities regulators, is developing an exam that anyone planning to call himself a financial planner will have to pass. Those already in the business will have three years to take the exam.

Such reforms will increase the likelihood that those giving financial advice know what they're talking about, but they won't fix the other problem that applies to advisers like Pat Lumbers. It's that Sarah doesn't pay him, Investors Group does. It's the same for most sellers of mutual funds. They like to consider themselves professionals, offering expert advice to their clients, as an accountant or a lawyer does. But the customer pays the lawyer or accountant directly. She doesn't pay the financial adviser directly, which means the adviser may have divided loyalties.

This is less of an issue with someone like Lumbers who represents a particular mutual fund company; his clients could have no doubt that he'll be disposed to put their money into Investors Group mutual funds. But what about the large majority of planners and brokers who present themselves as independent advisers? Suppose, for example, one of them decided that mutual funds are a bad way to invest because commissions, fees, and trading costs eat away too much of investors' returns. Or suppose he decided the market was about to crash, a crash so brutal and enduring as to invalidate the buy-and-hold philosophy and to require that all money be taken out of stocks and placed in safer havens. Most of the adviser's income is paid by mutual fund companies in the form of sales commissions and trailer fees. If he acted on his own convictions in either of these cases, he'd be impoverishing himself. A few advisers work for fees paid by their clients and could thus take clients' money out of equity mutual funds without slashing their own incomes. But most are, first and foremost, sellers of a product. Just as a vacuum cleaner salesman who became disillusioned with his product would have no option but to look for another occupation, so would a financial adviser who lost faith in mutual funds.

Many consumers don't understand that their financial adviser lives off fees received directly from the companies he's put their money into. Not surprisingly, the adviser will not want to put money into the funds of a company like Phillips, Hager & North, even though its funds are consistent performers with low management fees. That's because PH&N doesn't pay commissions or trailer fees; the adviser doesn't earn a penny by putting your money into one of its funds.

Despite this inherent conflict of interest, many advisers work hard for their clients and achieve excellent results. There are even some who stick up for clients even if it means biting the hand that feeds them. George Slutchuk (he pronounces it "Slewchuk") operates on Investors Group's Winnipeg home turf, but he doesn't work for them or for any other fund company. He has his own company, JGS Financial Planning Services Ltd., and manages between $50 million and $75 million, which would generate annual trailer fees of between $250,000 and $375,000 in addition to the 5% commissions he earns when he buys mutual fund units on behalf of his clients.

In 1997, Slutchuk put $600,000 belonging to 41 clients into a new American stock fund called Templeton Beacon. He chose this fund for one reason: it was managed by Michael Price, a big name in financial circles south of the border, where he is considered a top stock-picker. Templeton, he points out, sold the fund on the basis of Price's reputation, and Price was front and centre on the company's promotional materials. But Price left after only 18 months, and Templeton replaced him with an anonymous team of managers. "I didn't buy it because it was managed by a team, I bought specifically because of Michael Price," Slutchuk told me. He had taken the fund company at its word and bought an "investment product," a Price-managed fund; now the fund company was changing the product. The Coca-Cola company will always put Coke in its bottles, but a fund company will promise you Coke and then deliver a house brand – then expect you to drink it, whether you like it or not.

The same thing happened in 1996 to investors who bought the Fidelity True North Fund in response to a Fidelity ad blitz featuring its star manager Veronika Hirsch, who left after she ran afoul of the securities regulators. In that case, Fidelity gave refunds to those who wanted them and waived the deferred sales charges. Templeton refused to do the same for Slutchuk's clients. "There are no similarities between the departures of [Price and Hirsch] that would warrant us paying out the deferred sales charge," Tim Hague, Templeton's vice-president of marketing, told the *Winnipeg Free Press*. In a conference call with senior Templeton executives, Slutchuk was told he should have faith in Templeton because it is an old and respected company. Slutchuk replied that he wasn't buying the old and respected Templeton product, he was buying the new Michael Price product. Templeton offered to transfer his clients' money to any of its other funds. Slutchuk pulled the money out, paying about $30,000 in redemption charges himself, roughly what he'd earned in commissions when he bought into the Price fund in the first place.

Slutchuk doesn't feel beholden to any company and will not hesitate to move a client out of one. He does rely on mutual funds for his income, though, so he would be unlikely to move clients entirely into other investments, such as index participation units or individual stocks, since these would give him no ongoing income. That doesn't bother him because he's a fan of mutual funds, which he calls "the greatest invention for investing money for most people."

It bothers some critics of the industry, who urge that other ways be found of compensating advisers. A word that often comes up in discussions of how to improve the Canadian mutual fund industry is "unbundling" – separating the cost of advice from the cost of fund management. Why should payments to intermediaries, whose services may not even be required, be embedded in the cost of buying and owning funds? There's a wide choice of guidebooks to mutual funds, as well as a huge amount of information on them in daily newspapers, in specialized financial publications, and on-line. Many Canadians, having done their own research, may want to invest in a fund offered by a company that sells only through intermediaries, such as Fidelity, Mackenzie, or AIC. They're free to call a broker and place an order. But if they do, they'll be paying that broker every year for as long as the money is left in the fund for advice they neither sought nor obtained. These trailer fees range from 0.25% to 1%, depending on whether the investor chose the back-end or front-end load option. Trailer fees are especially important to consider for RRSP investors and others investing for the long haul because funds that pay them must charge higher MERs. As a rule of thumb, each percentage point of management expense ratio will reduce your money by 20% over 20 years.

Clearly, it would be better if the adviser were not paid by the fund company at all. How then would she be compensated for her advisory services? The client could pay her for her time, as he pays a lawyer or an accountant. Some financial planners already work this way, charging a fee for advising the client and designing a portfolio. If the client needs more help later, the adviser turns her meter on again, as a lawyer would.

Another system, increasingly popular in the United States among investors who need consistent monitoring of their investments, is to pay the adviser a flat 1% per year of the total portfolio. To make that work, assuming the adviser wanted to put his clients into mutual funds, there would have to be more PH&N-style no-load funds with low MERs devoid of trailer fees because it makes no sense, from the client's point of view, to pay 1% on top of service fees already embedded in funds. But among the many advantages of such a system is that it liberates the adviser entirely from the tyranny of mutual funds. He does not suffer a drop in income if he opts to put clients' money into index participation units or individual stocks. Should he still wish to take advantage of the convenience, diversification, and expert stock-picking offered by funds, he has no incentive to churn and every reason to choose the funds that are best for the client: there's no financial advantage to him in choosing one fund over another. And because the adviser would be paid directly by the client, instead of indirectly by the fund company out of money from the client, there would be no question about who the adviser was working for. This sort of change, much to be desired, will probably grow out of stiffer competition from on-line investment services and increased sophistication and knowledge on the part of consumers.

The slow process of reform, aimed at putting the interests of investors first, is already under way. It wasn't long ago, for example, that fund companies could reward intermediaries with lavish trips to exotic destinations. This sort of inducement, of course, diminished the likelihood that advisers would be objective in their recommendations to clients. After much criticism, the Investment Funds Institute of Canada, the industry association, decreed in 1996 that sales seminars must be held in continental North America and that participants must pay their own way.

That's why, when a Toronto financial planner named Rudi Carter travelled to Boston in 1999 to attend the Face to Face with Fidelity program, he paid his own travel and hotel expenses. The program includes attendance at the Fidelity Institute, which provides courses for financial advisers, updating them on the latest thinking and technology for running their practices. Then there are meetings with the managers who run Fidelity's Canadian equity funds out of Boston. Fidelity brings about 300 Canadian fund retailers to Boston every year as part of this program. Canadian companies such as Mackenzie and Trimark also run such courses, which count as part of the 30 hours of education that certified financial planners are required to take each year.

Paying your own way for courses in Boston is a far cry from travelling free to golf and lie on the beach in Maui, the sort of trip that fund companies used to offer friendly retailers. Still, it does help Fidelity in its strategy of building close relationships with the advisers who are their link to customers. "We're getting pitched all the time," says Carter, a partner in Financial Concept Group, a unit of Assante Corp. "Everybody's coming knocking on our doors and taking us for lunch, so just because we get pitched doesn't mean we're going to sell someone's fund." But is he more likely to recommend Fidelity as a result of the trip to Boston?

"I don't think there's any doubt. I was very impressed. I just felt they were so rigorous in their investment management. What really impressed me is how much they know about Canada. They have more people in Boston working on Canada than fund companies based in Canada do."

If John Vivash, who launched Fidelity in Canada in 1987, had had his way, Carter would never have been invited to Boston because Vivash, who thinks commissions and trailer fees are bad for investors, was intent on running Fidelity as a direct-to-the-consumer operation. In the United States, Fidelity is mainly a direct seller (although it also makes its funds available through advisers). And Fidelity funds in the States, like most American mutual funds, have lower fees than Canadian funds. "The big apprehension in the industry has been that either the banks or Americans like Fidelity would clean our clocks by having very low fees," Bob Jones of Investors Group told me. Ironically, Fidelity is cleaning a few clocks in Canada despite MERs that are about the same as the rest of the industry's. It's doing so because of the power of its brand and its success in winning the confidence of people like Carter.

Vivash is an innovator who likes to start things and then move on to start something else. He also likes to rock the boat. That was why, in the early 1990s when he was running the mutual fund arm of CIBC, he and Paul Starita, who was then at Royal Trust, decided that mutual fund units should be listed on a stock exchange instead of the current system in which they are bought from the issuer, either directly or through an intermediary. Such a change would make sales charges transparent, thereby increasing pressure to bring them down.

The intermediaries hated Vivash's idea, of course, because they love the deferred sales charge. It gives them a fat commission the client doesn't know about. Obviously, it's easier to keep sales charges high if they're hidden. That's also why bonds, which are sold on exchanges in some countries, are not listed on Canadian exchanges. Vivash says the big problem with mutual funds in Canada, now as when he was launching Fidelity, is that investors simply don't understand how much they're paying for them. "Why should you pay somebody a large commission to invest your money in a mutual fund which is going to charge another 3% to manage your money?" he asks. "It's just ludicrous." If the units were listed on the exchange, "you wouldn't pay any more to trade them than any $10 stock. So you could go to a discount broker and buy fund units for $30 to $40 a trade. And if you did that, why would you agree to pay a trailer fee? What ongoing service does the discount broker provide? Zero."

The Toronto Stock Exchange wanted nothing to do with Vivash's idea. The Montreal Stock Exchange was interested, though in the end nothing came of it. Still, having such a radical proposal on the table did serve one purpose: it made the competition nervous. Vivash's business philosophy is, he says, the same as that of the Quebec separatists: keep the opposition off balance. "That's why we put it forward. If it didn't work – well, it didn't work. None of the industry was in favour of it because it would have upset their distribution channel. The first question they ask when you come to them with a new idea is 'What will it do to my distribution channel?' Because they rent that channel, they don't own it."

Vivash was overruled in his desire to sell Fidelity funds direct to the consumer in Canada by senior executives in London, headquarters of Fidelity's international operations. Vivash's plan would have been best for investors, but would it have been best for Fidelity? Probably not. Then as now, the advice channel was where most of the action was in Canada. It was going to be hard enough to launch a foreign investment company without bucking the established distribution system as well.

Fidelity did have one advantage that no other American fund company would have had: name recognition. Anybody who had ever tuned in *Wall Street Week* or looked at the business section while on holiday in the United States had heard of Peter Lynch and his amazing success as manager of the Fidelity Magellan Fund. Just as some Americans on holiday in Canada take home Cuban cigars, a few Canadians in the United States had brought home the Fidelity Magellan Fund (which, like all foreign mutual funds, can't legally be sold in Canada). That was why, when Vivash spoke to a group of 300 people in southern Ontario just after opening for business, he discovered to his amazement that 30 of them already owned Fidelity funds they had bought in the States.

But the extent of that name recognition should not be exaggerated. In fact, Brian Henderson, Fidelity's marketing chief today, thinks Vivash encountered an unusual group of people. It surprises him that anybody in Canada had heard of Fidelity back in 1987, because six years after that he attended focus groups "with people who had $60,000 in Fidelity funds and had no idea what they owned – they didn't even know it was Fidelity their broker had just put them in." That explains as well as anything why fund companies love the intermediaries so much and why distribution is as important to them as investment management. It's because the intermediaries do amazing tricks such as raking in large amounts for Fidelity to manage from investors so clueless they've not heard of Fidelity even *after* it has their money.

I asked Starita why Fidelity had done so well in accumulating Canadian assets whereas Scudder, a direct-to-the-consumer firm, has limped along since it arrived in Canada from the United States in 1995, despite lower fees than Fidelity's and generally excellent performance. "That's easy," Starita said. "Fidelity has the best sales management in the industry, coupled with a recognizable brand and decent performance. Scudder was the sophisticated investors' product in the U.S. They never had to advertise. Scudder is a great old company and it has great performance. But that's not enough." In other words, decent performance plus great salesmanship adds up to success in the mutual fund business in Canada; great performance without salesmanship adds up to failure. Scudder ran ads pointing out that, by buying direct, investors could save money. But who did they expect to respond to those ads? Mr. Clueless, who's never even heard of the fund company that has his money? He's leaving all the decision-making to his broker. His broker wasn't going to call Scudder for him, because Scudder wasn't paying commissions.

Scudder's mistake was to overestimate the size of the well-informed-investor population. Fidelity does not make that mistake. It sells to the mass market, and it understands that the mass market is not sophisticated. In such an environment, the adviser channel is bound to be more lucrative than the direct channel. Distribution is important to all industries that sell mass-market products. There wouldn't be much of an oil industry without service stations to distribute its products. But imagine how much more important the distributors would be if most people didn't understand gasoline and weren't sure their cars needed it. If people needed to be educated and persuaded to try gasoline and to keep using it, the oil companies might well be sending service station owners on all-expenses-paid trips to Maui.

Fidelity, despite making the right choice about distribution, was not an overnight success. It chose an awkward time to start – October 19, 1987, also known as Black Monday, the day stock markets suffered their worst one-day percentage plunge ever, thereby scaring nervous investors away from mutual funds. Two years after Vivash had launched the Canadian operation, Fidelity had a measly $60 million under management. Things were so bad there was talk in Boston about pulling out of what seemed like inhospitable territory.

Fidelity's big problem was the one that caused Scudder grief a few years later: most Canadians make their mutual fund investments in their RRSPs, and the government says that most of those investments must be Canadian. (For years, the foreign limit both in individual RRSP accounts and in equity funds was 20%. It was raised to 25% for 2000 and will rise again to 30% in 2001.) Both Fidelity and Scudder were new to Canada and had no credibility in Canadian equities. To try to jump-start its Canadian equity effort, Fidelity transgressed its own policy – it recruited and promoted a star. Not that Fidelity has never had stars: in the 1960s, remember, Fidelity's Gerald Tsai became the first celebrity manager, and Peter Lynch later became the greatest mutual fund star ever. But they are the exceptions; the company's policy has long been to advertise its overall operation as the biggest and best in the world rather than to promote individual managers.

That policy was bypassed in 1996 when Vivash's successor as president of Fidelity Canada, Kevin Kelly, lured Veronika Hirsch away from AGF to manage the True North Fund. At the time, it seemed like a brilliant coup. Hirsch had been at AGF for only 10 months and the company had featured her in its $3-million RRSP-season ad campaign. The theme was Veronika's Secrets, a spin on Victoria's Secrets, the mail-order lingerie firm. In her short stay at AGF, she doubled the assets of the AGF Canadian Equity Fund and outperformed the TSE 300. AGF had made Hirsch a household name and now, or so it seemed, Fidelity could reap the benefits. She was getting $150,000 a year at AGF and had received a performance bonus of $75,000. Fidelity offered her a lot more and created a new fund, True North, for her to manage. It seemed a good plan until she got in trouble with securities officials over her personal investments. When the story broke, just weeks after she arrived at Fidelity, Hirsch was taken off True North. She later left the company.

David Denison, the current president of Fidelity Canada, looks pained when I raise the subject of Hirsch. He seems like a nice guy, so I acknowledge that he wasn't president then. He won't take the easy way out. "Veronika was in my time," he says. "Recruiting a star as opposed to grooming someone from within the organization [both Tsai and Lynch had been trained by Fidelity before emerging as stars] was a very big change for Fidelity. It was not the way we typically would handle a manager assignment, and I can say that it is not the way we will do it again. I think we've learned there is tremendous value in the way Fidelity has grown its portfolio managers. It takes time and patience but it's the way we will go. When you choose Fidelity, you're choosing a big organization and a consistent way of managing money and deep resources. If somebody does move off one of our funds, it's not 'Oh my God, what is Fidelity going to do now? That was a great person, that was the only reason I was owning the fund, should I sell?' In Fidelity that's not a big event." But he won't say Fidelity was wrong to hire Hirsch. After all, it couldn't have known she'd get in trouble for something she had done while working for someone else. "There were good reasons for us to do that in the Canadian market at that time. But it didn't turn out the way we wanted."

Had it not been for the 80% Canadian content rule, Fidelity probably never would have recruited Hirsch because Canadian equities wouldn't have been so all-important and there wouldn't have been the same sense of urgency. After she left, Fidelity went back to basics. It turned the fund over to one of its own Boston-based managers, Alan Radlo, an American, who was already managing a Canadian small-cap fund. He has managed True North ever since, keeping it in the second or first quartile of Canadian equity funds at all times while its assets have swelled to $1.6 billion. If Hirsch had stayed and achieved the same results, she would have remained a star and been hailed as a genius. Radlo, meanwhile, toils in obscurity, which is how Fidelity likes it.

For Denison, the classic replacement scenario occurred when Sally Walden left the Fidelity European Fund, the biggest and arguably the best European fund in Canada. Walden was no celebrity, but those Fidelity investors who take the time to peruse the literature the company sends out would have seen her pictured in annual reports as manager of the fund. She had started as an analyst, graduated to fund manager, and now heads a group of portfolio managers. In 1998 she was replaced by another Fidelity product, Thierry Serero, after the two of them had co-managed Fidelity European for a while. "It was a seamless proposition," Denison says, although so far the fund hasn't performed as well under Serero as it did under his mentor.

The president of Fidelity Canada occupies a windowless office in a downtown Toronto building that was taken over by the growing ranks of Fidelity employees when Bell Canada, trimming its payroll, no longer needed it. Denison is 47 years old and shaped like a pencil. He has the kind of physique those of us who pound the pavements in search of fitness recognize as belonging to a serious long-distance runner. "Do you run marathons?" I asked. He smiled and said that he used to, but with two young kids and the presidency of Fidelity he didn't have time to train for them any more. "I just don't want to make the sacrifice away from family that it takes to run a marathon. There's no way you can do it without having some of those 20-mile training runs on a Saturday or Sunday, and that takes a few hours in itself. And you don't feel that great after running 20 miles when you get home and the kids are jumping on your lap saying, 'Let's go to the beach.'"

Not that he's given up running entirely. "I do six miles a day, first thing in the morning at 5 o'clock. It's the only part of the day that I feel totally in control." Early in 1999, Toronto had an epic snowstorm that shut down the city and caused its excitable mayor to call in the army. The streets and sidewalks were piled with snow for days, which gave most Toronto runners a good excuse to take a break. Not Denison. "At 5 o'clock in the morning you don't have to worry about traffic. If the plow hasn't been there, usually a car or truck has been, and you just run in the tire ruts."

Running in tire ruts on sub-zero Toronto mornings may strike some as an odd hobby, but it shows that Fidelity Canada is led by a methodical and determined man. Still, Fidelity has a long way to go to supplant Investors, which has almost twice Fidelity's total of assets under management. Why did he tell the *Globe and Mail* reporter that Fidelity wanted to be number one?

"It's not very compelling to say we started the year number eight and we really want to be number six. It's obvious when you want a rallying cry that you try to set a stretch target for yourselves as an organization – hence number one. We are part of an organization that is number one in other markets, so we have an institutional view of ourselves as having the capability to achieve number one. It's not a pipe dream."

It would have seemed one in 1987, when Fidelity was struggling out of the gate. That measly $60 million had grown by early 2000 to $28.5 billion in assets under management. In 1999, for the second year in a row, Fidelity led the Canadian industry in net sales. This growth is the result of an early decision not to follow the example of another American company, Templeton, by being a niche player in the Canadian market. Templeton may run the largest single mutual fund in Canada, but Templeton Growth is a foreign stock fund and foreign stocks are Templeton's strength. So strong is Templeton in its chosen specialty that it has become the sixth-largest fund company in Canada, but because it has never been a major player in Canadian stocks it could never overtake Investors as the biggest. Fidelity has an impressive array of foreign funds and could also have built up a big Canadian business as a foreign specialist. But that's not how it got to be the biggest fund company in the world.

"To be really successful in this business you have to be seen as a strong domestic provider," Denison says. "That's something we've worked hard at over the last few years. We've moved from being a niche provider – the foreign company of choice, kind of a Templeton approach – to saying, 'Let's make a very strong commitment to the Canadian dimension of Fidelity and be seen as having terrific capability in Canadian equities.' That's where we've made the huge progress. Three years ago we had 19% of our assets in Canadian funds. Now we're at 43%. That's a big chunk of our growth."

Fidelity has a team of 37 analysts and portfolio managers in Boston working on Canada, including 14 analysts and three portfolio managers who work only on Canadian investments. What are they doing in Boston? Why aren't they in Canada, where they could have a close-up view of the Canadian economy? Because Fidelity thinks it can manage Canadian investments better from Boston than from Toronto.

Denison, a Montreal native, acknowledges that this bothers some Canadians. "But if we have the opportunity to explain to people why we do it that way, or if they actually go down and see how we manage money in Boston, it's no longer an issue, because we believe there's tremendous strength in having that group of people located in one spot. We've got 450 analysts and portfolio managers worldwide, and more than half of them are in Boston. What we get there is a cross-fertilization of ideas. It's a very challenging, fertile environment for people to analyze companies. So there's an oil and gas analyst who concentrates on Canadian companies, but he has the opportunity to talk to his counterparts who are covering the U.S. 'Here's the valuation model I'm using – how does that relate to the companies that you're following?' They're right down the hall, so they can have these conversations any time. All it means is they have to be in Toronto a fair bit of time [to talk to Toronto-based companies]."

With 5,000 employees, Fidelity is the largest employer in Boston. It generates a lot of business for Logan Airport. Not only are its own staff members flying off in all directions to do research, but a constant stream of senior executives arrive at Fidelity's offices to explain to Fidelity why it should own shares in their companies on behalf of its millions of unitholders. Most publicly traded Canadian companies make the Boston pilgrimage at least once a year, and they don't send just anybody. John Cleghorn, chairman of the Royal Bank, goes; so do Jean Monty of BCE and their counterparts at the other major Canadian companies. They are part of a huge crowd – the heads of about 5,000 companies make the trek each year.

Investors Group is number one in Canada, but it's a pipsqueak compared with Fidelity as a whole. Fidelity's US$1 trillion worth of assets under management worldwide is more than the market value of all the stocks on the TSE 300 index. That vast pool of money is the reason all those company chairmen use their expensive time travelling to Boston. Shareholders want to see shares go up, and that's more likely to happen if Fidelity chooses to own them than if it doesn't. The inevitable result of Fidelity's status as a major shareholder is that its managers gain influence over the operations of many businesses. Speaking to a Berlin audience a few years ago, Klaus Pohle, chief financial officer for Schering, a major German drug manufacturer, described how he made important decisions. "I go to Boston and visit Mrs. Firestone [Karen Firestone, a portfolio manager at Fidelity]," he said. "She tells me what to do."

It would be impossible for a company managing $1 trillion not to be powerful, but Fidelity appears to make an honest effort not to throw its weight around. As one of the largest shareholders in Air Canada, for example, it could have played an important role in the battle for control that followed the offer by Onex Corp. in August 1999 to buy the airline and merge it with Canadian Airlines. Fidelity, through different funds, quietly continued to accumulate Air Canada shares after Gerry Schwartz of Onex made his initial offer. But it took no public stand in favour of Onex's plan or in favour of Air Canada's defensive move, which eventually succeeded, to buy Canadian and merge it with Air Canada.

Fidelity inevitably has large accumulations of many stocks. As of early 2000, for example, it owns 15% of Lions Gate, the Vancouver movie company that is one of Alan Radlo's favourites, and almost 19% of Canwest Global. It can't own that much of Air Canada because a provision in the airline's charter prevents any person or organization from owning more than 10%. Quite apart from Air Canada's own rules, Canadian securities regulations restrict any one fund operator from owning more than 20% of a company's shares and also require that a fund company must file a report to regulators when its stake exceeds 10% of the shares. So when the Air Canada shares in all the Fidelity funds crept over 10% in the heat of the takeover battle, a routine press release was issued stating the fact.

Then Heather Whyte's phone started to ring. Whyte is a former financial journalist who was doing media relations for CIBC before she was lured away to become Fidelity Canada's vice-president of corporate communications. All the reporters who called her thought Fidelity was jumping into the fray, a reasonable assumption since the other major shareholder, the Caisse de dépôt et placement du Québec, had offered $300 million to help Air Canada fend off Onex's bid.

"Is Fidelity supporting Onex?" one reporter wanted to know.

"No," said Whyte.

"Is Fidelity backing Air Canada?" asked another.

"No," said Whyte.

"Why is Fidelity trying to take control of Air Canada?" asked a third.

"It isn't," said Whyte.

All the reporters heard the same story: "We're buying this for investment purposes only, that's what we do. It's not a strategic investment, it's what we do every day." Some Fidelity portfolio managers might have favoured the Air Canada plan, while others might have liked Schwartz's vision of a renewed airline industry under Onex's leadership. The point Whyte made to reporters was that Fidelity makes money for investors by doing research and then letting managers make their own decisions. Individual managers could have been buying, selling, or just holding Air Canada shares during the takeover fight; there was no such thing as an official Fidelity position. At the end of 1999, when the dust had settled, Fidelity still owned 10.2% of Air Canada and said in a filing to securities regulators that, depending on market conditions, its funds might buy more, given that the federal government was planning to raise the limit for any one shareholder to 15%.

It's no accident that Fidelity runs its investment operations from Boston while distribution (and advertising, which is part of distribution) is managed out of Toronto. The Fidelity investment management style, based on intensive research on individual companies, is the same regardless of a company's nationality. Distribution, though, is a local matter, which is why all presidents of Fidelity Canada have been Canadians. Like any successful multinational, Fidelity adapts to each market it enters. But Denison is sensitive to the fact that, because Fidelity chose to distribute through the locally dominant adviser channel when it entered Canada, Canadian consumers pay more to own a Fidelity fund than American consumers do.

The best way to fix that would be to do what John Vivash wanted to do in the first place: cut out the middleman. But there are other ways, says Denison. For example, some discount brokers now sell front-end-load funds with no commissions. (The commission on a front-load fund is negotiable between the seller and buyer. The discounters waive the commission entirely.) They also rebate some of the trailer fees they collect from the fund company to the consumer. "That gets you to the same point as having Fidelity cut the MER from the top," Denison says. Another system would award extra units in the funds to holders of large accounts, in effect cutting their management expenses. "If an investor's portfolio is 15 times bigger, why should he be paying 15 times more?" asks Denison. "Is his adviser doing 15 times more work?" In the United States, Fidelity has one set of funds with lower MERs for direct buyers and another with higher MERs for those who buy from intermediaries. Scudder has adopted this system in Canada. But Canada already has more than 3,000 mutual funds, far more per capita than the United States. "Do we want the universe of funds in Canada to be 6,000?" protests Denison. "Would that really benefit consumers?"

In the United States, a large part of the market wants to buy mutual funds direct without commissions, so Fidelity facilitates that. And because Americans are several years ahead of Canadians in recognizing the advantages of index funds, Fidelity U.S., for all its stock-picking prowess, now operates index funds as well as managed funds because its clients want them. It will do the same in Canada when

Canadians demand it, because Fidelity's most fundamental policy is not loyalty to financial intermediaries but domination of the marketplace. If, in a few years, millions of retired boomers are managing their own investment portfolios and demanding no-load, low-fee funds, Fidelity will provide them.

Fidelity's success in Canada distributing funds through fee-earning third parties doesn't mean it might not have been successful if it had chosen the direct route. Phillips, Hager & North has proven it can be done. By having very low fees, by refusing to pay a cent to middlemen, and by doing absolutely no advertising, PH&N has become the 16th-largest of 160 fund companies in Canada. I went to see Bob Hager to find out how he and his team have been so successful by being so different. Hager, the chairman, is the last founding member of the firm still in harness. The other two – Art Phillips, the former Vancouver mayor who married the TV star Carole Taylor, and Rudy North – have retired, the standard way to leave PH&N. It must be a good place to work because no manager in the 35-year history of the company has ever left to go somewhere else.

I passed Hager's office a few times during a couple of visits to PH&N; each time, he was staring out the window at the view, which, this being Vancouver, is spectacular. PH&N's office is high up in Waterfront Centre, one of the newer towers overlooking the Coal Harbour waterfront. From this perch, Hager can count the freighters loading lumber and wheat. He can estimate the size of the pile of sulphur waiting to be loaded for export. If there is a lot of snow on the North Shore mountains, he can consider whether Vancouver skiers might go there next weekend instead of driving up to Whistler, and whether that would be bad for the stock price of Intrawest Corp., which owns the ski operations at Whistler. In this way, if you spend a lot of time staring out the window, as Hager seems to, perhaps you can persuade yourself you're doing investment research.

Even if Hager is just daydreaming, there's nothing wrong with that – it's probably to the customer's benefit. Canadian mutual fund fees used to be lower than they are now because they were regulated by the securities commissions. Then, in the early 1980s, fees were deregulated and almost all the companies raised them. PH&N, which had been charging the maximum allowable at the time, didn't. Instead, Hager looked out the window and did nothing. As a result, the PH&N Canadian Equity Fund today has an MER of 1.07% (compared with, say, Fidelity True North's 2.47% or Altamira Equity's 2.36%). The PH&N Bond Fund charges a puny 0.56% (Manulife Cabot Diversified Bond charges 2%, almost four times as much).

These differences are even greater than they might appear because of the impact of compounding. Suppose you invested $10,000 in a fund whose stocks neither increased nor decreased in value after one year. The fund company would remove 2.5% and you'd be left with 97.5% of your original investment. The next year the company would take 2.5% of that 97.5%, and so on. If you stay in a fund for a long time, a lot of your potential earnings are diverted to fees. What's the difference between a PH&N fund and someone else's that has an MER higher by, say, a modest 0.81%? A lot. That difference can reduce the investor's overall return by 10% when it's compounded over 10 years. That's why fees are such a big deal, and why PH&N is so highly thought of by its customers and by experts who follow the industry closely.

Hager is old enough to remember the early days of the industry, the Bernie Cornfeld–style high-pressure sales tactics and the monstrous front-end loads. "On the investment side, it was all straight up," he recalls. "But the guys who sold mutual funds in those days were pretty aggressive. Cornfeld was reflective of a group of people that were selling funds." While Cornfeld was in Europe squiring French models and building IOS into a fund-selling machine, Hager was in Berkeley attending the University of California, working towards his MBA.

In the fall of 1964, the three partners set up PH&N as a pension management firm. To establish a track record to attract pension business, they started a mutual fund, the Phillips, Hager & North Fund, which specialized in American stocks. (It still exists, as the PH&N U.S. Equity Fund.) In its early years, it was sold only to family members and acquaintances. Despite the existence of that fund, PH&N wasn't really in the mutual fund business in the 1960s and 1970s, Hager says, because you needed a sales force to be in the business, and the fledgling firm had no sales force and no desire to have one.

Until the 1980s, it was a truism of the business that funds are sold, not bought. While a Canadian would voluntarily put money in a bank account, she would not put money in a mutual fund unless persuaded to do so by a Russ Isaac or a Pat Lumbers. As the success of Fidelity demonstrates, there's still truth in the truism; most funds still are sold rather than bought. But as the industry matured through the 1990s and Canadians became more knowledgeable about investing, more of them began putting money into funds on their own initiative. That set the stage for the success of PH&N.

Altamira, which had been the biggest direct seller before its troubles, sells itself through advertising and then waits for customers to buy. Because PH&N won't advertise, it has taken consumers longer to find it. How did they do so? Hager credits Gordon Pape, inventor of the mutual fund guidebook, and other journalists. He feels it's no coincidence that PH&N grew into a major player during the same period, the 1990s, in which book and newspaper publishers discovered personal finance. Pape's *Buyer's Guide to Mutual Funds* started in 1990, was a huge success, and spawned several imitators. Pape has long been a PH&N booster, and the 2000 edition of his book names it "fund company of the decade."

It was also during the 1990s that Jonathan Chevreau of the *National Post*, Michael Kane of the *Vancouver Sun*, Rob Carrick of the *Globe and Mail*, and other personal finance columnists began exposing flaws in the mutual fund industry. These writers know the impact of high fees on long-term returns and look approvingly on the handful of low-fee companies – Scudder, Perigee, and Bissett, as well as PH&N. That might explain why Hager was the only person I met while researching the industry who had anything good to say about journalists.

Jerry White, a radio personality and shareholder in Dundee Wealth Management, which owns Infinity Mutual Funds, was more typical of the industry's attitude. I attended a Toronto seminar at which White, who often speaks at events sponsored by mutual fund dealers, described journalists as "penniless bumpkin bozos who work in basements." (I hate to contradict such an eminent authority, but I'm a journalist and my workspace happens to be on the second floor. Pape does work out of his basement, but he's a multimillionaire.) Jim O'Donnell is another who takes a dim view of journalists. "To be writing about the fees all the time is ridiculous," he told me. "Write about the return. It's the reporters who complain about fees. They've got nothing else to write about."

Actually, they've got plenty else to write about, including funds with high fees *and* high returns – the Altamira e-business fund, for example, that returned 188% in its first year of operation with a relatively high MER of 2.79%. Nobody cares how fat the MER is if the net return is 188%, but the e-business fund is in a volatile sector, as investors discovered during the April 2000 correction, and there may be years when it is among the worst performers. You might not mind if you bought in before the fund went up 188%, but for those who bought in late, the high MER will hurt.

PH&N doesn't have an e-business fund and probably never will because it is not an innovator. It's a conservative investment manager that knows the North American equity and bond markets and delivers unspectacular, but above-average, returns. Its investment style derives from the fact that it is more of a pension fund manager than a mutual fund manager, and its big clients don't want undue risks taken with their employees' pension money. Despite the growth of its mutual fund business, PH&N still has more money in pensions and in pooled accounts for large investors than in public mutual funds. But all the money is managed in the same way, and the stocks in the PH&N Canadian Equity Fund are the same as those in the firm's corporate pension funds. "We don't make any big bets," says Hager. "So we are very seldom superstars but we seldom get into the glue either. Our aim is to be a second-quartile performer, minimum, all the time, or above median all the time, and if you do that over a long period, you end up in the top quartile. If nothing else we win by 1% just on the fees. That's a huge head start."

This may explain why Hager seems so relaxed, staring out the window doing investment research by checking which oil company's floating gas station in the harbour is getting the most business from passing boats. Not only does he not have to worry about middlemen, he has a major advantage when it comes to investment performance. Tom Bradley, PH&N's president, explains it this way: "Look at Bob Krembil," he says, referring to the respected portfolio manager who co-founded Trimark. Because it pays brokers and planners and runs expensive advertising campaigns, Trimark has to have higher fees than PH&N. "I think Bob Krembil is a terrific investor. But is he 1.5% smarter than we are over 10 years? He may be smarter, he may not be, but 1.5% is a lot. To earn our fee, we have to beat the TSE by 1%. He's got to beat it by 2.5%."

When I talked with Bradley, PH&N hadn't yet joined the rush to offer an RRSP-eligible clone fund to allow RRSP customers to bypass the foreign investment restriction. They have since launched one, though at the time Bradley wasn't sure something that exotic was PH&N's style. "But even if you don't think it's such a hot idea," I asked Bradley, "why wouldn't you do it just as a matter of good marketing?"

Bradley looked at me sternly. "Marketing?" There was a pause. "Marketing?" he repeated.

I decided to be helpful. "It means advertising and selling the, uh, product," I explained.

"I know what it means. But we don't do that here."

PH&N will happily manage your money but, he says, has no plans to advertise and otherwise behave like a "consumer products company." So how does PH&N get its products out to customers? One way is through brokers and planners who distribute PH&N funds free to keep some of their clients, who are Gordon Pape fans, happy. Then there are those of Pape's readers who don't bother with brokers and just send a cheque directly to PH&N. There's also the brother-in-law method. "We sell through referral," says Bradley. "You tell your brother-in-law about us." This only works if the brother-in-law has at least $25,000 to invest, the minimum to start an account. Dispensing with small accounts is another way to keep costs, and management fees, low, and PH&N has no plans to lower the minimum. If anything, it will increase it and let Fidelity and Investors Group look after the poor brothers-in-law.

PH&N's distribution model is Vanguard, the American company that has the lowest fees in the business and does almost no advertising. *Forbes* magazine called Vanguard a "low-cost religion" because its customers are so loyal. While the two companies have opposite investment management styles (Vanguard believes in indexing while PH&N believes in stock-picking), they both appeal to sophisticated, cost-conscious consumers. Bradley says PH&N customers have told him they like it that they never see a PH&N ad. When these customers watched Trimark's clever 1999 ad campaign showing herds of sheep walking in one direction while Trimark's independent thinkers went in the other, they could reflect happily on the fact that, as PH&N customers, no acting fees for sheep were being subtracted from their investments.

"Vanguard has proven that without any marketing you can become a brand by doing it the right way," says Bradley. That way means doing what mutual funds were invented to do: providing professional money management to the small investor as efficiently as possible. There is no sales pitch, no hype, and only 12 funds compared with Investors' 70 or Fidelity's 27. But it's not true, as some resentful financial planners would have it, that no-load means no service. PH&N provides trained financial planners to help its clients plan their investment portfolios. The hardest work these PH&N advisers have to do is with new clients who arrive with messed-up portfolios. "There's a lot of bad product out there," says Bradley. "In a way, that's our marketing campaign because we get a lot of disaffected people. Maybe their broker churned their account or they had 20 mutual funds at Dominion Securities or Nesbitt. Or they bought a whole bunch of DSC funds that they can't sell. We get a lot of those clients, and our advisers have to wade through all that."

I wondered why I hadn't seen such blunt talk in the literature PH&N sends to clients and prospective clients. "It's the culture," Bradley says. "Bob [Hager] is a low-key guy. He still manages pensions, and low-key works there." It also seems to work on the fund side, as the growth of PH&N's funds through the 1990s proves. Maybe it could work even better if the company were less self-effacing. Not that they are going to open storefront offices like

Altamira, or put Bob Hager on television, but Bradley does say he's instructed the advisers to be more outspoken when people phone in. "Up to now they have been quite low-key, letting the callers make up their own minds."

Bradley is low-key and soft-spoken himself, but he says things that are radical by industry standards. Just as most fund companies don't appreciate newspaper columnists who put the interests of their readers above those of the fund industry, they also don't much like the views of Glorianne Stromberg, a former member of the Ontario Securities Commission who wrote two reports criticizing the industry for exploiting ignorant investors. Bradley, though, is a fan, partly no doubt because criticisms like Stromberg's drive a lot of investors to companies like PH&N. "Stromberg hit it on the head," he enthuses. "The knowledge level of the people who are consuming the industry's product is so low. And that lack of knowledge gives the industry an ability to do things that aren't good for consumers. If there's a fee that you can bury somewhere, whether it's a bank or a mutual fund company or an insurance company, they'll do it. That's where we've been different."

Another way in which PH&N is different is in its system of investment management. Most companies have portfolio managers who rely on analysts, either in-house or working for brokerage firms, for advice on potential investments. PH&N's analysts are also its investment managers. So Dale Harrison, for example, the financial services industry analyst, makes the call on what banks and insurance companies to include in the Canadian Equity Fund. He doesn't need anyone else's approval (although stock buys are always discussed with other members of the team). Harrison, a 31-year-old with a history degree, is articulate and personable, potentially good television fodder, but as long as he stays at PH&N he'll never become a celebrity because there are no celebrities at PH&N.

If PH&N were going to promote a star (perish the thought), it would probably choose Ian Mottershead, whose Vintage Fund was the only equity fund in Canada to beat the TSE 300 index's return every year from 1994 to 1998. The fund, now closed to new investors, was named after Mottershead's passion for great wine, reflected in posters of vineyards and empty bottles of Château d'Yquem and other great wines on display in his office. This office doesn't have a view and, since views are a status symbol in Vancouver, Mottershead is sensitive about it and raises the subject himself. "I can't work next to a big window because I'm afraid of heights, you see." He's an expert on natural resources and given to such statements as "The Western Sedimentary Basin is gas-prone." He comes across more like an eccentric academic than like a button-down investment guy, but he's one of the shrewdest managers in the business. He likes natural gas companies because they are a "multi-year play. That is very much the kind of thing this firm is interested in. Multi-year, longer-term investments in top companies."

Mottershead is 58, ancient by industry standards, and speaks with a hint of Wales, where he was born and raised before moving to Vancouver at age 15. He went to Royal Military College, where he studied math, physics, economics, and political science before serving overseas in the Canadian Navy. He gets some of his best ideas not from annual reports but from offbeat stories in magazines like the *New Yorker*. He'd be great on TV, walking in the opposite direction from a herd of sheep, but it will never happen.

All the managers at PH&N are getting rich doing business exactly the way they want to – managing money, not distributing product. Nobody's head rolls if no new clients join up because it's nobody's job to recruit clients. "We don't feel a growth imperative," says Bradley. "If we do 2% better than the TSE and S&P, even if we add no new clients, we're delighted."

You have to hang around the fund industry for a year or two to understand how rare those words are. Most of the industry lives and breathes distribution. Here, for example, is Jean-Guy Gourdeau, senior vice-president of Investors Group: "We always viewed mutual funds in terms of how do we pursue distribution effectively." He's speaking for most fund operators.

For PH&N, however, investment management is everything, distribution nothing. Build a good fund, Hager and company believe, and the clients will come. If you can pull it off, it's the best distribution system of all.

CHAPTER FOUR

THE MYSTERIOUS ART OF INVESTMENT MANAGEMENT

Some visitors to the headquarters of AIC Ltd. are impressed by the acres of beautiful grounds whose lawns, flowers, and evergreens are meticulously groomed by a battalion of gardeners. Others are struck by the helicopter pad or the fish ponds or the animal statues gushing water or the elegant lobby with its gleaming marble floors and imposing bookcase holding a complete leather-bound set of the Harvard Classics. What caught my attention were the two parrots lazing in the warmth of the sun streaming into the atrium. The red one was inside his open cage; the green one sat atop his, preening and squawking about something, perhaps the fact that most AIC funds were down yet again that day.

"Never seen parrots before at a mutual fund company," I blurted. The receptionist's expression suggested she was accustomed to goofy comments from first-time visitors. "I knew AIC was different," I added.

"You can wait right over there," she said, gesturing towards a plush sofa. I plunked myself down to await scheduled audiences with two fund managers, Jonathan Wellum and Neil Murdoch, and the big boss himself, chairman and CEO Michael Lee-Chin.

To say AIC is different is to understate the fact. Even its location, in a private 30-acre park, overlooking a freeway in Burlington, Ontario, sets it apart. Most other mutual fund companies – Trimark, for example, 45 kilometres up the freeway in Toronto – operate out of conventional office towers in downtown financial districts and have offices that are comfortable but not lavish.

Michael Lee-Chin, one of nine children of a Jamaican sewing machine salesman, is obviously proud of the opulence his success has created. The fledgling firm he bought in 1987 has become the 12th-largest fund company in Canada, with assets under management of $12.2 billion. He's prouder still that this success has been won by adhering religiously to an investment style that is different from that of almost every other mutual fund company in Canada.

As I sat in the silent lobby, I tried unsuccessfully to recall the name of a bad movie about some cult that I had seen long ago on TV. The setting was a place like this: vast grounds in some remote suburb and a lavishly appointed building that was the domain of a charismatic leader. The term "cult" is usually associated with religion, but there are investment cults as well, the outstanding example being that of Warren Buffett, the billionaire from Omaha, Nebraska, considered by many the greatest investor in the world. When you visit AIC's offices, you are in the Canadian headquarters of Buffettism.

Religious language often creeps into conversations about investment style. Some fund managers "believe in" growth investing; others "have faith" that the practitioners of value investing will be redeemed after years of wandering in the desert. No two companies believe more strongly in their respective styles than AIC and Trimark. The odd thing is that when AIC or Trimark people talk about their investment philosophies, they sound similar. When you look at their portfolios and results, however, the similarity vanishes. Robert Krembil, who created Trimark's investment style, likes to say that investment managers at Trimark are "businessmen buying businesses" – that is, Trimark invests in companies it believes in rather than speculating on the direction in which the stock market is going to carry the shares of those companies in any given year. Lee-Chin tells the same story. He's also a businessman who buys businesses, and as long as those businesses are healthy he's happy. As for the unpredictable gyrations of the stock market, he lets the speculators worry about that.

That two companies with similar philosophies can get totally different results is a good example of why investment management is a mysterious art. Trimark Canadian, Trimark's flagship fund, is well diversified, its 60 stocks covering all sectors of the economy – resources, financial services, manufacturing, communications, and technology – with the heaviest concentration in resources. AIC's flagship, the AIC Advantage Fund, has only 23 companies, fewer than many amateur investors have in their portfolios, and features a strong concentration in the financial services industry. In 1997, AIC was flying high while Trimark's performance was collapsing. By 1999, fund retailers who had not already abandoned Trimark were loudly demanding that it forsake its obstinate faith in an investment style that wasn't working. But by the end of the year things had turned around – Trimark's performance was still mediocre, but mediocre was an improvement. The Trimark Canadian Fund finished 1999 up 16.7%, compared with the average Canadian equity fund's 21.7%. AIC, meanwhile, was floundering. AIC Advantage finished 1999 down 13.4%.

Someone with a million dollars to invest will generally interview a few money managers and choose one, usually for an annual fee of around 1.5% of the assets. Mutual funds give the investor who doesn't have a million bucks access to the same quality of professional management. While small investors can't interview managers personally, they can, and should, do enough research to decide if the fund's investment style suits them. Paying attention to investment style is all the more important in an era when certain tried-and-true notions – for example, that a company has to be profitable before its stock will rise in value – are no longer valid. In fact, as we'll see in the next chapter, millions of investors now doubt that active management is worth paying for at all. Don't buy businesses, they say, buy the stock market in the form of an index fund. You'll do better and save money too.

A desire to compare the investment styles of Trimark and AIC, so alike on the surface but so different under it, had already led me to Richard Charlton, an AIC exile who is the Buffett cult's most eloquent preacher. Charlton had been with Lee-Chin in the early days of AIC, the late 1980s; he was an officer of the company and worked in the sales branch, AIC Investment Planning (later renamed Berkshire Investment Group after Berkshire Hathaway, Warren Buffett's holding company). In 1996, he left to set up his own dealership as part of Fortune Financial Corp., a fund dealer turned manufacturer that had launched a new line of funds under the Infinity brand name. When I talked to Charlton, in 1999, Infinity Funds Management Inc., in which he was a shareholder, was being sued for $100 million by AIC on the grounds that its funds were copies of AIC's funds. Charlton thought that was pretty weird since AIC, as Lee-Chin never tires of explaining, took its investment philosophy directly from Buffett, and Buffett didn't sue AIC. The suit has since been dropped, but even while it was on, Charlton insisted that he and Lee-Chin were still the best of friends. (Infinity is now owned by Dundee Wealth Management, of which Charlton is a shareholder.)

Anybody who thinks investment people are boring hasn't met Charlton. Imagine an oversized Don Cherry with a dark complexion, a wardrobe that's just as expensive but more tasteful (including the shiniest Gucci loafers you've ever seen), and a Jamaican accent. Charlton is an outsider and proud of it. On the first page of his book, *Invest and Grow Rich!*, he describes his background: "I was born in Jamaica in 1950 to a mulatto father and a Sephardic-Jewish mother which meant that I was considered a white man." In Canada, though, he's considered black, which is fine with him as long as you don't forget he's also Jewish. When the Toronto journalist Ellen Roseman wrote that the people behind AIC were two Jamaicans, Lee-Chin and Charlton, "I gave her hell," Charlton recalls. "I asked her, 'Why didn't you say a black Chinese guy and a Jew from Jamaica?' I was just teasing."

Charlton's office in Oakville, a few miles down the road from AIC, is in a nondescript low-rise building. Inside, one is transported into the faux living room of a wealthy person with a taste for the ornate. The room has thick carpets, deep green wallpaper, and leather-covered furniture. Drawings on the wall depict red-jacketed Englishmen riding to hounds. On the table, four piles of magazines are carefully arranged so that the following titles are on top: the *Robb Report*, featuring stories on executive jets and the problems associated with giving away millions of dollars; *Sport-auto*, featuring a piece on the comparative merits of Mercedeses and Ferraris; *Queste*, "the international magazine for Rolls-Royce and Bentley owners"; and a brochure for those considering the purchase of a Leopard, a yacht whose manufacturers bill it as "king of the day cruisers."

Not being a Rolls or Bentley owner, I had not been aware of *Queste*. I asked the receptionist how it came to be there. "I think Mr. Charlton drives a Bentley," she said. One of my favourite book titles is *Where Are the Customers' Yachts? or A Good Hard Look at Wall Street*. The book, by Fred Schwed, Jr., published in 1940, gets its title from an old story about a visitor who's being shown around the New York financial district when his guide points to the yachts moored in the harbour, mentioning that they belong to bankers and brokers. "Where," the visitor asks innocently, "are the customers' yachts?"

Charlton ushered me into his office and sat me down in front of a coffee table. "Where," I asked, "are the customers' Bentleys?"

"Ha," he shouted in triumph, as if expecting that very question. He jabbed a finger at some client statements on the coffee table. "Take a look at those." One of them belongs to a client named Bill who lives in Gravenhurst, Ontario. All Bill's money is in AIC and Infinity mutual funds, and the bottom line is $4 million. If Bill needs a Bentley, he can cash in a few units and buy one. More statements with seven- and high-six-figure bottom lines are spread around. "I was just going through some of these," Charlton explains.

How did these clients become wealthy? By buying stocks of the companies favoured by Warren Buffett, businesses like Coke and Gillette and McDonald's. Or by buying shares of Berkshire Hathaway, Buffett's holding company, which owns huge amounts of these stocks. Or by buying AIC mutual funds, which own shares of Berkshire Hathaway as well as of the companies Berkshire Hathaway owns. Charlton grabs one statement. This particular client owns Berkshire Hathaway stock worth almost $1 million for which he paid $174,000 seven years earlier. And he has some Coke stock. It's down 24% from the previous year but is still worth $800,000, not bad considering he paid $40,000 for it. He also owns Gillette and the AIC Value Fund, whose holdings include Coke, Gillette, and Berkshire Hathaway. "What are the chances you could ever walk into a brokerage office and see an account like that?" Charlton exclaims. "Probably next to none. When those shares doubled, or long before, what would the broker have done? Convinced you to sell."

This client's account is a good illustration of the Buffett principle of buying and holding a small number of companies purchased when their value was not fully appreciated by the market. A Buffett company typically has a powerful brand that dominates the market-place for some simple mass-market product, such as a soft drink or a newspaper or a razor blade, a product that's used up quickly and therefore always in demand. Charlton's client has only four stocks and one mutual fund, which holds the same stocks. That's not diversification, that's focus – Buffett's style is sometimes called "focus investing." Another element of Buffettism is tax efficiency. Eventually, Charlton's client or his heirs are going to have to pay capital gains taxes, but the client hasn't had to yet because he hasn't sold anything. And because AIC doesn't turn over its portfolios much, its clients rarely get hit with taxable distributions. A more typical fund whose manager trades frequently creates a hefty tax burden on people investing outside their RRSPs. When a company advertises that $10,000 invested in its fund in 1954 is worth $4 million today, that's $4 million before taxes.

Like many loyal followers of the Oracle of Omaha, Charlton makes a pilgrimage every year to the Berkshire Hathaway annual meeting, which has been described by Mary Buffett, a former daughter-in-law of the great man, as "like going to Mecca." Charlton has made 13 visits to these meetings in Omaha, where Buffett, one of the world's richest men, still lives in the house he bought 40 years ago for $31,500. Over the years, Charlton got to know Mildred and Donald Othmer, his favourite examples of successful investing. The Othmers, natives of Omaha, had placed $25,000 apiece with Buffett in the 1960s. That $50,000 stake was worth $750 million by the time they died in the late 1990s. Hardly anyone knew how wealthy they were, and they amazed their friends by leaving $340 million to several charitable organizations, including Polytechnic University in

Brooklyn, where Donald Othmer had taught chemical engineering, and Planned Parenthood.

Buffett's achievement is proof that active management at its best will hugely outperform the market. If you had $10,000 in 1965, and you were smart enough to hand it over to Buffett, you'd have had $50 million by 1999. The same sum invested in the 500 top American stocks of the Standard and Poor's index would have grown to a paltry $500,000. Of course, hardly anyone knew about Buffett in 1965, and many people who got in early did so only because they lived in Omaha; thanks to Buffett, 40 Omaha families are worth more than $100 million each. As for the superiority of active investing over passive, during the same period some money managers underperformed the S&P 500. But Charlton has no interest in indexing. For him there is only one kind of investing, the Buffett kind: buying good companies and keeping them. To him investing with Buffett, or in a Buffett-style fund such as AIC or Infinity, will always be better than buying an index fund or a fund managed by someone who trades stocks rather than buys businesses.

That's why the statements on Charlton's coffee table don't show any investments in mutual funds run by companies other than AIC and his own Infinity. "I could not conceive of allowing anyone who didn't think like us to touch our clients' money," Charlton proclaims. "Buffett has given us this framework. He is the second-richest man in America. He has made us very, very wealthy. He has made our mutual funds phenomenally successful. Why would we ever allow anyone to touch our clients' life savings who was not committed to these simple buy-and-hold, tax deferral, compound-interest investment principles? We're not buying a stock and hoping it goes up, so we can sell it and go back and buy something else and hope it goes up. The genius fund manager, he looks like an idiot to us. I have a hard time believing that Wall Street pays millions of dollars to these assholes.

"What makes you rich is not trading stocks, it's buying into a company like Wal-Mart. Five years ago there wasn't one Wal-Mart store in Canada. Today there are 300. It's the largest and most successful retail organization in Canada. I'm a simple guy. Twenty years from now there will be more Wal-Mart stores, and the stock market will have no choice but to give you a higher valuation if the business is worth it."

Charlton is right when he zeroes in on simplicity as the chief appeal of Buffett-style investing. In an era of day traders, Buffett is a decade trader. And in an age in which stocks of companies that don't make any money and whose businesses most people can't understand soar to incredible heights overnight, and come back to earth just as quickly, Buffett owns companies that everyone understands and that always make money, decade after decade. The profitability of Buffett's companies reassures investors that the inevitable downturns in their stock prices will be short-lived.

There's one significant difference between Buffett and Charlton: Buffett genuinely likes the products of the companies he owns. He always drinks Coke with his lunch and dinner. Charlton, whose clients, directly and through their AIC units, own a big chunk of Mackenzie stock, says he would not be caught dead with a Mackenzie mutual fund. "I don't even think they should be in business," he says. At the same time he likes owning Mackenzie and other financial stocks because "you can't help but make money in a good wealth management company." The reason, of course, is the steady income from fees that makes money management "the ultimate business" and pays for Charlton's Bentley and Guccis.

In AIC's Burlington lobby, the luxurious surroundings belie the fact that these are bad times in Buffettland. The clue was on the statement of that Charlton client whose Coke shares have been dropping. Coke isn't the only Buffett stock in the doldrums, and Berkshire Hathaway, whose share price had climbed from US$300 in 1980 to $84,000 in 1998, tumbled in 1999, ending the year at $51,000. That's still a phenomenal price for a single share and underlines again the democratizing power of mutual funds. Most people could not afford to buy even one Berkshire Hathaway "A" share, but they can own part of one by investing in an AIC mutual fund.

In 1999, however, Berkshire Hathaway's problems were hurting AIC's funds. The flagship, AIC Advantage, dropped 13.4% in a year in which the TSE 300 index was up 31.7%. Berkshire Hathaway wasn't the only AIC stock that was floundering; so were the Canadian financial services stocks that made up much of the portfolio.

Could this poor performance be what Jonathan Wellum is hiding from? Wellum joined AIC in 1990 and did so well that the industry inflicted the Fund Manager of the Year award on him in both 1995 and 1997. Once was bad enough; twice was fatal. A wise investor would have cashed out of Wellum's Advantage Fund the instant the dreaded award was announced. But the hordes stayed in, oblivious to the inevitable crash. In fact, so many of them wanted in that the Advantage Fund bumped up against the 10% limit on ownership on some of the stocks it owned and AIC had to start a clone, Advantage II, to accommodate the new cash pouring in at a rate of $15 million a day. By mid-1999, however, investors were fleeing both funds. In the good days, Wellum was happy to tell his story in interviews. Now he won't return phone calls and, although AIC's public relations manager has set up an appointment, he's nowhere to be found. I decide to interview the green parrot instead.

The parrot makes rude noises as I approach. Wellum and the bird are not the only ones at AIC who prefer to avoid media attention. AIC has been known to have lawyers call senior executives at newspapers when reporters ask embarrassing questions. When Keith Kawalsky covered a meeting of AIC investors at Toronto's Hummingbird Centre in 1999 for *Canadian Business* magazine, he was swarmed by security guards demanding to know what he was doing there. The people who run AIC are really smart, no doubt. So why do they do such dumb things? Probably because they are outsiders, and outsiders tend to be shy and over-sensitive. A headline in the *Globe and Mail* in 1999 reflected AIC's isolation in the mutual fund business: "AIC's disadvantage: no street friends." The street, of course, is Bay Street, and its denizens tend to view AIC, with its fancy headquarters out in the boondocks, with a mixture of envy and disdain. "AIC is an accident waiting to happen," one fund manager told me, referring to the firm's heavy concentration in volatile financial stocks.

AIC's success accounts for the envy; its uncommon investment style explains the disdain. Then there's the fact that the three people who run its funds – Lee-Chin, Wellum, and Murdoch – have never worked on Bay Street and had no experience in managing money before coming to AIC. Lee-Chin is an engineer who became a fund dealer; Wellum has a master's degree in theology and worked as an auditor; Murdoch was a lawyer specializing in bankruptcy before being recruited by an old law school friend, Kris Astaphan, AIC's lawyer. (If Astaphan's name is familiar, it's because his brother was the sprinter Ben Johnson's medical adviser.) Not being cozy with the street didn't matter when AIC was flying high. But in 1999, with its funds sagging, its outsider status was a disadvantage. AIC's weakness is the same as Buffett's: it owns so much of certain stocks that it's hard to sell them without doing serious damage to their value. Buffett, for example, owns $13 billion worth of Coca-Cola, and if word got out that he was even thinking of selling, the stock price would collapse. Even if Buffett decides he'd rather drink root beer, he's stuck with his Coke stock.

In AIC's case, just the knowledge that it was suffering net redemptions and might have to cash in some shares to meet those redemptions was said in the summer of 1999 to be depressing the share price of the grocery chain Loblaw Cos., one of its big holdings. If you are popular with the street, investment houses will sometimes put up their own capital to help you move a large block of shares without disturbing their price. But, as Andrew Willis reported in the *Globe and Mail*, the street wasn't in any mood to help, because the AIC outsiders hadn't been playing by its rules, which state that you apportion your stock trades, with their 4-cent-per-share commissions, among a number of dealers. Instead AIC used to do most of its trading through one dealer, First Marathon, in return for a lower commission. According to a company spokesman, AIC now follows normal industry practices.

Clearly, the AIC people are nonconformists. No doubt they have interesting things to say. But was this petulant parrot the only creature who'd speak to me? Just as it was starting to seem so, Neil Murdoch arrived to usher me into his office. A boyish, smiling 39-year-old who this day was dressed in T-shirt and casual slacks,

Murdoch manages several funds, including the AIC Value Fund (an American equity fund) and the AIC World Equity Fund. The Value Fund, predictably in a bad year for Buffett, was struggling (it finished 1999 down 10.7%, in the bottom quartile of all American funds sold in Canada), while World Equity was having a mediocre year (it finished up 15.7%, well below the 32.3% average gain for its group). But Murdoch doesn't come across like an officer on a ship that's going down. Instead, he's full of enthusiasm for the AIC way.

It was only because Lee-Chin's investment philosophy was the same as his own, he says, that he decided to forsake the joys of bankruptcy to run mutual funds for AIC. He greatly appreciates the difference between AIC and other companies, a difference brought home to him when he was in Europe visiting potential investments with some other fund managers. "One of the companies was France Telecom, which is 10% of the French index. I was chatting with a woman who runs some European funds for another company and I said, 'This is a company we would never own.' She agrees it's not a very good company, but she says, 'I own it.'

"'If it's not a very good company, why do you own it?'

"'Because it's 10% of the index and I have to own it. I'm an active manager but I have to be close to the index.'"

This manager is known in the industry as a "closet indexer," a bad thing to be. Closet indexing means pretending to be a stock-picking manager when you're really putting together a portfolio not much different from whatever index is the benchmark for your category of fund. Why would a manager do that? Because investors get upset when their funds underperform the index, and they call their dealers and complain. The dealers call the mutual fund companies and complain.

The problem with investing in a closet index fund is that you're paying an MER of more than 2% when you could own a real index fund for less than half that, and index participation units for even less. The only reason for tolerating an MER above 1% is to give yourself a chance to outperform the index, the way AIC Advantage did in the 10 years ending in 1999, when it had an average annual compound return of 17.3% (compared with 8.5% for the TSE 300 index).

On the other hand, a closet index fund will probably never bomb as badly as AIC Advantage did during three of those years – 1990, 1994, and 1999. So going your own way, as AIC does, means that you will outperform if you are good but also that, almost inevitably, there will be times when you underperform. The buy-and-hold investor has done well with AIC Advantage, but someone who bought it recently isn't pleased.

Buffettists like Murdoch don't like to discuss investment in these terms. For them, the market is just the place you go to buy and sell shares. It is of no interest in itself. AIC doesn't worry about what the market is doing or what a particular index is doing, it just worries about its investments. Other fund companies may say the same thing but they don't really mean it, in Murdoch's opinion. "When we're talking to new people for the portfolio management department or outside analysts to try to get them to think the way we do, it's hard. Very few people in the industry think that way. Most people in our industry look at buying and selling pieces of paper. We don't do that. We *invest*. We try to buy the best businesses in strong industries. And while they may not be spared in a downturn, because everybody gets sideswiped, they are the ones that will come back better because they are generating real wealth. As long as they're chugging along at 12% to 15% growth a year, that's a value somebody's going to recognize and pay for."

Bankruptcy work was good preparation for portfolio management, Murdoch says, because "you had to go into the nuts and bolts of a business. You had to decide whether you should shut down a whole operation or just a piece of it. Being on the factory floor was good experience for doing the AIC type of portfolio management." As an investor, he still visits the factory floor, and sometimes that can get interesting. On one of his European trips he visited Pik Salami, in Szeged, in southern Hungary. Murdoch knew the meat-packing business from his bankruptcy days and was in his element as he chatted with Pik's chief financial officer next to a row of carcasses on a conveyor system. Suddenly the conveyor belt started up unexpectedly, missing Murdoch but knocking the CFO down and injuring him badly enough that his suit was covered in his own blood. AIC did not add Pik to its portfolio.

It wasn't the errant conveyor belt that made Murdoch pass on Pik; it was that the salami maker wasn't a "generator of wealth" in the way of a classic Buffett company like Wal-Mart or Coca-Cola. It is pointed out to Murdoch that there are outfits in AIC's portfolios, like the investment dealer First Marathon in the Advantage Fund and Wesco Financial Corp. in the Value Fund, that don't look much like Buffett companies either. What famous brands or powerful franchises do these obscure companies own? Murdoch concedes that First Marathon is "closer to the edge" of the definition but adds that it's a small part of the portfolio. By this time, however, I'm concluding that the real difference between AIC and the rest of the crowd is not the kind of companies it chooses but the small number of them. This is not a minor difference. It means AIC's managers have enormous confidence in the select handful of stocks they invest their clients' money in. When you buy an AIC fund you know exactly what you're getting: the services of professional stock-pickers who have the courage of their convictions. AIC has its critics but no one has ever called it a closet indexer.

Mike Lee-Chin's success is a testament to the power of the written word. It was a chapter on Warren Buffett in a 1980 book called *The Money Masters*, by John Train, that gave Lee-Chin the investment philosophy that would be the foundation of AIC's success. Twenty years have not dimmed the relevance of Train's piece on Buffett, and dipping into any page of it can help the reader understand what Lee-Chin is trying to do. In the third paragraph, for example, Train writes: "A masterfully competent investor (like an art collector) should buy what is out of fashion and thus hard to resell quickly, and indeed he should buy a lot of it, prepared to be patient with any particular holding. If he's right, the values will be recognized and his purchase gain liquidity in due course. Buffett . . . likes to own a dozen or so securities and characterizes traditional diversification as the 'Noah's Ark approach.' You buy two of everything in sight and end up with a zoo instead of a portfolio."

This approach made sense to someone trained as an engineer who had difficulty understanding the stock market because it did not appear to behave rationally. "But I could train myself to understand what are the characteristics of a great business. To me that was rational. So I locked on to Buffett's methodology because that methodology was rational. It was something I could practise."

Lee-Chin is telling me this in his well-appointed office in the company of his young secretary. She had started to leave when the interview began, but Lee-Chin called her back, saying, "I want you to listen to this." In many years of interviewing important people, this is a first for me. Sometimes the public relations person will sit in on an interview, but never the secretary. Maybe he wants her to learn more about the AIC investment philosophy in case she ever has to manage a portfolio.

Lee-Chin is comfortable talking about investment but uncomfortable talking about himself. Trying to get him to reveal something personal is like trying to get a small animal to react by poking it with a stick. Lee-Chin is big and, at 49, lean and fit. He came to Canada as a student and graduated from Hamilton's McMaster University in 1974 with a degree in civil engineering. Then he went back home to Jamaica and worked as an engineer for two years for the Jamaican government. He would have stayed, he says, had it not been for "my then wife, Vera – she's Canadian and she missed her parents. Being a citizen of the world, it didn't matter to me where I was, so I came back to facilitate her."

"So your ex-wife is responsible for AIC?"

Lee-Chin laughs. "She's responsible, exactly. Don't put that in there or she may say, 'Give me half.'"

With no engineering job available, Lee-Chin went to work in Hamilton selling mutual funds for Investors Group. Later he switched to a dealer called Regal Capital Planners, where he became a branch manager. He was a natural salesman and built up a lucrative client list that included a good number of doctors, a group notorious for its lack of investment skills. Lee-Chin prospered as a fund dealer, cutting a fine figure as he wheeled about Hamilton in his Ferrari, but he was starting to see that the sales side of the business wasn't the best place to be. These were the days before trailer fees; salespeople depended entirely on sales commissions. "You ate what you killed," Lee-Chin recalls, meaning that if your doctors weren't in a mood to invest you might not be able to afford spare parts for your Ferrari. Living off the kill was fine when people wanted mutual funds, but it wasn't fine in the early 1980s when interest rates went through the roof and even doctors had sense enough to forget about stocks and put their money in bank deposits offering no-risk returns of over 20%.

In 1982, Lee-Chin had a revelation. At the time, Mackenzie Financial Corp., the fund company Jim O'Donnell was helping to build with the help of salesmen like Lee-Chin, had a small office above a Harvey's restaurant on Bloor Street in the centre of Toronto. Then Mackenzie moved into a much larger office and spent $100,000 to renovate it. Lee-Chin did some hard thinking: "Interest rates had gone to 23.75% prime, and we in the field who were selling securities were starving, yet Mackenzie was able to move from 800 square feet to 10,000 square feet and spend $100,000. We who were protecting their assets, we were dying on the vine."

Lee-Chin's deep, hearty laugh fills the room: "I decided I wanted to be on the Mackenzie side of the fence. Because I realized the importance of having a business that has an annuitized type of cash-flow stream." An "annuitized type of cash-flow stream" is a polite way of saying that, even when salespeople are starving and investors are gaping in horror as their life savings shrivel up, Mackenzie still rakes in profits because it takes a cut of the money it manages whether its funds go up or down.

Lee-Chin decided to be an owner and not just one of the dealers. As a start, he borrowed $500,000 to buy 1% of Mackenzie as a personal investment. The opportunity to buy Advantage Investment Counsel (AIC) came four years later. The company, then based in Kitchener, was running a balanced mutual fund that had a minuscule $800,000 in assets. One of its owners, Mario Frankovich, whom Lee-Chin had known in university, came to him for help in improving sales. Instead, Lee-Chin offered to buy control of the company. So as not to be totally dependent on independent dealers, he started his own sales division, now called Berkshire Investment Group.

Lee-Chin keeps in shape by running and lifting weights. In fact, the gym has played an important part in the history of AIC. It was in the McMaster weight room that he met Frankovich and, in 1990, discovered Jonathan Wellum. The flashy Lee-Chin and the bashful Wellum, a chiropractor's son who teaches Sunday school at a Baptist church, were sometimes described as an odd couple, but they were one of the most effective partnerships in the industry. Wellum took over management of AIC Advantage from Lee-Chin in 1995 and delivered returns of 30.7%, 66.5%, and 43.3% before coming back to earth with a thud in 1998 and 1999. He handed the fund back to Lee-Chin in 1999, when he left to form his own investment management business (although he continues to manage three other AIC funds).

If all funds were like AIC Advantage, the buy-and-hold philosophy would be unchallengeable. Over the 10 years starting in 1990, the fund had three awful years, two mediocre years, and five sensational years. The result is a 10-year return of 17.78%, 10th best for that period of any Canadian fund. So AIC Advantage is a good fund but it's also a volatile one, and investors with low risk tolerance paid for their profits with a lot of sleepless nights. It's questionable whether the fund is a Buffett-style investment vehicle or a specialty fund, since 60% of its holdings are in the financial services sector. Buffett is not diversified, but neither is he dependent on one sector, nor are his investments as volatile as AIC's. In fact, 1999 was the first year since 1980 that Buffett failed to beat the market index, something that happens regularly to AIC.

Lee-Chin and Wellum have always replied to this sort of criticism by saying they are implementing Buffett's philosophy in their own way. They were among the first to understand that the aging of the boomers would make wealth management a growth industry. The result is that AIC is the largest shareholder of two of its chief competitors, Mackenzie and Trimark, as well as having important holdings in the insurance and brokerage businesses. In 1999, technology was hot and financial services were not, so AIC had a bad year, but a bad year doesn't faze a Buffettist. Because Buffett has proved that buying good companies and holding on to them works, AIC's managers have supreme confidence that all will turn out well in the end. "When the market drops, we can be resolute and hold on to our stocks in part because of him," Wellum said in an interview in 1998, before he climbed into his shell. "I won't lose my cool and liquidate great firms when the market falls."

A piece of Buffett scripture, about 200 words long, appears in every AIC annual and quarterly report. In it, the oracle points out that nobody could have predicted such major events of recent decades as the Vietnam war, the breakup of the Soviet Union, the surge in oil prices, or wild fluctuations in interest rates. And yet none of that made any difference to an investment strategy based on "purchases of fine businesses at sensible prices." Buffett goes on to say that other world-shaking economic and political events are sure to occur in future, yet "we will neither try to predict these nor profit from them" because sound businesses will succeed despite "external surprises." The most memorable sentence in this passage is this: "Fear is the foe of the faddist, but the friend to the fundamentalist."

In investment terms, a fundamentalist is someone concerned about whether a company makes any money, or whether it owes too much. As the new century dawned, the frustrating thing for many portfolio managers, not just AIC's, was that a handful of companies, including some with questionable fundamentals, were driving the indexes upward, while the stocks of solid businesses with sound fundamentals languished. For a young investor armed with an Internet trading account, the study of fundamentals seemed "about as useful as studying Latin in school," the fund expert Duff Young observed in his *Globe and Mail* column.

But Lee-Chin doesn't care if he seems out of step. Like Buffett, he is not surprised if the market doesn't always put high values on the stocks he chooses. "Having a philosophy," he explains, "does two things for you. It tells us what we should do and what we should not do. Our investment philosophy has kept us out of trouble, and it has led us to do things that in the long run have done very well."

Is AIC an accident waiting to happen because its funds are not diversified? No, says Lee-Chin, because diversification is not safer. "If you own a lot of junk, your business risk is not less, but if you own one good company that is bulletproof, your business risk is very nominal. I guess it depends on how you define safety. If you define safety as minimizing short-term volatility, then diversifying will be safer. But if you define safety as protection against permanent losses, then owning a strong business that is in a great industry and is not highly levered, that's your safety."

For Lee-Chin, short-term volatility in good stocks is an opportunity. Fear is the friend of the fundamentalist. Because he has confidence that his investments are sound, he takes advantage of temporary low prices to buy more. "These are opportunities for us because the businesses that we own are going to be here for a very long time. So if the speculators turf those businesses out at cheap prices, we are very eager to accept them."

There are a couple of problems with that idea. One is that AIC already owns all it is allowed to own of its favourite mutual fund companies, Trimark and Mackenzie. Another is that a manager can't go bargain-hunting when his investors are pulling their money out. But while the Advantage Fund was shrinking, AIC did take advantage of the sale on Mackenzie stock to buy some for its own corporate account. Lee-Chin dismissed stories that appeared in late 1999 that his company was having problems meeting redemptions, pointing out that a lot of the money was just being switched from the Advantage funds to other AIC funds. As for an alleged liquidity crisis (meaning that AIC wouldn't be able to sell enough stock quickly enough to pay off clients who were cashing out), that never existed, Lee-Chin insisted. The two Advantage funds had more than $1 billion in highly liquid American stocks, such as Berkshire Hathaway, that it could sell without affecting their price, before it would have to bail out of its less liquid Canadian holdings.

Because AIC is different, Lee-Chin believes, it attracts criticism. "If you're doing something non-traditional, you always open yourself up to suspicion," he says. "We are not downtown on Bay Street. And we are successful at what we do. Our success magnifies our competitors' failings."

That's not an outsider's paranoia, it's reality. AIC does get more criticism and less credit than it deserves. It was the first fund company to figure out that the industry it was part of was going to be a huge winner. That was brilliant. AIC doesn't believe in diversification, which is sacrilege in the mutual fund industry but also courageous. Most telling of all, AIC gets results. Levi Folk and Richard Webb, editors of the *Fund Counsel* newsletter, analyzed the performance of all the equity funds offered by the major Canadian fund families over the five-year period to the end of 1999. They used an asset-weighted system so that the results would not be skewed by a sensational result in a small fund. In other words, they got a number that showed the return on the average dollar invested in a company rather than the return of the average fund within that company. In this analysis, AIC led all fund families with an average return of 24.8%. Trimark was near the bottom with an average return of 11.5%.

Magazine articles about Lee-Chin usually note his penchant for expensive cars. I mention that I've read he has two Ferraris and a Rolls.

"That was then. I don't have two Ferraris and a Rolls now."

"How many Ferraris and Rollses do you have now?"

Lee-Chin sighs and looks at his secretary with a expression that says, "You see, what did I tell you about these writers?"

"So what are you driving now?" I persist.

"Can we leave that out? What does it say about personality? I don't think you can draw a conclusion about someone from what car he drives. I could drive a Volkswagen."

"If you drove one of the new Volkswagen Bugs, that would be interesting."

"Would it make a statement as to my personality? Would it?"

"Yes."

Lee-Chin gives up. "I drive a Mercedes."

As the 12th-largest fund company, AIC is competing head-to-head against the other major powers in the industry, such as Trimark (number five) and Mackenzie (number three). Yet it's the largest shareholder in both these companies, which gives it a say in how they conduct their business, something that was particularly relevant in 1998 and 1999 when Trimark was going through a disastrous period. As a shareholder, AIC wants Trimark and Mackenzie to do well, but as a competitor it both does and doesn't want them to do well. It wants them to do well so the AIC funds that own their stocks will prosper, but it doesn't, or so I assume, want the public to decide

Mackenzie and Trimark funds are better than AIC's. So how does AIC deal with all these conflicts of interest?

Rumours had circulated that AIC was involved in Trimark's 1999 decision to get rid of its top Canadian equity manager, Vito Maida, whose strategy of loading up on undervalued resource stocks was dragging down the performance of its funds. "We definitely didn't do that, because I sat in on all the meetings we had with Trimark as part of the portfolio management team," Neil Murdoch had told me. "Whether it's Trimark, Loblaws, or Thomson, we would not get involved in day-to-day business such as getting rid of a manager."

What sort of issues would it get involved in? Murdoch explains that, as a shareholder of the Toronto-Dominion Bank, for example, AIC might have expressed an opinion as to whether it should spin off its Waterhouse brokerage subsidiary (as it did). But it wouldn't have anything to say about whether the bank should close some branches. The former is a major strategic issue; the latter is day-to-day management.

For Lee-Chin, visiting his competitors at Trimark to find out why their stock is sagging is not awkward. "When we go in as portfolio managers to a company like Trimark we don't see ourselves as being competitors at that point in time. Our focus is to help them. Because if we help Trimark it's going to come back to us in terms of appreciation of the stock and therefore appreciation of our funds.

"We want Trimark to do well. We want them to do very well. And if they do so well that people sell AIC to buy Trimark, that's okay, because the AIC funds will do well and people will buy AIC again."

At this, Lee-Chin laughs heartily, appreciating the irony of it. As I leave, he is still laughing.

Arthur Labatt is not laughing. We're sitting in his office, 56 floors up in First Canadian Place, several months before the May 2000 deal that would see Amvescap PLC, the British owner of AIM Funds Management Ltd., buy Trimark and combine its mutual fund operations with those of AIM. This transaction was worth $400 million each to Labatt and Bob Krembil, the two co-founders of Trimark. At the time of our interview, Labatt was still chairman of Trimark (his only role now is as a board member of the merged company), and he was talking to me about Vito Maida without ever once uttering Vito Maida's name, referring to him instead as "a certain manager." In 1997, this certain manager thought resource stocks would go up, so he loaded the Canadian equity funds he was managing with resource stocks. They didn't go up. The banks went up, but Trimark didn't own those. As a result, Trimark's funds were in the tank, the dealers were in open revolt, and customers were hauling truckloads of money out the door. This happened during what was supposed to be a great bull market. And still the certain manager stayed the course. During the worst of it, the fiscal year ending March 31, 1999, Trimark's assets under management shrank by $4.1 billion, more than the total assets of most fund companies. (Total redemptions were an astronomical $6.9 billion, while new sales were $2.8 billion.) And so, finally, in February 1999, Labatt and his partner Bob Krembil asked the manager to stop coming to work. Why did it take so long? Well, Labatt tells me, there were other portfolio managers, not just the certain one; it was supposed to be a team, and you would have expected the other team members to say something or do something. The certain manager's "strength and conviction was so strong," he says, shaking his head in anger and frustration.

Trimark's offices are elegant and comfortable but not nearly as plush as AIC's. "If you're in the investment management business you don't want to portray any kind of opulence, but you do want to give the impression you're here for the long haul," Labatt explained. Labatt is a scion of the old-money family that founded the brewery, so it's easy for him to forgo opulence. Unlike Michael Lee-Chin, he's got nothing to prove.

Trimark's head office is 49 storeys above the much smaller quarters it leased in this same building when it opened for business in 1981. Back then the phones were on cardboard boxes, and Labatt and Krembil often answered them. Now Trimark has 800 employees. The lobby display of three Philippine ceramic granary jars, each a bit larger than the last, is an unusual touch. The Asian theme is carried over to Labatt's own office, where a photo shows him and his daughter at a Buddhist temple in Korea, where she is studying art while her husband works as a management consultant. Shots of Labatt's six grandchildren add to the homey atmosphere.

The long-haul notion applies to Trimark's investment management style as well. Trimark is a value manager, meaning it looks for companies whose stock is selling for less than it's worth. That requires poring over all the reports down to the last footnote, grilling the managers, sounding out competitors, customers, suppliers, even former employees – and then waiting patiently for a year, or two, or five, until the market finally discovers the value Trimark discovered first. A value investor, by definition, is a contrarian, which is why the 1999 television campaign showing herds of sheep going one way and Trimark's value investor going the other was appropriate. The herd was composed of growth investors, the kind who look for companies with above-average earnings growth rather than ones with unsung value. In 1998, growth-style funds had outperformed value-style funds by 11%, so it took nerve for Trimark to run those ads when it did.

During and after the ad campaign, well into 1999, the rest of the industry watched in horrified fascination as Trimark continued its free fall. This wasn't, after all, just any fund company, this was Trimark, and Labatt and Krembil were two of the most respected people in the business. They had been the ideal combination to build a fund company when they joined forces in 1981. Labatt, with a warm and friendly personality, was a good businessman and a natural salesman who, like Jim O'Donnell, was good at establishing close relationships with dealers. Krembil, reticent and shy, had a reputation as an expert stock-picker whose value style could be relied upon to preserve his investors' assets while delivering above-average long-term performance. That reputation was the basis on which the company became so successful that, by the mid-1990s, it was the second biggest in the country (after Investors Group). Labatt and Krembil took Trimark public in 1992; that made them both so rich that in 1999 they were included on a published list of Toronto's wealthiest people.

Through 1998 and 1999, however, Trimark's ongoing woes and its refusal to change were hot topics of discussion. By February, when Maida made his exit, Trimark had slipped from second place to fourth, its assets having declined by 10%. Some argued that Trimark had abandoned the trademark Krembil style, at least in the large Canadian funds managed by Maida, who had made a bet that the resource sector as a whole was due to surge. Krembil had always said he was a businessman buying individual businesses – just what Michael Lee-Chin says – not the kind of investor who tries to predict in advance which way the market is going to carry a particular industrial sector.

Others said the problem wasn't that Trimark had changed its style but that it hadn't changed it enough. Why, they wondered, didn't it set up some new funds based on different investment philosophies, so that unhappy investors could switch instead of pulling out? Mackenzie had done that a few years earlier when its Industrial line of funds was in trouble. It added three new fund brands – Ivy, Universal, and Cundill – using different investment styles, so that customers could switch from one to another without leaving Mackenzie. I spoke to the CEO of another major firm whose theory was that Trimark had suffered from Krembil's hubris. "They wouldn't try something new; they were captive to one style. Mackenzie did the right thing by diversifying by style. Trimark was committed to value, and that led them to be heavy on resources because the prices of those stocks were so low."

Trimark didn't listen to all the unsolicited advice. Its system had paid off in the past because it had stuck with it, and not just in the good times. Moreover, Labatt believed, it was unfair to suggest he couldn't adapt to changing circumstances when he'd done so throughout his career. As a young man, he would have preferred to go into the family beer business, but he knew the family intended to sell (which it did in 1964) so he became a chartered accountant instead. That led to a job with McLeod Young Weir, a brokerage house, which eventually took him to Paris, where he spent three years as a salesman covering France, Switzerland, Belgium, and Luxembourg. By 1979, he was back in Canada as president of Bolton Tremblay Inc., an investment management company.

By then Labatt was aware of the investing prowess of Bob Krembil. He'd observed Krembil during an 18-month period starting in 1973 when the market "didn't crash, it just kept going down and down and down." During that miserable time, most funds in Canada and the United States were suffering net redemptions. So was the Taurus Fund, managed by Krembil; but it was also one of a small handful that rose in value despite the poor overall performance of the stock market.

In 1977, Commercial Union, the insurance company for which Krembil was working, decided to sell its mutual funds. It offered them to Krembil and his associate, Russell Morrison. They declined, saying they were money managers, not businessmen. Labatt talked Bolton Tremblay into buying the funds, and Krembil went with them. By 1980, Labatt and Krembil had figured out, as Michael Lee-Chin would some years later, that the best-paying job in the fund industry is company owner. He and Krembil tried to get Lorne Webster, who controlled the company that controlled Bolton Tremblay, to let them come in as partners. They talked about it for six months, but in the end Webster said no. "He'd had it with us," Labatt recalls. "He sort of forced our hand."

So, along with a third partner, Mike Axford (now retired), Labatt and Krembil started Trimark in September 1981, a launch date almost as inauspicious as Fidelity Canada's debut on Black Monday. This was the era of soaring interest rates, a time when most investors thought it was nuts to risk money in equities because you could get 19% risk-free by buying Canada Savings Bonds. To get off the ground they amassed not quite $1 million, much of it from Labatt's relatives. Their goal was to see that modest sum grow into a sizable investment pool, perhaps someday as much as $100 million. Given the lack of demand for the product they were selling, that seemed unlikely. But they persevered through the bad times, interest rates came down, and then the boomers started investing. By the end of 1982, they had $35 million to manage, almost enough to break even. By the end of 1983, they had $125 million. As the 1990s drew to an end, even after three bad years, Trimark had $24.5 billion under its wing.

Like the other founders of the industry in Canada, Labatt and Krembil were in the right place at exactly the right time; the result has been success far beyond their expectations. But as 1999 wore on, Labatt, 66, was impatient for a turnaround so that he could enter retirement knowing the company he'd founded was headed in the right direction. And towards the end of the year, things were looking up just a bit – some new managers were on board, new funds had been launched, and some of the old ones had revived. Despite all that, more money was leaving than was coming in, a trend that continued into the 2000 RRSP season. Months after a certain manager had departed, most investors were still steering clear of Trimark. I ask Labatt if he thinks he let the downward spiral go on for too long before intervening.

"In retrospect, yes, we did. But it's Bob's call, he's head of the investment side. I can argue, but I've known him since 1973 and worked with him since 1977, and it's been a wonderful long-term relationship. I have great respect for his judgment. But it did go on too long. I think the manager backed himself into a corner a bit by some of his dramatic moves. By doing that he backed Bob into a corner, because they both had to defend their positions all the time and that's not good, to always be in a defensive posture."

The "dramatic moves" included Maida's big bet on gold in the summer of 1997. Maida at the time was managing the Trimark Canadian Equity, Trimark RSP Equity, and Trimark Select Canadian Growth funds, a total of about $7 billion in assets. Gold certificates were 5% of the portfolios of each of these funds. Trimark's official line was that the gold was simply an alternative to cash, of which the funds were also holding an ample amount. Trimark's critics, including dealers and financial planners, weren't buying it. Their investors had bought Trimark Canadian because they wanted an actively managed Canadian stock fund, not a play on a volatile commodity like gold. How did gold fit in with the philosophy of "buying good businesses"? How for that matter did holding a large cash position, at a time when the overall market was moving upward? Then there was the question of whether loading up on undervalued resource companies really was value investing. Just because a company is undervalued doesn't mean it's worth owning.

I ask Labatt whether Trimark had strayed from its discipline and bought cheap companies rather than good ones. "Bob would argue that we didn't change our style, but a particular manager who had such strong conviction was slanted that way. There's no question about it."

Jade Hemeon, who used to write about mutual funds for the *Toronto Star* and who now has the demanding job of handling public relations for a company in trouble, is sitting in on the interview. As a reporter, she would have been happy to quote the chairman of Trimark admitting that Trimark had screwed up; as Trimark's image polisher, she's not happy, and she interrupts to say that in fact Trimark didn't buy poor quality.

"I don't think we felt that we were buying poor quality," Labatt agrees.

"The timing didn't work out, but they are quality companies and a lot of them are still in those portfolios," Hemeon adds.

Labatt is not satisfied to leave it at that. "I think, Jade, though, they were not as high quality as some of the growth companies we were not buying at that point."

Poor Jade. She's trying her best to accentuate the positive, but the chairman of the company keeps telling it as he sees it. I observe that there is a big difference between a major company like Bombardier, a global leader in its field, and some of the obscure resource companies jammed into Trimark's portfolios. Bombardier is quality (although it's no longer undervalued); Trimark's resource companies are undervalued, but it's questionable whether all of them are quality.

"They were quality in the sense that the resource companies we were buying had very little debt and very high cash positions," Labatt explains. "So within their industry they were strong players. But because of their size and the nature of the industry they were in, it would be hard to stack them up against a Nortel or a BCE."

No wonder investment management is so difficult for amateur investors to figure out. The experts can't figure it out either. It's hard for a company to stick rigorously to a philosophy, and it's not even clear whether sticking rigorously to a philosophy is good. It's one thing to have a policy of confining yourself to buying good businesses cheap when you've got $1 million to manage, quite another when you've got $24 billion. There may not be enough stock of enough good cheap companies to absorb that much money. Trimark's investment style seems to have changed subtly without the people at the top being prepared to face up to what was happening. Here's what an investment manager at another company says: "Trimark used to buy quality companies but was very rigorous in what it paid for them. And once it found that quality, it just kept buying it. So Trimark did very well for a number of years buying growth at a reasonable price. Then it got very big and it was difficult to manoeuvre that portfolio, very tough to find stocks it could buy enough of at that nice cheap price. And then managers began to leave and they brought in some individuals who weren't always looking for the best company, just for the cheapest value company. Look at the stocks Trimark owns now, compared with what it used to own. Sixty per cent of the portfolio is in resource stocks – lots of resource stocks and not just the best ones. Those stocks are cheap but they aren't necessarily good companies. If Trimark had stuck to its original model, buying quality growing companies at a reasonable price, I think it would have had a great couple of years in 1998 and 1999, because that was a good growth-type market."

Investment management is founded in investment philosophy but relies on investment skill, and Trimark's bad years were preceded by the loss of some highly skilled managers. In the mid-1990s, Bill Kanko, Dennis Staritt, and Dina DeGeer all left to go elsewhere (Kanko has since returned). These people were key parts of the portfolio management team Krembil had assembled. They were also millionaires as a result of owning Trimark shares before the company went public. John Caspar, the erudite Vancouver broker we met in Chapter One, thinks their departure had much to do with Trimark's troubles. "It's interesting to note the correlation between the off years and the loss of their management team," he says. "It's hard to believe that would be coincidental."

Caspar doesn't buy the argument that Trimark's investing style simply stopped working. True, value investing wasn't being rewarded, but Caspar thinks Trimark is more a growth investor than a value investor. For him, the company's problems are evidence of the importance of the manager, evidence being Kanko's continued success after leaving Trimark for Mackenzie. "The fact is these [portfolio managers] are adding value. The mistake people make is they think they're buying a mutual fund, but they're actually buying a manager. So you'd better know what is going on. If you're monitoring your investments, it's reasonable to ask whether you should continue to hold a fund if the management team has left."

During 1998 and 1999, thousands of advisers were suggesting to clients that it might no longer be wise to hold Trimark funds. The timing of Trimark's downturn couldn't have been worse. While it was floundering, newer names such as Fidelity, C.I., AIM, and Synergy were getting good performance and good press. Many of Trimark's clients had been invested for several years, so deferred sales charges were not a strong deterrent to cashing out. Moreover, mutual fund sales had slowed down, so the intermediaries weren't collecting commissions at the rate they once had. Selling Trimark and buying something else not only seemed to be in the client's best interest, it was also a quick way for financial advisers to earn a badly needed 5% commission. In this environment, says the former fund company chairman Paul Starita, Trimark was a sitting duck.

"When the independent broker turns on you, you're dead meat," Starita says. "In Trimark's case, the performance is modest or lacklustre. Their clients have been in those funds for seven or eight years, they have done quite well, and there was very little business in the last 18 months. Imagine you're a rep sitting back, saying, 'I need to make a living this year. I can't sell anything new, what should I do?' What I do is I churn my account. And Trimark was the victim. I feel sorry for those guys but they got killed."

Arthur Labatt points to another reason: a lot of financial planners are joining together into national distribution organizations that have launched their own funds. "So even if our performance had been middle-of-the-road to good, we would have had a lot of redemptions. They were taking people out of Trimark and putting them into their own product. And of course if the performance is not good, they have an excuse to do some trading and earn another 5%. That's very compelling. We got hit with all that at the same time."

Not all brokers and planners turned on Trimark; indeed, some had good words to say about the "certain manager" as resource stocks started to rise while bank stocks started to fall in 1999. Chris Tidd, a veteran mutual fund specialist at Odlum Brown, a Vancouver brokerage house, calls Maida a hero. "He made all the right calls, and my criticism is that Trimark stopped being managed by Arthur Labatt and Bob Krembil and started being managed by their wholesalers [Trimark employees who represent the company to brokers and planners]. All of a sudden, they were all on Krembil's case, saying, 'This guy's unsaleable.'"

Maida was incommunicado for an entire year following his departure. And after talking to a raft of knowledgeable outsiders, I was still confused about Trimark's investment style. Is it a value investor or a growth investor or a bit of both? Or is its style what some managers call Garp? That's not the hero of a John Irving novel – it stands for "growth at a reasonable price." The obvious person to ask was Krembil but, like Labatt, he's close to retirement, and his views are well known in any case. Here's what he said in a magazine interview in 1996: "We put our emphasis on the companies and we really search for business opportunities. It's a lot of hard work and study . . . and if you do all that study why not take advantage of that and have a decent holding? If you have too many names, your efforts get diluted." That would explain why the Trimark Fund, an international fund managed by Krembil until he was replaced by Bill Kanko in 1999, always has about 50 stocks, more than an AIC fund but a lot fewer than a typical fund in the same category. Green Line International Equity, for example, has about 120 stocks.

Trimark's future depends on the team of young managers it has recently recruited, so Keith Graham seemed like a good person to talk about investment philosophy. Graham is one of seven people Trimark raided from the Ontario Teachers Pension Plan Board, whose multibillion-dollar portfolio, while he was there, consistently turned in better results than the TSE 300 index, not to mention Trimark's Canadian funds. In fact, the teachers' Canadian equity portfolio beat the TSE 300 index's total return every year from 1994 to 1998. That's impressive, given that only one Canadian mutual fund, the PH&N Vintage Fund (run by Ian Mottershead and closed to new investors), achieved the same feat.

Vito Maida had also come to Trimark from a large public-sector pension fund. These pension funds are important sources of talent for the mutual fund industry, because portfolio managers who work there get experience investing huge amounts of money and yet get paid less than they can make at a mutual fund company. Graham and Geoff MacDonald arrived at Trimark in 1998 to start two new funds, one for small-cap stocks and one for resources. Then, when Maida got the boot, they took over the struggling RSP Equity Fund, a massive diversified Canadian stock fund.

Graham is a hefty fellow just short of 40 years old who grew up in Canada and then moved to the United States, where he worked as a broker for Fidelity (which in the United States is a seller of stocks and funds, not only a fund manager). He started out in Dallas and then worked in Atlanta, Boston, and Baltimore, eventually becoming a vice-president, at 27 one of the youngest Fidelity had ever had. But he wanted to manage money, and when you start out on the sales side for Fidelity, says Graham, you get typecast. It's hard to cross to the investment management side. So he came back to Canada, got an MBA, and went to work for the Ontario Teachers Pension Plan Board. After his success there, he got lots of offers from mutual fund companies. He and MacDonald were thinking about starting their own fund company instead. Then Trimark came calling. "This is the only company I was interested in working for," he says. "The people here think the same as I do about investment, they have integrity, and the company has financial stability and a great brand name. It was an easy decision."

By fall of 1999, it was looking like the right decision for Trimark as well: the RSP Equity Fund was up 27.2% to the end of August. It finished the year up only 16.2%, however, below average for its category. Unlike the case at Altamira, where new managers totally revamped the Equity Fund after the departure of Frank Mersch, Graham did only fine-tuning on the Trimark RSP Equity Fund because he thought Maida's only mistake was bad timing. "Vito is probably one of the greatest pure investors there ever was. It was circumstance that he became the lightning rod for things at Trimark. In hindsight everything he's said has come true." (Maida got another chance to display his investment skills in February 2000, when he launched his own firm, the appropriately named Patient Capital Management Inc., to manage money for wealthy individuals, institutions, and charities.)

As I spoke with Graham in his modest office, he kept surprising me. I expected the standard pitch about what a great investment equities are and how Canadians should just hand their money over and not worry about the inevitable fluctuations in the market. Instead, Graham said they *should* be worried. He's worried – not about Trimark, which he is sure will again beat the competition, but about the investment climate in general. "I am not convinced that in 10 years people will ever want to own mutual funds again, because the market will go down and they'll lose money," he told me.

Graham feels the same frustration people like Wayne Deans and Michael Lee-Chin must feel watching their carefully assembled portfolios languish while index funds are up almost every day. Graham would love a chance to display his talents in a market like that of the 1970s, when Bob Krembil proved that knowledge and skill really do matter. Krembil makes sure that new recruits hear the story of how the market fell 40% over the 1970s while his Taurus Fund went up tenfold during the same period. "That's a stock-picker's market," Graham says wistfully. "These markets today are not stock-pickers' markets. It's just buy anything with dot-com, and no one cares that it doesn't make a product and it doesn't have sales, it's worth $100 billion anyway. That's insanity. You can't invest in that."

For the amateur investor, the problem with a stock-picker's market is that if you aren't smart enough to be in the Taurus Fund at the right time, you lose. So if Graham gets his wish and the market takes a dive, it's going to be bad news for everybody who bought index funds and closet index funds and index participation units. Trimark, on the other hand, will look good again, at least in Graham's scenario. "I think the financial markets are in for some rocky times over the next 10 to 20 years," he says. "That's good for Trimark, because those are the times when good investing will win out."

So what exactly is good investing? Graham calls himself a "fundamental manager." For him, good investing means what it means for Bob Krembil: buying good businesses, businesses that are fundamentally sound, when the price is right. For example, in the latter part of the 1990s, the American market was roaring ahead while Japan was in the doldrums. The stocks of some companies went up just because they were American; others were penalized for being Japanese. Sony and General Electric both had similar businesses and growth rates. Sony had sales of $60 billion, GE $98 billion. Yet in the spring of 1999, the market had placed a value on GE 10 times higher than that of Sony. It made no sense. Sony is an excellent business whose products are in demand all over the world. Trimark started buying Sony in 1992; by 1999 it was up 144%, but it was still good value and Trimark was still buying.

This kind of investing is "amazingly simple," Graham says. When he buys a stock, he pretends he's buying the whole company. He adds up the total value of all the shares outstanding and decides if everything the company has – its plants, its brand, its cash flow – is a good deal at that price. "What am I paying and what am I getting? That's what I want to know. It's that simple."

Trimark used to run a TV ad showing a team of investment managers visiting a crummy little company in some fly-infested backwater. The manager of the company was surprised that so many people had come so far just to visit his crummy little company. (As an investor, I was surprised too. Why didn't Trimark send just one person and pass the savings on to their investors in the form of lower MERs?) Graham is one of those people who visit managers of companies small and large. The rest of the time he's at his desk, studying and doing complicated things with numbers on his computer. He never stops. "If I had nothing else to do, I would read annual reports for fun," he says. "At home and on vacation. My wife reads a murder mystery and I read the U.S. Tobacco Company annual report. It's fun to me, it's my hobby. The number one skill needed to succeed at investing long-term is curiosity. If you're a naturally curious person, asking questions, that's how you learn." When the family goes shopping on the weekend, Graham wanders about, analyzing the store layout. He'll hunt down the manager and discuss business. "I live, eat, breathe, sleep, and think investing," he says. "I drive my wife crazy."

Visiting the premises of a prospective investment is an art, not a science. "It's the vibes, it's what kind of car does the boss drive, how much does he pay himself? Is the factory clean? How long have the people worked there? What do the customers have to say? All the companies we see are customers of other companies, and we always ask their opinion."

Many investors don't understand that this type of research might not result in the kind of gains they were able to make recently by buying, say, units of a NASDAQ index fund. They probably should have owned some NASDAQ index units, but it would be risky to put a high percentage of one's assets in a NASDAQ fund. A portfolio manager always balances risk and return because, says Graham, "the best way to make money is not to lose any in the first place." Buying good companies at good prices is a way to do that. For example, he bought a big holding in Viceroy Homes for the small-cap fund he runs. "When we started buying it, we were getting it for less than the cash on the balance sheet. The company had the brand name, it made money, it had no debt, it had been in business many years. That's a good investment."

What worries Graham is that many investors lack the patience to wait for good investments to pay off. They have forgotten, or never knew, that any return above about 5%, which you can get on a treasury bill or GIC, involves risk. "People have forgotten risk and are just thinking about return. I think risk will come back and bite them." He even questions the basic thesis of every financial planner and seminar speaker, namely that equities will outperform over the long term. "If you're starting up here" – he raises his hand over his head – "and your term is out here" – he moves his hand a shorter distance in front of him – "that's not true. We've seen the greatest bull run in history, and I would argue now is not the time to be plowing money into the stock market. Yet that's what everybody's doing."

This is frank talk from someone whose business is collecting assets to invest in the stock market. But if you send him your money, he'll invest it in the best businesses he can find. Unlike Maida, he doesn't believe in holding large amounts of cash in an equity fund. "I am being given money by investors to invest in the market, not to hold cash. That's a market call and I don't make market calls." In other words, he won't hold cash in anticipation of a fluctuation in the overall market that might drag all stocks down temporarily. If you want apples, don't buy oranges; if you want cash, don't buy an equity fund. All Graham can do to protect his investors from a down-turn is to look for the best 50 Canadian companies to invest in. "Even if the whole market collapses, those 50 will go down less than the other 50."

While he's investing your money, though, he'll be worrying about whether you should have sent it in. "If you look through hundreds of years of market history, at market tops is when the public owns the most financial assets, at market bottoms the public owns the least. Not so long ago people understood that the stock market was risky. Now if you don't have your money in the stock market, you're made to feel you're a fool."

Is Graham saying that maybe people should be putting money into boring, safe stuff like Canada Savings Bonds instead of equity mutual funds?

"Yes, they should."

That may be the most radical advice I heard from any fund manager. But if it makes Trimark investors nervous, here's some news that should cheer them up: most of Graham's own money is in the funds he manages.

Chances are that Keith Graham and the other investors in the funds he's managing for Trimark won't do as well as the teachers did when he was managing their pension funds. The reason is that Trimark sells its funds through intermediaries who have to be paid. As a result, Trimark's investors pay higher management expense ratios than the teachers do in their pension fund. And high MERs, as we have seen, eat away at long-term returns.

The issue of MERs is an awkward one for Trimark, because it's the only major fund company to offer separate but virtually iden-tical funds for investors paying a front-end commission and for those paying the deferred sales charge (DSC), payable only if the fund is sold within six years. On the front-end-load fund, the customer is responsible for paying the commission, which is negotiable between him and the dealer. But on the DSC equivalent, Trimark has to pay 4.9% of the amount invested to the dealer, so it extracts a higher MER. Obviously, the DSC fund is going to underperform its front-end-load equivalent by approximately the amount of the extra MER.

Trimark got pushed into setting up DSC funds because there are so few Chris Tidds among mutual fund dealers. Tidd, the Vancouver broker and Vito Maida fan, has been around since before the DSC was concocted. He hates it. He won't sell DSC funds because he doesn't want his customers staying in bad investments just to avoid paying commissions. Instead he charges them a 1% front-end commission. Trimark would be happy to see all its funds sold that way, but most dealers won't stand for it. "We dragged our heels before even bringing out a back-end-load fund, but it was what all the brokers and planners wanted," Labatt told me. Some advisers conveniently forget to tell their customers that the DSC fund has a higher MER; Trimark, to its credit, explains this clearly in its latest prospectus.

Trimark's original funds, Trimark Fund (international) and Trimark Canadian, still have the same MERs they had at the beginning, 1.52%. These are well below average, which means that, for investors capable of figuring this out, Trimark is offering a good deal. The problem is that most advisers don't want their clients to get a good deal. Instead, Labatt said, financial advisers complain when clients bug them to sell Trimark's low-MER funds instead of the identical high-MER ones. The intermediaries would like Trimark to get rid of the low-MER funds because, says Labatt, the fact that consumers have a choice "puts the intermediaries on the spot." That's not going to happen. Those two funds represent the 20-year track record that Trimark's reputation is based on. Not only are they are going to remain, Labatt expects increased interest in them as consumers become more cost-conscious.

Through Trimark's tough times, the most frequently heard criticism was the lack of variety in its offerings. All its funds were based on the idea, as explained in a Trimark brochure, that "we don't chase 'hot investments,' but look for securities that have inherent value and are out of favour – and therefore attractively priced." This was not a popular investment style when, month after month, the hot investments kept getting hotter and the undervalued stocks stayed undervalued. Not only did all the funds operate according to that one style, but Trimark's array of funds was comparatively limited. Until 1999, it did not have an American equity fund, thus forcing even its most loyal customers to go elsewhere to invest in the world's largest economy. (AIC also had a limited selection, but it was offering three different American funds by the end of 1999.)

The money kept fleeing, and by the summer of 1999, it was time for something dramatic. Finally, in June, Trimark made a move. It hired a star manager, Kiki Delaney, to run a new fund, the Trimark Enterprise Fund. Delaney did not come to Trimark as an employee; she ran the fund through her company, C.A. Delaney Capital Management Ltd. Her partner in that company, Lynn Miller, became the manager of a second new fund, the Trimark Enterprise Small Cap Fund. This move was reminiscent of Fidelity's acquisition of Veronika Hirsch after AGF had spent a fortune building her up as a star. Spectrum United, which is owned by Sun Life, had invested heavily in Delaney, who looked good on TV riding a tractor across a grain field in a chic outfit. And putting her in the limelight had paid off for Spectrum United. The assets in Spectrum United Canadian Equity had grown from $147 million when she took it over in October 1992 to $1.4 billion by the time she left in 1999. But her departure, leaving behind thousands of investors who had invested not in a fund but in a manager, was just the sort of thing that is souring some Canadians on mutual funds.

I attended the press conference Trimark called in Toronto to announce the acquisition of Delaney. She was being beamed in from Victoria, where she was starting a nationwide road show to promote the two new Enterprise funds.

"What would you advise an investor who had put money into your fund at Spectrum to do now?" somebody asked her.

"I would definitely say come on over," she replied. "I believe absolutely our record stands up and it behooves people to make the switch."

What she neglected to say was that almost all the investors who had entrusted their money to her at Spectrum United would have to pay deferred sales charges if they pulled out. Someone who had invested, say, $20,000, a couple of years earlier would lose $1,000 to sales charges if he followed Delaney to Trimark. (There would also be the matter of the capital gains tax.) Would it be worth it? Rudy Luukko, a fund analyst, took a close look at Delaney's record at Spectrum United. For the fund she was managing, the longest period attributable entirely to her was that ending April 30, 1999. During those five years, her fund's compound annual return was 10.9%, compared with 12.7% for her benchmark, the TSE 300 index. Delaney's investors trailed the index – surprise – by approximately the amount of the MER on her fund. Luukko concluded that Delaney's high profile was mainly due to one great year, her first full one, when the fund rose 42.9%, compared with the index's 32.5%. The rest of the time she underperformed. In fact, her record at Spectrum United wasn't nearly as good as that of Trimark's new non-star manager, Keith Graham, when he was at the teachers' pension fund.

As it turned out, Spectrum United Canadian Equity, under Delaney's successor, Doug Mahaffey, ended the year with a 26% increase, better than the average fund in its class. Delaney's new Trimark Enterprise Fund, meanwhile, had a 15.2% return in its first six months, also above average. It all goes to prove that even a famous fund manager can give bad advice, which Delaney did by urging Spectrum United investors to follow her to Trimark. As Luukko acidly pointed out in the *National Post*, a 5% deferred sales charge is "a lot to pay for historical below-index performance."

The Delaney episode raises another issue for mutual fund investors. If it's true that you invest in a manager and not a fund, then the investor had better find out something about the relationship between the manager and the fund. Is he a freelancer like Delaney? If so, he may not be around for long. Or is he on staff? Does he own a stake in the company, as quite a few fund managers do? Those are the ones least likely to jump ship.

The most puzzling thing about the acquisition of Delaney was that it did nothing to satisfy those who thought Trimark should diversify its investment style. Delaney was not about to start a growth fund or a sector rotation fund or a momentum fund because she wasn't that kind of investor. She's a value investor, like the other Trimark managers. She does intensive research looking for good deals, a good deal being defined as "the most growth for the least price." She did say, however, in what sounded like it could be a knock at a certain manager, that "buying deep and dirty value on its own is not good enough."

The hiring of Delaney was part of an evolving strategy under which Trimark would offer investors not a choice of investment style but a choice of managers. Whereas previously Maida had been lead manager on all the diversified Canadian funds, now Trimark was offering four diversified funds with four different management teams, all committed to the value philosophy. This new policy also alleviated the embarrassing issue of identical high-MER and low-MER Canadian funds. The low-MER Trimark Canadian Fund now had its own distinct management team and thus could be expected to perform differently from the other funds for reasons other than lower fees.

Krembil, also in Victoria for the Kiki Delaney press conference, did not look happy drumming his fingers on the table as reporters asked him to explain how he expected Trimark customers to differentiate among a bunch of funds using different managers to implement the same style. "I can't think of any long-term record that isn't the product of a bottom-up approach," he said. In other words, he wouldn't hire a manager with a different style, because it's his company and for him there is only one style. (Bottom-up, by the way, is another way of saying you buy a company only because it's a good business and not for some other reason, such as that its stock is going up.) Any style differences among the funds, Krembil said, would be discernible only as "shades of grey."

Shades of grey – it might have been a catchy slogan for Trimark's annual general meeting a couple of weeks later, but the promotion people had already picked "Trimark is strong." That was news to the share-holders who had escaped a steamy Toronto summer afternoon for the air-conditioned comfort of the Royal York Hotel. Their shares, which had been worth $29.75 in March 1998, were now worth $18. Krembil took the podium to respond to critics who thought Trimark needed different investment styles. He said he'd never endanger the Trimark brand by becoming a "Heinz 57" kind of company. He referred several times to the importance of building the brand as Trimark's best strategy in an increasingly competitive business environment.

No shareholder stood up to ask why the brand, already one of the best known in Canada, didn't prevent customers from hauling an incredible $6.9 billion out of Trimark funds in the year ended March 31, 1999. Krembil apparently does not understand that investors are becoming more sophisticated and less impressed by advertising hype. The companies with the biggest increases in assets in 1999 were ones like Synergy, C.I., AIM, and Talvest. Their success had little to do with brand recognition (almost non-existent) or tele-vision ads. Investors put money in those companies because those companies were making money for investors. The same thing is hap-pening in the United States. "The three most important things in fund flows are performance, performance, performance," Charles Biderman, president of a California investment research company, informed the *Wall Street Journal*.

Trimark had decided to be a value investor because it thought that was the only method that worked in the long run. But the pain continued, and Trimark suffered another $1.5 billion in net redemp-tions in the fiscal year ended March 2000. The deal combining Trimark and AIM was a way to solve the redemptions problem. The new company, with Krembil staying on as chairman and chief invest-ment officer, would continue to offer Trimark's value funds. But investors weary of the value style would be able to switch to one of AIM's growth or momentum funds without taking their money out of the newly merged company. Labatt could now move on to retire-ment confident that he was leaving Trimark in good shape.

Despite all the redemptions, it hadn't been in such terrible shape even before the merger with AIM. While Trimark's unitholders were watching their investments shrink or stagnate, the company itself was making pots of money. Even after the plunge in assets, fiscal 1999 was its most profitable year since it became a public company. How could this happen? Some of the fleeing customers had to pay deferred sales charges, which added to revenues, and the thousands of advisers who'd stopped selling Trimark funds weren't getting commissions, which reduced expenses.

Remember Steve Wynn, the casino owner? Well, Trimark owned a big casino, and even if it was less crowded than it used to be, it was still crowded. The $23.5 billion under management was enough to produce half a billion dollars in management fees. The best of times, the worst of times – even in the most trying year imaginable, a mutual fund company is still a wonderful money machine.

CHAPTER FIVE

WHAT DO FUND MANAGERS DO?

On a balmy January evening in Victoria, 800 people in a ballroom of the Empress Hotel are happily flipping pennies. It's a bit of a surprise to find such boisterous activity in this dignified hotel best known for the afternoon teas it has been serving for the past 90 years. But Ted Cadsby has a point to prove.

Cadsby, instigator of the mass coin toss, is one of the more unusual people in Canada's mutual fund industry. Although many people in the business have liberal arts backgrounds, not many have degrees in philosophy, Cadsby's subject at Queen's University. And even in the investment business, a young person's turf, it's unusual for a 32-year-old to be put in command of a major fund company. Yet that's how old Cadsby was in 1998 when he took charge of CIBC Securities Inc., the seventh-largest fund company in Canada, with $21 billion of assets under management.

Why has a serious young man who should be tending to the $21 billion under his care got all these potential buyers of CIBC mutual funds flipping coins? It's the routine Cadsby uses whenever he speaks about his favourite subject: the management of mutual funds and the superiority, in his opinion, of index funds to actively managed ones. This opinion – heresy in most of the industry – is the most unconventional thing of all about Cadsby. The industry's pitch, offered by almost all companies and dealers, is that investors should buy mutual funds because mutual funds give them professional money management. In other words, one of the most important things the industry has to sell is the brains of its portfolio managers.

Brains are also involved in choosing the stocks that go into an index, but they don't work as hard as an active fund manager's. The main index in Canada, the TSE 300, contains 300 of the biggest companies trading on the Toronto Stock Exchange, accounting for about 85% of the total value of all Canadian stocks. A committee of the exchange makes decisions about adding or deleting stocks from the index. To stay in the index, stocks must meet certain criteria, such as being in good financial health and being actively traded, but the selection process is much less rigorous than that employed by active managers. And while an active manager will make his own decision about how much of a given stock to put in his portfolio, that decision is made passively by the index, which is "weighted" according to the market capitalization of the stocks on it. In other words, each stock is not 1/300 of the index. The bigger stocks constitute a bigger percentage of the index and the smaller ones a lower percentage. As a result, the price movements of the stocks of the biggest companies have the most impact on the index.

The manager of an index fund does not have to make decisions about what companies to buy or sell because the index committee makes those decisions for her. She does have to make sure her fund accurately tracks the index, but she need not know anything about the companies in her portfolio. She just buys all the stocks on the index. Even if Bre-X is in the TSE 300 and the manager has a queasy feeling about Bre-X, she has to buy it. An active manager, on the other hand, has many reasons for choosing a stock, but whether the stock is in an index should not be one of them.

Cadsby arrived, as he always does, with a bagful of pennies, and everyone got one as they came in. "Let's pretend that every one of you is a manager of a mutual fund," he tells the assembly. "Would each manager please stand up, and have your penny in your hand."

Eight hundred money managers stand, pennies at the ready.

"Now everybody flip."

Eight hundred people flip. "Everyone who flipped heads did better than the index for one year and everyone who flipped tails did worse than the index," he says. "Will the underperformers please sit down."

Four hundred people, more or less, sit down.

To those left standing, he says, "Let's see if we can get another year of good performance out of you."

After five flips, only a handful are left standing, and Cadsby is effusive in his praise. "Now you're really recognized in the industry," he says. "After five years of outperformance, you've all had write-ups in the newspaper featuring you as very skilled managers."

After 11 flips, one person is left standing, the only one whose penny has not yet come down tails. This is Cadsby's way of driving home his point that, through pure luck, one person out of 800 can obtain results that are far above average. In his view, the implications of his coin-flipping game for Canadian investors trying to choose among more than 3,000 different mutual funds are huge. In a given year some mutual fund managers will outperform the index, but most won't do any better than the majority of this gathering of Victorians, who were seated after one or two coin tosses. As for the handful of fund managers who do outperform, Cadsby has the audacity to suggest that their success may be due more to luck than to skill. As a philosophy graduate, he's trained in logic, and logic prompts him to ask whether there's any difference between a successful money manager, even one who's had 11 good years in a row, and a coin-flipper who flips heads 11 times in a row. There are, after all, thousands of money managers. Probability suggests that at least one or two would have many successive years of above-average returns. "Who is to say that Peter Lynch and Warren Buffett aren't just very lucky coin-flippers rather than skilled managers?" Cadsby asks. "Mathematically, it's very difficult to differentiate." His conclusion? Since one's chances of picking a fund that will consistently do better than the index are slim, and since most funds underperform the index, why not just buy the index?

John Vivash is one of the few people in the industry who agree with Cadsby. After years of running mutual fund companies that offered actively managed funds, Vivash, now a consultant, concluded that most portfolio managers have "delusions of adequacy." Of course, nobody likes to be told that what he does all day is not necessary, and the proposition is especially hard to swallow for fund managers, who tend to be smart and hard-working. Nevertheless, the appeal of index funds is growing rapidly. Americans, as usual when it comes to investment trends, are well ahead of Canadians. Almost half of the new money going into equity funds in the United States now goes to index funds. As of November 1999, Americans had $240 billion invested in index funds, as much as the U.S. government spends on national defence in a year. In Canada, although most companies don't even offer index funds, they are the fastest-growing segment of the industry: 21% of new equity fund sales in 1999 were in index funds, compared with only 7% in 1998. One of the important decisions a fund investor has to make is whether to use actively managed funds, index funds, or a mix of the two.

Is active management worth paying for? To answer that question, it helps to know what "active management" actually means. Synergy Asset Management, a mutual fund company in downtown Toronto, has an approach to active management that's unique in the industry. Synergy's offices, ironically, are in the same prestigious Toronto complex, First Canadian Place, as Trimark's. It's ironic because when it comes to investment style, Synergy is Trimark's opposite. Trimark is wedded to a single approach, value investing, whereas Synergy was founded to implement Joe Canavan's belief that the best way to get consistent above-average performance is to integrate four distinct investment styles.

Canavan is a 38-year-old dynamo, a younger version of Jim O'Donnell, one of the industry's early movers and shakers. Although Canavan is more outgoing than the reserved O'Donnell, both are gifted salesmen with a deep intellectual interest in financial markets (and a penchant for drawing lines to explain their ideas). Both have a knack for innovation and for turning small mutual fund businesses into bigger ones. Canavan, a former broker to rock stars and CEOs, joined Fidelity in 1989, two years after it arrived in Canada. Fidelity was stagnating with a measly $60 million in assets. Canavan and another talented persuader, John Simpson, split the country up between them, hit the road visiting brokers and planners, and four years later had helped lure $6 billion of Canadians' savings into Fidelity's care.

In 1994, Canavan found himself in need of employment; all he will say is that he disagreed with his bosses at Fidelity "over the direction of the firm." He persuaded GT Global, an international fund firm based in Liechtenstein, that it needed a Canadian branch. GT under Canavan did two things no other Canadian fund company had done. First, it introduced what Canavan calls "theme funds," dedicated to investing in such areas as health care and telecommunications. Second, it introduced the first mutual fund in Canada using the momentum investment style. This innovation on the investment side, combined with Canavan's salesmanship, led to rapid growth for GT Global.

In 1997, Canavan decided he had "one last company to build." He surprised the industry by walking out of GT (which has since been absorbed by AIM Management, the same British-owned fund company that later merged with Trimark). In Chapter One, we heard from Canavan that 90% of mutual funds in Canada are "crap." How could he be sure his new Synergy funds would be among the non-crappy minority? In a small glass-walled office affording a view of most of Synergy's 50 employees, he grabs pen and paper and illustrates the insight on which Synergy is based. It's the same story he's told hundreds of times as he travels the country wining and dining the financial advisers and brokers who sell his funds.

At Fidelity he found there were times when growth, that company's favoured style, doesn't work so well. He draws a line showing growth investing going up and then down. He also knew, from his experience at GT Global, that the momentum style has its ups and downs. He draws more lines showing ups and downs. Then there's Trimark's beloved value style. "Value is a great way to make money," he enthuses, "but boy, is it cyclical! In the last two years, if you've been a value investor you've been in pain, you've been losing money, you've been drinking Digel, you've been losing sleep." He draws another line going up and then down. "And small cap – I really think small cap is fantastic and the returns over 10 years are stunning. But the volatility! It's a roller-coaster ride." More lines, up and down, up and down, looking more like the Alps than a roller coaster. "In small cap, from the peak to the trough to the peak can be four years."

Four years of suffering for a cause may be noble, even character-building, but is small-cap investing, or any other kind of investing, worth suffering for? Canavan didn't think so. Why not, he wondered, offer customers four funds, for the momentum, growth, value, and small-cap investing styles? Why not give the funds a legal structure that allows investors to switch from one to another without triggering capital gains? And, to cover all bases, why not have a fifth fund embodying all four investment styles? To turn that novel idea into reality, why not hire the most ambitious young managers you can find, give them a piece of the action, and tell them their bonuses depend on beating the benchmark for their particular investment style?

Blending the four investment styles, Canavan says, reduces risk and boosts returns at the same time. To Canavan, risk is almost as important an issue as return. He doesn't want Synergy investors to get a 20% average return by being up 30% one year and down 10% the next. Some investors can tolerate that kind of volatility, but most can't, and financial advisers hate it. "That's why we use a lot of risk technology within a portfolio to make sure we spread the risk. Where some funds will take a 10% position in some small-cap company that they can't get out of, or load up on the hot stock of the day, we can't and won't do that. It's part of our philosophy to manage the risk as much as the return."

One part of managing risk is to avoid becoming dependent on a star manager. While Trimark was splashing Kiki Delaney's smile all over Canadian newspapers, Synergy was running sober-looking ads showing David Picton's Synergy momentum fund, up 31% since inception, without even mentioning Picton. It's not that Canavan isn't thrilled with David Picton's success; he simply doesn't want to see any of his managers become so prominent that the company's future is compromised. "There's a point where you're taking a risk by having one person at the forefront. If he gets hit by a truck or becomes not so good at his job, there's a business risk." The consensus in the industry is that the era of the star manager is over; the success of index funds is one of the reasons. This is especially true in the U.S., where the Standard and Poor's 500 stock index has outperformed most active funds for several years. "The tyranny of the S&P 500 has made it an impossible environment for a fund manager to be a star in," John Rekenthaler, research director at Morningstar, the leading fund-tracking company, told the *Wall Street Journal*.

What does a fund manager do all day? To find out, I got up early one morning and went to see Picton. If one searched for a manager who embodied everything that the fund industry says is good about active management, one would probably end up with Picton, who runs the Synergy Momentum Class. Picton is no closet indexer; he's a disciplined investor who uses computer technology and his own highly trained brain to identify the stocks most likely to rise in value. The results? In each of the two years that Picton's fund has been in business, it has whipped the TSE 300 and most of the competition. And its gaudy returns were net of a fat MER of 2.95%, well above average. Performance is worth paying for, the industry tells us, and defenders of high MERs must wish they had dozens of Pictons to point to.

Picton comes down to rescue me from the lobby of First Canadian Place, where I'm stranded because the elevator won't take visitors to the 36th floor outside normal office hours. It's 7 a.m., and Picton has been at work since 6:30. He likes a bit of quiet time to check on breaking financial news before the phone starts ringing at 8. On this day the monitor tuned to CNBC-TV (an American business channel) on the wall behind his desk is too snowy to look at, so he brings up the Bloomberg business news site on the Internet. He checks the markets in Asia and Europe ("The Europe index is tanking") and ponders the big business story of the day: Global Crossing Ltd., a Bermuda-based telecom company, is merging with U.S. West Inc., a US$37-billion deal that would create a new telecom giant. "It could affect the valuation of Teleglobe," Picton says, referring to Montreal-based Teleglobe Inc., the major Canadian competitor.

Don't be fooled by the word "momentum" in the name of Picton's fund. For casual readers of the business pages, it conjures up an image of the day trader who doesn't know or care what business a company is in but will hitch a ride on its stock if it's moving up. That's gambling, not investing, no different than betting on a hot shooter in a crap game. It's not what Picton does, although a rising stock price is one of his decision-making criteria. Canavan, who brought momentum investing to Canada from the United States, has a nice image to explain it. Think of the value investor and the momentum investor as two travellers about to board the same train. The value investor gets to the station 20 minutes before departure and waits for the train to leave. The momentum investor arrives at the last second, not hopping aboard until the train is chugging out of the station.

Far from having a day trader's ignorance about the companies he invests in, Picton knows everything important there is to know about them. The Synergy office seethes with information. Picton has a cluttered workspace decorated with drawings by his three young children. Because the space is open concept, the managers chat among themselves. Computers churn out data all day, as do the TV monitors; and starting at 8 a.m. Picton's phone rings nonstop as brokerage analysts, company executives, and others call to chat. What does he do with all this information? He applies it to his decision-making process on stocks that his computer software has already flagged as fitting into his momentum system.

He grabs a computer printout showing financial details on stocks that meet his criteria. Picton monitors 100 Canadian stocks, looking for those worth climbing aboard. His software winnows these down to about 40, this day including companies as varied as Alberta Energy, Open Text, and Sears Canada. "The software makes the most important trade-off in fund management," explains Picton. "And that is: how much risk am I going to take and how much reward do I want to get out of this portfolio?" He uses the technology to analyze every combination of the eligible stocks in terms of risk and return. He draws a vertical line down the left side of a sheet of paper and connects it to a horizontal line across the bottom. The vertical line is

return, the horizontal line is risk. The top left corner of the paper –
maximum return and minimum risk – is where he wants to be. He
calls this "the efficient frontier." Picton's computer screens all the
stocks on the market, looking for those with four characteristics:

- accelerating earnings and/or revenues
- earnings forecasts being revised upward by analysts
- better-than-expected earnings
- stock price outperforming the market or other similar stocks

These criteria are what he means by momentum.

How does Picton's reliance on the four criteria differentiate him
from the value investor? "The value investor, if he's got any brains,
would look for something incredibly cheap where he could visualize
how the earnings are going to increase eventually. I don't want to
have to visualize. I want to *see* the earnings and sales growing, and I
want to see them growing at a faster rate. I want to see that acceleration – not just an increase but an increase in the increase. That's the
real key difference."

The value investor insists she's buying a business, not a stock,
certain that if the business is a good one the market eventually will
recognize its merits. The momentum investor wants good businesses
too, but only when their earnings are rising at an accelerated clip and
the market has already begun to take notice. A risky strategy? Not
particularly. Note that three of Picton's four criteria revolve around
earnings. That automatically excludes high-flying technology stocks
with no earnings. Because he adheres religiously to his discipline,
Picton can't buy, for example, money-losing Ballard Power, even if
he is convinced that the fuel cell company's stock has nowhere to go
but up. "I'm going to miss concepts like Ballard," he admits. "You can
make a lot of money on concepts, but my guess is that nine out of
ten never pan out."

Today Picton's computer is telling him to buy TD Bank. Its
"momentum rank" is fifth, way up from 53rd just three months ago.
It's making this recommendation even though the stock price has just
hit a new high. The computer is so hot on TD that it's recommending

it constitute 8% of the portfolio. Picton thinks that's too much. "There's always this subjective trade-off you're making between what the computer says, what your due diligence has found, and finally the overall state of the market. There's a computer-assisted part of [decision-making] but there's a subjective part as well. That's the whole art of portfolio management. There's no formula. It's all trading off risk versus return potential."

As Picton explains all this, the office is starting to hum. The occupant of the closest desk, Suzanne Pennington, a value manager who runs the Canadian Value Class, arrives. (Synergy designates its funds as "classes" because, technically, they are all one fund with different classes – momentum, value, growth, and small cap. That way, if an investor thinks momentum is losing steam and value is about to have its day in the sun, he can switch money from Picton's portfolio to Pennington's without having to pay capital gains tax.) Pennington starts talking about her weekend adventures as a soccer mom, but Picton changes the subject. "Suzanne, you should look at Sherritt," he says, referring to Sherritt International, the conglomerate run by Kiki Delaney's husband, Ian, which is currently trading at $3.75.

"I looked at it last week," she replies. "I think we're going to get it weaker."

The crucial concept in momentum investing is positive change, which TD is experiencing as it establishes a beachhead in discount brokerage. Fast-rising earnings, upward changes in forecasts, and happy earnings surprises are all positive changes, and positive changes are attention-getters. "What you want to do," explains Picton, "is change people's opinions, re-evaluate what they think of a stock. When they do that re-evaluation, that's when you get your most exciting moves in a stock." And that's when Picton wants to climb aboard the train.

A tower in Toronto's financial district is a long way from Castlegar, a mining and sawmill town on the banks of the Columbia River about halfway between Vancouver and Calgary, where Picton grew up. The 35-year-old son of a truck driver, he has a scruffy beard, a ready smile, a deep, confident voice, and a knack for explaining complex concepts clearly. Synergy Momentum is Picton's first crack at money management but he was already well known in the small world of "the street" before he came over to Canavan's fledgling company. After graduating in commerce from the University of British Columbia, he got a job at Dominion Securities in Vancouver. A year and a half later, he moved to Toronto to do quantitative research for Dominion. "That means using computer models to predict what stock prices are going to do. But before you ever get to that stage, you have to do a whole bunch of research into what actually drives stock prices and come up with theories and do testing to see if those theories have actually worked in real life. I interviewed fund managers and found they had totally different ways of investing. And they all were quite adamant that their way was the way to do it."

In his testing, he found that value investing and growth investing both work well over the long term, providing the managers stick to their guns, which can be hard to do when things aren't going well. He decided his own preference was for the momentum style, partly because he saw it as a way to make his mark in Canada, where it was relatively unknown and where a momentum fund would stand out in an overcrowded market.

Picton thinks Canada is too dominated by the "cult of value." Speakers at investment seminars pay endless tribute to Benjamin Graham, founder of value investing, and his most successful students, Warren Buffett and John Templeton. The same seminars usually offer "a portfolio manager telling why his version of value is good. Over the years everyone heard the same thing and they all loaded up on value. And then we came along with a totally different message." Canadians were obviously ready for Synergy's message: by April 2000, after just over two years in business, it had assets under management of $760 million, and new money was coming in at a rate of $5 million a day.

Momentum investing has an alluring simplicity. "If a company is cheap or expensive doesn't really matter," Picton says. "It is fundamental change for the better that's driving these stocks. Momentum does not mean you're buying the flavour of the day, high flyers, the great new story. I really don't like to buy stories. I like to buy positive fundamental change."

Momentum investing is old news in the United States, but few Canadian managers have adopted it. That's surprising given that the momentum style has been more successful in recent years than the value method, and is easier to implement. A value manager has to dig and dig and dig. "Sometimes there's something buried within the financial statements," Picton says, "for example, that the company has this other operation that's worth a lot and that people aren't aware of." Companies like Trimark and Fidelity, which have their own teams of analysts, have the manpower to dig out such facts. This is where a start-up company like Synergy that can't afford its own in-house analysts seems to be at a disadvantage. But because he's using the momentum style, Picton says, he doesn't feel at all disadvantaged. The information he needs on such things as earnings growth is not hidden in company reports. It's so readily available that it pops out automatically when he runs his computer program.

Things that preoccupy other managers don't matter much to a momentum manager. For example, Michael Lee-Chin buys financial companies for his AIC funds because he thinks aging boomers will increasingly need financial services. Vito Maida, on the other hand, avoided financial stocks because he thought they were overpriced. But Picton will buy a stock if it meets his criteria, regardless of its price or the industry it's in. In January 1998, as one of his first buys for the newly launched fund, he bought National Bank, not because it was cheap or because he thought boomers would be flocking to its branches but because its earnings were better than expected and analysts were revising their forecasts upward. Five months after he bought it, the stock was up 35%. Picton pays attention to the industry a company is in only insofar as he wants diversity in the portfolio. Depending on the economic cycle, the screen might be turning up mostly resource or high-tech stocks. He won't allow the portfolio to get too concentrated in any one area. Screening stocks to find ones that meet the criteria is only the first step in stock selection. If a stock rates high on his list and he's considering it, he'll meet the managers of the company and study the fundamentals, just as a bottom-up manager does, to ensure that the outfit has the capital and strategy to sustain momentum. "I want to meet them, not so I can get their rosy projections but just to get a better understanding of why there is momentum in this company. Did they actually do something or was it a fluke?"

Meeting management is more important than ever, Picton says, because of the increasing importance of technology stocks. "I definitely want to spend a little more time to understand what business they're in, what niche they're in." If he decides to buy, there's the critical question of how much to buy. Synergy Momentum has only about 40 stocks, and Picton puts a lot of effort into having the right blend. "It's not good enough to just go out and buy Royal Bank. It's better to buy Royal Bank in the right proportion so I get enough momentum but I don't have a huge risk profile. Say I like a little company, Patheon, a [drug] company that meets my momentum criteria. It's small, illiquid, it's got a bit of volatility, therefore a bit more risky. I can't buy a large position because in terms of a risk/reward profile it's very difficult to justify. So I'll tone down my Patheon weighting. I'll still own the stock but in such a way that I'm controlling the risk parameters in my portfolio."

Maybe it's just lucky coin-flipping, but Synergy Momentum has brought nothing but joy to its investors since it opened for business. In 1998, its first year, it returned 20.2%, the best performance among 300 Canadian equity funds in a year in which the average fund lost 3% and the TSE 300 fell by 1.6%. This debut was so spectacular that not one of six experts polled by the *Globe and Mail* at the beginning of 1999 for their top fund picks chose Synergy Momentum. Undeterred, Picton managed it to a 42.9% increase in 1999, when the TSE 300 index gained 31.7%. The *Globe*, to its credit, did a post-mortem on its experts' picks a year later. Of 36 choices, only 10 were in the top quartile of funds; 18, exactly half, were in the fourth quartile. Fourth quartile is a polite way of saying bottom of the heap. If that's the best the experts can do, perhaps Ted Cadsby is right when he suggests it's futile to try to forecast which funds will beat the index. An amateur, throwing darts at the weekly fund charts pinned up on a wall, could hardly do worse than the experts.

David Picton, it soon becomes clear, is good at multi-tasking. While he's talking to me, he's also observing stock prices on his monitor, taking and placing calls, and chatting with Suzanne Pennington, Andrew McCreath (who runs the Growth Class), and Michael Mahoney (who manages a global fund). Canavan is wandering about and the sales and administrative staff are also out here in this same space. Other fund managers have private offices where tranquillity reigns. Picton's work environment has the charged atmosphere of a newspaper office on deadline. He likes being in constant contact with other managers because, in addition to the Momentum Class, he also manages the Style Management Class, which mixes stocks chosen by the four different investment styles. Depending on the market, Picton's momentum picks often overlap with those of the other managers. In 1998, for example, he had a "huge overlap" with McCreath's growth portfolio, and in 1999 he got interested in some of the same stocks that are in Suzanne Pennington's value portfolio.

Picton trades ideas regularly with Mahoney, the global manager, because Synergy's policy is to maximize foreign content in its Canadian funds. (A Canadian fund as of 2000 can have 25% foreign content and still be 100% RRSP-eligible. By 2001, the foreign content limit will be raised to 30%. An investor who chooses Canadian funds that use full foreign content and also includes fully foreign funds to a total of 30% of the overall book value of an RRSP will be able to bring the foreign portion of that RRSP up to 51% without resorting to high-priced clone funds.) Some companies don't put much foreign content in their Canadian funds, believing that, if a fund is sold as Canadian, that's what it should be. Picton disagrees. First of all, he points out, foreign markets have persistently outperformed Canada's, so why be puritanical and not boost your returns by including foreign stocks? Second, "By buying companies in industries that aren't avail-able in the Canadian marketplace and that act differently, you also help the risk side of the equation. You boost returns and you cut risk, so it's imprudent to not run full foreign content."

Out of Cadsby's 800 coin-tossers in Victoria, 200 were still in business after two tosses, which is all Picton has had so far. Whether he's a genius or just lucky will be determined by how he handles the torrent of cash coming his way, since it's harder to make big gains in a big fund. The managers of the largest Canadian funds, ones with several billion in assets, will usually dispute this, but Canavan says they're out to lunch. "If a portfolio manager says size is not an issue because he happens to run a big fund, there is a way to trip him up and really get to the truth. Just say this to him: 'We have a family of funds and we'd like you to be one of the portfolio managers. We'll pay you $1 million for every 1% by which you beat your benchmark. So if you beat it by 12%, we'll pay you $12 million.'

"'Okay,' says this portfolio manager, 'what's the catch?'

"'No catch. But you do have to make one choice. You have to choose between Fund A that has $5 billion and Fund B that has $500 million.'"

Canavan concludes: "You show me the manager who picks Fund A and I'll show you a fund manager who's not long for the business. That's a real issue in Canada. Some funds are too big, but people won't admit it because there is revenue to be had."

Canavan vows that won't happen at Synergy and promises to cap his Canadian funds (it won't be necessary with the global funds, which aren't restricted to the small Canadian equity market). "There's a point of diminishing returns for each investment style," Canavan explains. "It's not a science yet but I think for value investing it's $3 billion, for growth it's about $1.8 billion, for momentum it's $1.6 to $1.8 billion, and for small cap it's about $800 million. That's where we'd probably close our funds off."

A small fund is more flexible and versatile than a big one. Picton says he can "cut a mistake" (bail out of a major holding that's gone bad) in one or two days, whereas a big fund with a huge number of shares might take three months to unload them all. On this day, Picton is taking advantage of the momentum fund's smallness to do some "pairs trading." A typical pair is Quebecor and Quebecor Printing, majority-owned by Quebecor, or Nortel and Bell Canada, which, at the time, was the major shareholder of Nortel. These stocks usually trade at a certain relationship to each other, but sometimes a temporary fluctuation creates an opportunity to make a quick buck. Picton gets on the phone and buys 2,000 shares of Nortel. Then he calls an analyst to talk about Ventra Group Inc., an auto parts maker that interests him. He interrupts the call to sell Nortel, which has gone up $1.25; then he buys BCE, which has gone up 25 cents. So he's made a quick $2,000 while doing something else on the phone. It's a small transaction, not worth the time of the manager of, say, the Ivy Canadian Fund with its $5.5 billion in assets, because its impact on that fund's performance would be imperceptible. Even for Synergy Momentum, which at the time had $30 million, it won't help much, and Picton says it's not a big part of his portfolio management. Then again, "you're always trying to squeeze every eighth and quarter you can out of the game."

(By April 2000, the fund's assets had swelled to $400 million, so a $2,000 deal was even less likely to be worthwhile. I called Picton to see if he was still doing pairs trading, and he said yes, but it was a different kind where he would hold the stocks for weeks or even months. "Once you've identified a situation, is there an even better way of buying that situation because of temporary changing relationships in a pair? Sometimes you'll find a stock that has great momentum and there might be another way you can buy it even cheaper. Bell/Nortel was a great pairs trade where you wanted to have Nortel but you knew you could buy it at a discount to its market value within Bell. So that's the way I do it – find a great stock and then look for another alternative that gives you exposure to that stock at a better price. I don't like the Bell businesses but I loved the Nortel holding. So in the case of that one you were using two stocks to buy Nortel and that was a really good pairs trade.")

At 11 a.m. it's time for the "gauntlet meeting," named, Picton tells me, after a Clint Eastwood movie, *The Gauntlet*. "Clint has this prisoner he has to get to jail. The prisoner knows too much about all the corrupt cops in town. So in the final scene, there's Clint in a

Winnebago. All these cops are trying to stop this Winnebago, machine guns are pumping it full of lead. That's running the gauntlet. We do the same thing with stocks. If I'm planning to buy a stock, I have to justify why the company fits the momentum style. Everybody takes their shots at it."

The meeting takes place in a boardroom whose picture windows afford a view through the smog of other downtown towers and, beyond them, tree-lined Toronto streets to the east. About a dozen people, including managers and the wholesalers who service the financial advisers, are gathered around a table. Canavan and Picton are at either end. The meeting starts with some chat about general economic issues. The U.S. Federal Reserve is scheduled tomorrow to announce its "bias" concerning interest rates. "I think he'll announce a tightening bias," says Picton, meaning he thinks Federal Reserve chairman Alan Greenspan will indicate that he may raise interest rates to slow down the economy. Everybody in the investment business worries about what Greenspan might say, because any indication of change in U.S. monetary policy can cause turmoil in the markets. There's more discussion about this, with everyone talking about what "he" might do. The other gossip is that Mark Maxwell, a bank analyst with CIBC World Markets, the international investment banking subsidiary of CIBC, is leaving to set up a money management firm in partnership with Jonathan Wellum, with AIC mutual funds as a major client.

"He loves National Bank," somebody says.

"See if AIC owns National Bank," says someone else.

As it turns out, AIC doesn't. But Maxwell's move hasn't been announced publicly yet and so these people know before anyone outside the business that a rival fund company with $12.4 billion at its disposal might be on the verge of getting interested in National Bank, possibly putting upward pressure on the stock. It's an illustration of the fact that, despite the proliferation of information available to everybody, the street still gets the news first.

The main investment issue up for discussion is Ventra, which Picton is considering for his portfolio. The auto parts manufacturer and distributor in Oakville, Ontario, sounds like a good deal. It's got steadily rising revenues and profits and excellent international diversification, with 26 manufacturing operations in Canada, the United States, Germany, Mexico, Spain, Argentina, Brazil, and China. "The reason I'm intrigued about the stock is that they came out with a huge positive earnings surprise the other day," Picton says. "They were supposed to do 13 cents [per share] versus 12, and they did 18. Big margin [profit] improvements are taking place. Estimates keep going up. Forty-two became 48 for this year, 52 became 62 to 65 for next year.

"The hair on this stock is that these guys will have a great quarter and then they'll screw something up. That's why the stock still trades at only seven and a half to eight times earnings. It's a very cheap company, but I believe they're on the right track – they've done enough acquisitions that the momentum is certainly sustainable. There's upsides to the estimates: they think they can get their gross margins up from 18% to 23%, which would be in line with other auto companies. That would double their net return from about 3% to 6% and that's not in people's numbers yet. There's a big opportunity here. U.S. auto parts companies are up 25% in the past four to six weeks, part of a cyclical rally. Our guys in Canada have done nothing. Ventra's moved from $3.90 to $4.25 so it's up about 10%." ("Hair," by the way, means a negative, a bit of street slang that sounds strange coming from a guy who sports a hairy chin.)

The other managers start asking questions.

"Are they international?"

"Yes. Their biggest customer is Volkswagen, and they have huge exposure to the Mercedes A class, which is sold through a division in Germany. I think the global exposure is a key in the outsourcing environment we're in."

"What about capacity?"

"Yeah, a fair amount, they're actually trying to cut less profitable businesses to get more profitable. They've never had that mentality in the past."

"Who's the comp?" (Short for competition.)

"Their biggest comp is Dura [Dura Automotive Systems, Inc., an American manufacturer listed on the NASDAQ exchange]. That makes a bit of a problem. Dura can't buy these guys, they'd have an antitrust problem on the jacks." (Jacks are one of Ventra's major products.) "The Canadian comps trade at 14 times '99 [earnings], Ventra trades at 9 times. There's also an upside on the plastics side. They made an acquisition that gives them exterior mouldings, and they now have a painting capacity they never had in the past."

Picton answers a few more questions, but nobody at the table has any problems with Picton buying Ventra. This is hardly the equivalent of rogue cops machine-gunning Clint Eastwood's Winnebago, though Picton assures me that this meeting can get pretty rough. Maybe the other managers are receptive to Ventra because it's one of those stocks that fit all the investment styles: it's got momentum, it's growing fast, it's a small-cap company (about $300 million), and it's cheap enough to catch the attention of a value manager.

As the meeting continues, the managers range over a variety of topics: Japanese demographics, wireless data transmission, Australian nickel mining, rising demand for natural gas, the future of U.S. bond yields, the state of the Chinese currency and of the euro, and the shortage of stocks to buy. When it's over, Picton takes me to see the Relax Room, a windowless space with a couple of chairs and a comfy couch where he keeps his guitar. Around noon most days he comes here, closes the door, and strums a few tunes. "It's amazing what it does," he says. "Kind of takes your head to a different space. Gives you a little energizer. I come here on bad and good days. On good days, you've got this frenetic energy, and you want to dissipate a little of that, get to that balance point where you're in the zone, your mind is very clear. It's not good to think, 'I'm the king of the world, I can do no wrong,' or to think, 'I'm the worst investor in the world.' Either way, the guitar helps me to find balance."

He needed the solace of his guitar in the fall of 1999 when his fund's investment in Ventra started to turn sour. The company was in trouble: it was late delivering on a big jack contract because some machinery didn't arrive on time; it had to use a lot of overtime to meet some other contracts; and overhead and shipping costs rose. I called Picton about 10 months after the meeting at which the Ventra buy was approved. By then the stock, which he had bought for an average price of about $4, was trading at $1.85, or less than six times earnings, an even greater bargain by the standards of value investors. Picton told me he had dumped it about four months after he bought it. "After that meeting, I started to accumulate the stock. The next quarter [management] did not deliver on the continued acceleration and I became an immediate seller."

It took about a month "to bleed that one out" because a lot of other fund managers were trying to unload Ventra at the same time. Picton is philosophical about the loss, knowing that no manager is always right. "You see the criteria you like in a stock – most times they live up to it, sometimes they don't. When they don't, off they go to the value buyer or whoever will take it from you. Ventra met my criteria, and most times when a company reports a positive earnings surprise, chances are they're going to follow it up with another positive earnings surprise because they've turned something around in their operation and it's going to continue to get better. This is one of those exceptions where it was a one-quarter wonder."

The Ventra misadventure demonstrates that certain stocks are usually cheap for a reason. "The cheap companies usually have hair. So when they deliver the positive surprise, you have to put up with that. The great companies, when they deliver the positive surprise, usually are already very expensive and continue to go higher." But inconsistent performance in a stock can create buying opportunities Picton will seize. After his mishap with Ventra, he acquired Mitel for similar reasons. "You've got a great semiconductor company trading at a huge discount that's just come off a great positive surprise and no one believes it. In fact, what allows you to buy at a good price is that so many people are saying it's not going to last. That stock was $12 a quarter and a half ago and it just closed at $42.50. Sometimes it goes your way."

A system based on buying companies with accelerating earnings and stock prices starting to move should always be effective, right? Wrong, says Picton. Sometimes stock prices will move before the jump in earnings takes place, and so the momentum manager gets left out. Before he started managing the Synergy fund, Picton did his historical research and discovered that 1993-94 would have been a

WHAT DO FUND MANAGERS DO? • 157

terrible time for momentum managers. "Almost overnight you went from an interest-sensitive, growth stock market to a heavy resource market. In that transition there is no way a momentum guy can be there right away. You're still looking for companies that are showing price momentum and acceleration, and it takes a little while before resource companies start to show those fundamental trends. So the stocks bottom and then begin to move higher. The value guys have been buying them all the way down, and they're the ones who participate in the first leg of the resource rally. The momentum guy cannot be there because he has to see the turn take place."

During that 1993-94 period, the upward revisions in analysts' forecasts that Picton relies on didn't happen until three to six months after the stocks had started to move. For those six months, the index beat a momentum portfolio. That's why Picton, aggressive manager that he is, is also a defensive manager. He doesn't always do what his computer, screening for the best momentum stocks, tells him to do because that might leave him with not enough eggs in his basket. When the market has a sudden change of direction, he says, "you don't want to get pasted."

David Picton knows that, no matter how careful he is, there will be times when Synergy Momentum goes down instead of up. But he's convinced that a well-conceived investment discipline and the determination to stick with it will see him through those times. His advice to mutual fund buyers is to be wary of putting money into mutual funds whose managers lack a disciplined approach. "Try to have them pin down what their discipline is, so that it's easy to see in their portfolio how all the stocks meet that discipline. That's the tricky part of the Canadian marketplace. In Canada there are a whole bunch of funds in the middle. They can't really tell you what style they are. They offer a product, they say they're going to buy 'good quality stocks that are growing at a reasonable price, companies with good management, etc.' But that doesn't tell you what stocks they're going to buy. They can't articulate their discipline. When the market goes down and you don't have a discipline to fall back on, it must be a lonely place to be."

Running a mutual fund in the volatile markets of the Internet age is like living in a pressure cooker, reason enough to want to hide in a dark room and strum your guitar. But running mutual funds isn't all Picton has to do. He also has to sell them. Over lunch at the Duke of Westminster, a brokers' haunt in the basement of First Canadian Place, he tells me he's about to embark on a road show to sell financial advisers on Synergy funds. "Before, it was wholesalers who did the selling. Now the advisers want to meet the portfolio manager. They want to see the person who's managing the money." Even vacations can be stressful. In August 1998, he took his family to Castlegar. The stock market promptly had a meltdown, and he spent his vacation on the phone to Toronto. Sometimes he gets nostalgic for the nice quiet job he used to have at Dominion Securities, doing quantitative research. "I wasn't responsible for managing a big chunk of money, so I could go home and not worry."

But when you've been entrusted with millions of dollars of people's wealth, "that's pretty tough to leave behind. You've got an obligation. Unfortunately in this market, people are more 'What have you done for me lately?' than ever. Your personal reputation is on the line. So if you take a few weeks off and you miss a few things, you're hurting your personal reputation."

That's why Picton stays reachable, even on holiday. At the same time, he predicts that fund managers and other people in high-stress jobs are going to start taking three-month vacations, without cell-phones, to replenish their brains and their energies. Sue Coleman, a veteran fund manager, surprised Bay Street by taking a year off work starting in 1999. She needed a rest but it was going to be tough, she said in an interview in *Report on Business Magazine*, because "the market is very addictive. It's far more addictive than anything anybody could put up their nose. I've got to break that . . . The daily hit. I'm going to miss that." My impression is that Coleman speaks for a lot of money managers, though Picton isn't one of them. "When Friday comes along and it's the weekend, do I miss the market? Absolutely not. I hope the move to 24-hour trading gets kiboshed. I don't want to trade 24 hours a day. I want the market to close, I want to leave it behind on the weekend. Except," he adds, "I might do a bit of research."

Money managers are well compensated for all the worrying they do. Picton made about $300,000 in salary and bonus in 1999, around the average for investment professionals. If he keeps trouncing the index and drawing millions of dollars of new money into his funds, he can expect that to increase handsomely. Still, there are times when he wonders whether it's worth it. On the freeway home one day after the market had behaved badly, he noticed a man driving a truck in the next lane. "The guy was stalled in traffic, but he had the music turned up and he was enjoying a cigarette. He seemed to be really content. At that moment, I almost wished I could trade places with him. He was going home that night, not taking his work with him."

The split in the mutual fund industry between proponents of active management and advocates of indexing is an ideological schism, comparable in its modest way to ideological schisms between right and left in politics or the rupture of Western Christianity in the 16th century. The indexers are the radicals, challengers to an entrenched orthodoxy, and the split involves not just ideas but also money and power. A lot is at stake. If indexing becomes the predominant mode of mutual fund management, many mutual fund companies will go out of business, because few investors will be interested in whatever special approach they offer.

The only difference between one company's index fund and another's is the size of the MER; barring a failure by a fund to track the index accurately, the fund with the lower MER will have the higher return. An index fund is a commodity comparable to a deposit account. A handful of large banks dominate the business of deposit accounts because they can offer superior access and economies of scale; they will dominate the business of index funds for the same reasons. If index funds continue to grow in popularity, the banks will be the winners. The losers will be thousands of money managers and financial advisers who make a living creating and selling actively managed funds.

The rise of index funds has created "fear and loathing in the fund management community," Paul Kedrosky, who teaches business at the University of British Columbia, wrote in the *National Post*. But those managers who think index funds are somehow "unsporting" miss the point, Kedrosky says. "It is a tenet of efficient market theory that no matter how many hours fund managers spend interviewing CEOs, customers, suppliers, and so on, the market will end up smarter than they are. In other words, in an efficient market there is an excellent chance that some index-buying personal computer will make 95% of fund managers look like fools. Why not take advantage of it?"

In talking to people about index funds, I found that proponents on both sides argued their cases passionately and sincerely. But could it be merely coincidence that intellectual positions tended to coincide with economic self-interest? Ted Cadsby, the most eloquent proponent of index funds in Canada (he's written a book on the subject), heads a mutual fund company that specializes in them. On the other side are fund managers whose jobs are threatened by index funds, and financial advisers who would see their incomes plummet or disappear entirely if index funds became predominant. Index funds are a low-margin product that pays only small fees to intermediaries.

People who had been intimately involved in actively managed funds tend to have positive things to say about index funds, once they're no longer in actively managed funds. Peter Lynch is the most successful fund manager ever. In his 13 years at the helm of the flagship of the world's largest fund company, he built the Fidelity Magellan Fund into the biggest and the most consistently successful fund in the world. If you think active management at its best doesn't trounce the index, you probably don't know that $1,000 invested in Fidelity Magellan when Lynch took it over in 1977 was worth $28,000 when he quit in 1990.

Three years after his retirement, however, Lynch wrote a book called *Beating the Street* in which he reproduced evidence from Michael Lipper, an American authority on mutual funds, showing that over the previous 10 years, the S&P 500 had outperformed the average fund eight times. Over the previous 30 years, actively managed funds had only a slight edge. Perhaps the recent success of index funds is just a self-fulfilling prophecy, Lynch suggests: as more institutions invest in indexes, more money goes into the stocks that make up the indexes, causing those stocks to rise in price and index funds to outperform the competition. Lynch concludes: "All the time and effort that people devote to picking the right fund, the hot hand, the great manager, have in most cases led to no advantage. Unless you were fortunate enough to pick one of the few funds that consistently beat the averages . . . your research came to naught. There's something to be said for the dart-board method of investing: buy the whole dart board."

Fund managers who, unlike Lynch, still have to go home at night and worry about the money they have been entrusted with are much less sanguine about the index fund phenomenon. Remember the tulip mania in Holland, when formerly cautious Dutchmen went into debt to invest in tulip bulbs, only to be wiped out when that investment bubble burst? Keith Graham, Trimark's worried manager, thinks index funds are just such a bubble. "It scares me more and more. People are going home at night, checking their funds on the computer, saying, 'This one is underperforming, I'm going to buy index funds.' When 99% of the people own index funds, there's nobody left to buy. The bubble bursts and it all comes crashing down." In other words, once all the potential shareholders own the same basket of stocks, demand for these stocks evaporates and their prices collapse.

Graham's fears highlight the essential difference between index investing and active management: when you buy an index fund, you buy the market or what is supposed to be (but sometimes isn't) a representative cross-section of it. When you buy a managed fund run according to a strict investment discipline, you're buying a collection of businesses chosen because they have certain characteristics that appeal to the fund manager. Such a collection of businesses can go down in value even when the indexes are going up, as investors in the funds of AIC and Trimark have found. But if the whole market crashes, chances are that a carefully chosen collection of businesses will go down less than the market as a whole.

Of course, it's possible for an active manager to beat the index even in a rising market, as David Picton has proven every year (all two of them) that he's been managing mutual funds. Still, his success puts him among a small minority of managers, in both Canada and the United States. In 1999, only 7 of the 30 largest Canadian funds matched or beat the TSE 300 index. Even big funds with low MERs, such as MD Equity and PH&N Canadian Equity, were demolished by the index. Which big funds did better than the index in 1999? Ones like Altamira Equity and AIM Canada Growth, whose managers loaded up on high-flying tech stocks. It's understandable that most managers, whose mandate includes prudence as well as performance, would be wary of overexposure to technology stocks, so perhaps they should not even have been expected to do as well as the index in an unusual year such as 1999.

But underperformance is not just a recent phenomenon. Since 1983, in only five years have more than half of Canadian actively managed funds outperformed the TSE 300. And in only one year, 1993, did more than half of American equity funds outperform the S&P 500. These numbers lead some observers to make disparaging remarks about the abilities of professional fund managers. "In what other profession," Michael Mauboussin, an investment strategist at Credit Suisse First Boston, asked in an interview in the on-line magazine *Slate*, "can the average guy on the street do better than 70 percent of those who are supposed to be the very best at what they do?"

While "the average guy" and an index fund are not one and the same, it does seem that the average guy can buy an index fund and beat the professionals most of the time. And Mauboussin is right that this appears to make professional investment managers more dispensable than other kinds of professionals. If you've been charged with a crime, you need a lawyer; if you have a complex tax situation, you had better find an accountant. But when it comes to investing, you can buy an index fund and do pretty well for yourself. This, not surprisingly, is galling to fund managers whose expertise is vastly greater than the average guy's. Wayne Deans, the former Fund Manager of the Year we met in Chapter One, is typically scornful of index investing. "Indexing," he told me, "is a very, very dangerous thing to do because you've got to choose the right index. Just because the TSE concocts a group of 300 stocks, why is that the benchmark? I have no idea. It makes no sense to me."

Deans points out that Bre-X was in the TSE 300 index for a while and did not turn out to be a good investment. Of course, being in an actively managed fund was no protection against owning Bre-X either because actively managed funds, including Deans's, owned Bre-X. However, Deans's unitholders were among those who made money on the stock because Deans had the sense to dump most of it before it crashed. An index fund manager, on the other hand, had no choice but to wait stupidly for the stock's value to dissipate until it automatically fell out of the index.

So garbage sometimes finds its way into the index. Does that invalidate index investing? Bob Jones, who built Investors Group into the largest Canadian fund company by offering actively managed funds, doesn't think so. "Bre-X was only a small percentage of the index, and as an investor, you had made the decision that if you could match the TSE 300 you would be well satisfied," he said, with the objectivity that comes from being no longer actively involved in the mutual fund business. Investors Group still doesn't offer index funds, and Jones doesn't expect indexing will ever fully replace active management. But, like Lynch, he's prepared to concede that "there is a case to be made" for index funds.

Let's look at that case more closely. The most important point is that index funds are the most efficient way to invest in mutual funds. Because they don't have to pay smart guys like David Picton (the cost of active management adds from 0.8% to a full 1% to the MER of a mutual fund), index funds can offer lower MERs. Moreover, the stocks within an index are bought and sold much less often than those in an actively managed fund, so investors lose less money to brokerage commissions. These trading costs are included in the gross return and are not part of the MER, so investors rarely give them any thought. But Keith Ambachtsheer, an expert on pension funds, has calculated that they can eat up all of the value that an active manager adds to a portfolio. Finally, again because they trade their stocks less often, index funds incur fewer capital gains and those who own them outside their RRSPs pay less in taxes. When I asked the fund guru Gordon Pape how he responded to the advice in the title of the book *Stop Buying Mutual Funds*, he pointed to the cost advantages of indexing (this despite the fact his own books are mainly about actively managed funds). "When you can buy an index fund based on the S&P 500 on a no-load basis and pay an MER of less than 1%," Pape said, "I defy anyone to put together a stock portfolio that's going to be cheaper and is going to do better."

Because the low cost of index funds is their major advantage, it makes no sense for investors to pay high MERs to invest in funds run by closet indexers, those timorous managers who mimic the index for fear of underperforming it. Managers like Michael Lee-Chin and Bob Krembil, who have absolute confidence in a particular investment philosophy and who also happen to own the mutual fund companies they manage money for, are unlikely to become closet indexers. But many others lack the sense of security needed to act on their convictions. They're like the one AIC's Neil Murdoch met in Paris, the manager who had France Telecom in her portfolio even though she didn't like France Telecom, because that company was an important part of her benchmark index and she didn't want to do worse than the index.

The only way to beat the index is to be different from the index, thereby running the risk that the index will beat you. Because of fierce competition in the industry, managers are more afraid than ever of that eventuality. They know their customers have a huge variety of funds to choose from and that they monitor the performance of their investments closely. These investors are demanding but not totally unreasonable; they don't necessarily expect their fund to return 322% (as Talvest China Plus did in the year ended February 29, 2000) but they do get annoyed when it trails the index by 10% or more. When they get annoyed, they withdraw their money; when that happens, a fund manager's employer's revenues go down and so does the manager's bonus. Often the penalty for doing worse than the index is greater than the reward for doing better.

Closet indexing, the mutual fund industry's dirty little secret, is most advanced in the States. Morningstar, the fund-tracking company, uses a measure called "R-squared" to reveal the correlation between a fund and its benchmark index. If a fund has an R-squared of 90, it means that 90% of its ups and downs are explicable by similar movements in the index. Morningstar found that for the three years ended in August 1999, the average actively managed fund in the United States had an R-squared of 74, compared with only 58 five years earlier. And among the large-cap funds – the most popular ones, which specialize in the biggest companies – the R-squared was 86, up from 71 five years before. Robert Sanborn, an active manager who runs the Oakmark Fund, calls closet indexing "a big rip-off." His fund, which has a low R-squared, was a top performer in the early part of the 1990s but has been badly beaten by the S&P 500 index in recent years. He thinks investors should buy index funds or funds that ignore the index, but should never buy closet index funds. "Having a guy manage a closet index fund, charging active fees, is a very poor value," he told the *New York Times*.

The reason Sanborn has been having such a hard time beating the index is the same reason index investing is more popular in the States than in Canada: the American market is more "efficient" than the Canadian market, which makes it harder for the manager to make a difference. It's more efficient because the United States has more mutual funds (12,000 of them) and more pension funds and there-fore more portfolio managers sifting at the same time through more information. The result is that in 1998, only 14% of American equity funds beat the S&P 500, whereas 41% of Canadian equity funds beat the TSE 300. (In 1999, 38% of American equity finds beat the S&P 500, compared with only 19% of all Canadian equity funds that beat the TSE 300, but then 1999, because three stocks dominated the TSE 300, was atypical.)

In fact, there's nothing new about the American industry's inabil-ity to outperform the market. A 1962 study commissioned by the Securities and Exchange Commission found that even as far back as the 1950s mutual funds had done worse than the overall stock market. The American market is so efficient that in 1998 Ted Cadsby took the radical step of shutting down the CIBC's actively managed American equity fund and replacing it with the whole dartboard: an index fund based on the Wilshire 5000 index, which represents 97% of all publicly traded companies in the United States and which, in recent years, has done better than the S&P 500. (The bank's RRSP-eligible American index fund is based on the S&P 500 because an RRSP-eligible foreign fund has to use derivatives, and there are no derivatives on the Wilshire. If you don't know what a derivative is, read Chapter Six.)

CIBC still offers managed Canadian funds because the less efficient Canadian market still offers scope for managers to outperform. Cadsby, passionate advocate of indexing that he is, recommends that investors find actively managed funds for as much as half of their Canadian holdings. But the managed part of the portfolio should complement the indexed part, which means it has to be different. And that means it can't consist of closet index funds.

The best way to find out if a fund is a closet indexer is to check if it has a high R-squared. As of April 2000, Morningstar's Canadian operation was measuring the R-squared of Canadian funds. Investors can check Morningstar's website for information; alternatively, they can look at the annual report of an actively managed fund, which lists the stocks it holds, and compare it with the annual report of an index fund. If many of the same stocks are in each in similar proportions, the actively managed fund may qualify as a closet index fund. The next step would be to analyze recent returns of the fund and compare them with those of the index. If the managed fund consistently trails the index by roughly the amount of its MER, that probably confirms its closet index status.

By mixing index funds with well-chosen managed ones, the investor in the Canadian market obtains diversification that indexing alone doesn't provide. In 1999 and 2000, if your only Canadian investment was an index fund that tracked the TSE 300, you owed almost your entire gain to three stocks: BCE, Nortel, and JDS Uniphase Corp., the fibre-optic manufacturer formed in 1999 from the merger of JDS Fitel Inc. of Nepean, Ontario, and Uniphase Corp. of San Jose, California. Because each stock in the index is weighted according to its market value, the performance of the most valuable ones drives the index. So while the TSE 300 was up 30%, the TSE 297, without the big three, gained only 3%. Few fund managers would want to be as heavily exposed to a single stock as the TSE 300 was to Nortel (an actively managed fund is allowed to have only a maximum of 10% of its portfolio in a single stock, while Nortel was

18% of the index), but not having enough Nortel made it hard for a fund to keep up with the index.

In fact, the dominance of Nortel in 1999 and 2000 offered another way to detect closet indexers. It was debatable whether Nortel was overvalued, but it was not undervalued and would have no place in a portfolio managed according to the value style. So a fund that claimed to be a value fund but had Nortel among its holdings had forsaken its discipline rather than be left behind by the index.

Not being a value manager, Picton had no problems owning Nortel. He was also helped by his policy of not keeping much cash in his portfolio. "I might let cash build up for a day or a week but essentially our mandate is to remain fully invested," he says. "I believe there are a lot of [managers] who have been caught with too much cash. This is one of the reasons index funds have done so well. Indexes by their very nature have no cash. We've been in a bull market for seven years now, where you've been penalized for cash positions except for a couple of months. In the long run, cash hurts you."

That seven-year bull market is one of two major reasons that index funds had become such a prominent part of the mutual fund industry by the end of the 1990s. The other is a man named John Bogle, who started the first index fund, based on the S&P 500, in 1975. Bogle was convinced he could beat the stock-pickers simply by mimicking the index and keeping costs low. This notion was dismissed as "Bogle's folly" by critics in the fund industry who said it was a recipe for perpetual mediocrity. But 12 million "Bogleheads," as his devoted investors are called, have had the last laugh. By the end of 1999, Vanguard Group, the company Bogle started, was managing $500 billion in assets from its base in a Philadelphia suburb and was hauling in more cash than any other company, including Fidelity. Vanguard has more money under management than all the mutual fund companies in Canada combined. If current trends continue, it will replace Fidelity as the largest fund company in the world in 2003.

If Vanguard is a "low-cost religion," Bogle is its high priest. Bogle, who retired in 1999, used to fine his staff members a dollar if they referred to Vanguard funds as "products." Calling investors "customers" also triggered a one-dollar fine. To Bogle, a customer was someone who "buys the latest thing in a white sale, transferring allegiance from store to store as prices change." He didn't want customers, he wanted "clients" or "shareholders" who would have a lasting relationships with Vanguard. "Products" and "customers" are marketing words, and Bogle despises the marketing culture that dominates the mutual fund industry. Vanguard runs almost no advertising. Yet it is on the verge of becoming the biggest company in a furiously competitive industry. Thomas Easton, writing in *Forbes* magazine in 1999, reflected on just how astonishing this achievement is: "Can you imagine," he asked, "a world in which AT&T or General Motors or Procter & Gamble is still a market leader but does not advertise?"

Vanguard does not advertise because Bogle's fundamental principle is to minimize expenses. As a student at Princeton in 1951, he wrote a thesis on the mutual fund industry, which at the time was charging high sales commissions. He was appalled by what he considered the profligate way in which the industry spent money that rightfully belonged to the investor and became convinced that a fund company dedicated to keeping costs down could do a better job of serving investors. It wasn't until 1974 that Bogle began to put these ideas into practice, after being fired from his job as CEO of Wellington Management, a fund company with actively managed funds and high costs.

Bogle takes the "mutual" part of "mutual fund" seriously, which is why he set up Vanguard as a non-profit organization owned by the investors in its funds. That way the profit motive would not get in the way of low fees. Despite that advantage, though, Vanguard's debut was a flop and the skepticism of Bogle's critics seemed justified. In those days, the stock-pickers were doing better than the index, and Bogle's index fund was a dog. For six years in a row, investors redeemed more Vanguard shares than they bought. Bogle's response to the poor sales was to fire his sales force and make the funds no-load. "Cost is everything," he said. "You can reduce cost, give more to your investor. Just take less for yourself." In that spirit,

Bogle always flew coach when travelling on Vanguard business. And, even as the tide turned and millions of dollars began flowing into his funds, he was relentless in his criticism of the rest of the industry. "Croupier, croupier, croupier, where is thy rake?" was how he once summed up the industry's attitude to expense ratios.

The average MER on Vanguard's 100 funds is about 1% lower than the industry average. In other words, based on $500 billion of assets, some $5 billion a year that otherwise would be eaten up in expenses stays in the accounts of the Bogleheads. As an example, the MER on the company's flagship fund, the Vanguard 500, is only 0.18%, compared with the average American fund's 1.44%. In Canada, an MER of 1.44% would be praised as wonderfully low, but American consumers are more demanding, and one reason they have been flocking to Vanguard and other index funds is that they've become increasingly conscious of how fees eat into returns. In 1999, the New York Times used the following example in a story about fees. Assume two investors each invested $10,000 in 1989. One chose the Vanguard 500 Fund and the other chose the Average Equity Fund. Be highly optimistic and assume also that for the next 20 years both funds have annual returns before expenses of 10%. If that happens, the Vanguard investor in 2009 would have $992,763 while the Average investor would have $848,120, a difference of $144,643. Numbers like that, and the priceless publicity they attract, have made Bogle a hero to consumers and a pain to competitors. To make the competitors' pain even worse, the Vanguard 500 has been one of the top-performing funds in the United States for much of the 1990s.

In the United States, Bogle created index funds because he wanted to offer his clients low costs. In Canada, CIBC Securities Inc. created index funds in 1996 because just about anything would be better than its actively managed funds. Most of CIBC's funds at the time were consistent fourth-quartile performers. That was when Paul Starita promised that if CIBC's funds weren't among the top 50% in performance, the company would pay a rebate to investors, a promise that cost the bank $1 million. Ted Cadsby thinks CIBC's early performance problems were the result of having its funds managed in-house by the same people who were managing pension money. These managers were used to risk-averse, patient clients and did not understand that mutual fund investors, especially the kind who bought the no-load funds the bank was selling, were impatient clients who would move elsewhere if short-term results were poor. The other problem was that the funds were being sold in bank branches by people who knew more about GICs and mortgages than about mutual funds.

John Vivash, who had come over from Fidelity in 1990 to try to rescue CIBC's floundering fund business, discovered that the branches didn't really want their customers to buy CIBC mutual funds. "If a customer wrote a cheque to Investors Group, nobody cared," Vivash recalls, "but if he wrote a cheque to CIBC Securities, everybody was upset because they saw it as cannibalization of their deposit base." He had to undertake a propaganda campaign within the bank to persuade CIBC employees that cannibalization was good because customers were going to invest in mutual funds anyway, so they might as well invest in ones that produced management fees for CIBC.

What was bad was not cannibalization but "disintermediation," industry jargon for what happens when money is moved from a CIBC deposit account to an Investors Group mutual fund account. At the time, however, branch managers were paid according to their deposit base, not according to their success selling mutual funds, so they hated to see money move from a CIBC deposit to a CIBC mutual fund. Senior bank management had made the error of starting a mutual fund business without getting key staff in the field onside. To his horror, Vivash discovered that "one very successful customer representative at a small-town branch in southern Alberta was actually told by her manager, 'If you sell any more mutual funds, you're out the door.'" (Now performance is graded according to assets managed, including mutual funds.)

To get his point across, Vivash had T-shirts made for CIBC employees with the word "disintermediation" in a circle with a line through it; he also handed out anti-disintermediation bumper stickers. Eventually, however, the bank's customers, especially affluent baby boomers moving from their spending to their savings years, got the point across better than any T-shirt could do. They moved millions of dollars of savings out of low-interest deposits and entrusted the money to companies like Trimark and Mackenzie that took mutual funds seriously, thus demonstrating to the bank that it had better take mutual funds seriously too.

Just as Starita had done at Royal Trust, Vivash decided the way to kick-start a large financial institution's mutual fund program was through money market funds. The bank already had a small money market fund, but customers didn't see it as being as safe as a deposit account. To get over that problem, Vivash started a money market fund invested solely in government treasury bills, which everyone knows are safe. He called it the Canadian Treasury Bill Fund. Even that was too radical for some CIBC lifers. Vivash recalls meeting a customer service representative in Sault Ste. Marie and asking if she was selling the Treasury Bill Fund, started three months earlier. "She looked me straight in the eye and said, 'Oh no, Mr. Vivash, I'm waiting a few more months to see if it works.' That's what I call caution."

It may have taken some bank employees a while to get it, but the T-bill fund was such a success that Vivash started a second one. It was called the Premium T-bill Fund and had an MER of 0.5%, half that of the regular T-bill fund, and a minimum investment of $250,000. "People looked at us like we were crazy," recalls Vivash. And it does seem crazy. Why would someone with that kind of money give up half a percentage point when it's simple to buy a treasury bill directly, from either a bank or a stockbroker, with no management fee? The typical user of this fund, replies Vivash, was the treasurer of a company or a wealthy individual. "He didn't want to have to talk to anybody every 30, 60, or 90 days to do the rollover. He wanted somebody else to manage it for him and still be able to get the money at any time. So the product took off like a rocket. Within a year we had $2.5 billion in our money market funds and we were number one by probably $1.5 billion."

The surprising success of the Premium T-bill Fund demonstrated that even relatively sophisticated investors are willing to pay for the convenience of a mutual fund. It also proved that a fund company could make money selling a fund with a low MER. This lesson was not lost on the bank when it shifted its focus to index funds. Switching the CIBC American equity fund from actively managed to index was brave because the MER had to be reduced from 2.3% to 0.9%, which cost CIBC Securities a few million in revenue. It also demonstrated the strength of CIBC's commitment to indexing, because the old fund wasn't that bad. Managed by T.A.L. Investment Counsel, it was a steady second-quartile performer. "We did a lot of research, and it seemed obvious that in the long term there was no way management was going to consistently beat the index," Cadsby explains. "We will more than make up for lost revenue in incremental assets and higher sales that we'll generate by doing the right thing for the customer."

Cadsby is a brainy guy who talks a mile a minute and favours a preppy fashion style. You'd peg him for an academic rather than a Bay Street money manager, but he's well qualified for his job. In addition to the philosophy degree, he's got an MBA and is a chartered financial analyst. And although he's an enthusiast for the benefits of indexing, he knows there's a major impediment to his dream of CIBC as the "Vanguard of Canada," with millions of Cadsbyheads emulating the Bogleheads to the south. Vanguard is a non-profit organization that keeps its fees just high enough to cover costs. CIBC, on the other hand, will never be mistaken for a non-profit organization. It has an expensive branch network to support and shareholders who expect dividends. So while Vanguard charges 0.18% to all investors, the best the CIBC can do is 0.25% for those willing to put $500,000 into CIBC's index funds. That's not a large group, and most buyers of CIBC index funds pay MERs of 0.9%, five times as much as a Vanguard investor. Vanguard's current CEO, John Brennan, has said expansion outside the United States is a possibility, which means Vanguard may arrive in Canada some day. Until that happens, however, the closest to a Vanguard-style MER in Canada is the 0.25% that TD Asset Management charges on its TD eFunds, sold only on the Internet.

CIBC, however, is now fully onside as a believer in mutual funds, and Cadsby runs one of the more innovative fund companies. One of its innovations was the launch in 1999 of a NASDAQ index fund, the first in Canada. Even Vanguard, the ultimate indexer, has declined to offer a NASDAQ fund, believing it would attract too many speculative investors rather than the buy-and-hold types Vanguard wants. Cadsby, however, thinks that with NASDAQ now the home of some of the biggest American companies, it's no longer just a speculative market. CIBC won't, however, be launching an index fund based on the Canadian Venture Exchange (CDNX), formed in 1999 from the merger of the Vancouver and Alberta exchanges. The new exchange, home to fledgling technology companies, was outperforming every other exchange in North America in the first part of 2000, so an index fund that tracked it would probably have been a good seller. But the shares of CDNX companies don't trade in sufficient volume to make an index fund based on them technically possible.

Only 10% of CIBC's funds are sold through intermediaries, most of whom are not big fans of index funds. Perhaps that's why Cadsby is more critical of the middlemen than other executives who are completely dependent on them. Most do a good job, he says, but he has also met quite a few investors who haven't received good advice. "They don't understand that their broker might recommend something that he or she has a financial incentive to recommend. The advice they are getting can be skewed. You talk to people who have brokers or planners – they say they have this fund or that fund and you wonder why, then you say to yourself, 'I know why. A broker sold it to them.' You try to sell them on indexing, and they say their broker told them he can pick funds that do better than the index. You realize there's still a lot of education to occur."

And it will occur, partly for demographic reasons. As the population ages, and the boomers start to wind down their careers, they'll get more involved in directing their own finances. "Retirees have more time to learn," Cadsby says. "That's why I see the indexing trend getting bigger, not smaller. As people get more knowledgeable there will be greater demand. It's going to be one of the biggest challenges facing the active side of the business."

Sellers of index funds will also face challenges as investors educate themselves about an even more economical alternative to actively managed funds: index participation units. An index participation unit is a mutual fund that acts like a stock. It's a 21st-century indexed version of the investment trusts, precursor to the modern mutual fund, described in Chapter Two. Examples are the i60 units that represent ownership of the 60 blue-chip stocks on the Toronto Stock Exchange and "Spiders" (S&P 500 Depositary Receipts, or SPDRs), which track the S&P 500 index. IPUs are traded on exchanges just like any other stock. That makes them more liquid than a mutual fund, since they can be bought and sold any time the market is open. A mutual fund, on the other hand, is bought or sold only at the end of the market day at whatever price it's worth at that time.

The biggest advantage of IPUs is their low cost. The MER on i60 units, for example, is only 0.17%, not only less than that of any index fund sold in Canada but less than the MER on a Vanguard index fund. Since the major difference between one index fund and another is the amount of the MER, fee structure is a major factor in favour of IPUs as opposed to index funds. On the other hand, the investor has to pay a commission to buy and sell IPUs, whereas index funds are no-load. If there's a lot of buying and selling, commissions will eat up the gains from the lower MER. But the more adventurous investor will accept commissions as the price to pay for having a mutual fund that acts like a stock. Unlike fund units, i60s can be bought on margin or sold short in anticipation of a decline in the stock market.

The no-load status isn't the only advantage of index funds over IPUs. In a fund, the dividends earned by the underlying stocks are automatically reinvested in more units, whereas the IPU pays them directly to the investor, a disadvantage that also partly offsets the lower fees on the IPU. Although you could use the dividends to buy more units, the cost of commissions makes it uneconomical to buy IPUs in very small amounts.

Finally, there is the issue of just what one is investing in when one buys an index fund or an IPU. The i60 units, the only IPUs currently available in Canada, track the S&P/TSE 60, an index of 60 large stocks created for the TSE by Standard and Poor's. So if you buy i60s, you're buying a portfolio of only 60 stocks. Most Canadian index funds, in contrast, track the TSE 300, which includes 300 stocks. Research shows that the S&P/TSE 60, had it existed for 12 years (it was created in 1999), would have beaten the TSE 300 nine times. But if the point of indexing is to buy the market rather than individual stocks on it, the TSE 300 comes closer to meeting that objective.

Investors interested in IPUs that track foreign indexes have a lot more to choose from. An IPU based on the NASDAQ index trades on the American Stock Exchange, where you can also buy World Equity Benchmark Shares (WEBS), which allow you to invest in different foreign stock markets. Barclays Global Investors, the multinational company that manages the i60 units in Canada, plans to introduce 50 more exchange-traded index instruments, and there will probably be more to come after that. There are 600 different stock indexes in the world, tracking such exotic segments of the global economy as Bulgarian bonds and stocks in companies whose activities conform to the dictates of Islam.

Perhaps there's a reason to own a Bulgarian bond index, but sleeping peacefully is not one of them, which brings up the issue of risk and index funds. A fund that tracks a broad index, such as the Wilshire 5000, is probably less risky than one that tracks some very narrow segment. But is a Canadian index fund that tracks the TSE 300 a low-risk investment? That's where Picton and Cadsby disagree. For Picton, the issue is not whether the TSE 300 beats most actively managed funds. He accepts that the "median portfolio manager" will probably deliver a return about the same as the index's less management fees. "So the index does tend to beat over time the majority of portfolio managers." The real issue, however, is whether a portfolio based on the TSE 300 index, as the index was in much of 1999 and 2000, is one a reasonable person would want to own, given the dominant position in it of Nortel. "If you were given $1 million today," he asked me in March 2000, "would you go and put $350,000 of that, 35%, into one stock with a P/E ratio of 110? And if you did, could you sleep at night?" For Picton, the only reasonable answer is no. He calls the TSE 300 "a ridiculous portfolio. No one should use that as a benchmark, and no one should advocate a strategy where you put 35% of someone's portfolio into a high-tech, high-multiple stock. It's dumb. Right now we're having a lot of success against index funds because who would build a portfolio that looks that ridiculous? No one."

Cadsby demurs. "There's a point where it becomes imprudent to hold so much of one stock, but I don't think we're there with Nortel. Some of the biggest indexes around the world have much heavier weightings in a few companies than the TSE does: for example, the Hang Seng in Hong Kong, the CAC 40 in France. If you're not going to market-weight it, what weight are you going to attribute to Nortel? If you give it a lesser weight, then you're back into active management. The market weight is the least arbitrary. If Nortel ever got to be 40% or 50% it would be more disconcerting." In that eventuality, Cadsby said, he wouldn't stray from the index, but he might write a letter to unitholders advising them to reconsider their risk tolerance.

But isn't 32% disconcerting enough? That was Nortel's weight on the TSE 300 in March 2000, if you included BCE's 40% ownership of Nortel at that time. And the i60s had an even more disconcerting concentration of Nortel. What this argument really revolves around is the concept of risk-adjusted return, a concept so important that 99% of investors have never heard of it. The concept requires the investor to analyze an investment's return by asking a simple question: How much risk was undertaken to produce it? The idea is that it's better to earn 5% from a GIC in a Canadian bank than to earn 50% from an investment in Albanian currency futures. Such a statement appears at first to defy common sense. Why would it ever be better to earn 5% than 50%? Because the risk you took to get the 50% was so great that a premium of 10 times over the no-risk bank deposit was too small. Now whether that analysis is right also depends on who's doing the investing. If the investor truly enjoys living dangerously, jumping from planes and skiing double-blacks when not speculating in Albanian currency, then maybe the 50% return would be acceptable. If, on the other hand, holding the investment made the investor a nervous wreck, then it wasn't enough.

Picton thinks the TSE 300's risk-adjusted return in 1999 was too low. In other words, investors took on so much risk by owning the CIBC Canadian Index Fund that they deserved better than the 30.4% it returned. A better return would have been the 26.1% earned in the same year by investors in the Synergy Style Management Class, managed by none other than David Picton. Because this fund combines four different investment styles, it's never going to do as well as, say, a momentum fund in a hot year for momentum stocks. But it was less volatile than the TSE 300, so the risk-adjusted return was better.

Picton is right that the TSE 300, as it was in early 2000, was a risky investment because it was overly dominated by Nortel, a stock capable in today's jittery markets of losing 40% of its value in a matter of hours. On the other hand, active managers have to take risks, too, all the more because their performance is always being compared with that of the index. Because of the higher costs of actively managed funds, they have to beat the index by 2% or 3% just to post the same net return.

On the subject of risk, John Bogle wrote a paper for the *Journal of Portfolio Management* showing that from 1991 to 1996 the average S&P 500 index fund returned 15% with a "standard deviation" (a measure of risk) of 9%. The average actively managed large-cap fund returned 13% during that period with a higher standard deviation of 11%. In other words, the index funds took less risk to earn better returns. Conclusion? Most index funds are less risky than most actively managed funds most of the time. But much depends on the characteristics of the index and on the fund it's being compared with. Nobody should assume that TSE 300 index funds or i60 units are less likely to suffer a sudden plunge than the typical diversified actively managed Canadian equity fund. They aren't.

Critics of indexing concede that playing the index works well in a bull market led by the big stocks that make up an index such as the TSE 300. But wait until the next big hurt, they say, because that's when index funds will fall hardest of all. And it's true that index funds tend to do worse than actively managed funds in falling markets, though not much worse. In the market's big tumble in the late summer of 1998, for example, the TSE 300 (less an index fund's 0.9% MER) dropped 25.7% while the average Canadian equity fund lost 22.2% – a difference in favour of active funds of 3.5%. But during the same period in the United States, which also experienced a severe market correction, the S&P 500 bettered the average American equity fund by 3.2%. So underperformance in down markets is not reason enough to avoid index funds.

Another alleged advantage of actively managed funds is the ability of managers to forecast fluctuations in the market and dump stocks for cash in anticipation of a downturn. But few managers have success in timing the market, and the fund companies themselves often tell us it's impossible. In their literature, they love to cite studies such as the one that found that in the 70 years ending in 1995, 99% of the gains occurred during 4% of the time. For every manager who's been in cash at the right time there are others, like Vito Maida, whose funds performed poorly in part because they held too much cash in a rising market. Moreover, many equity managers have a policy of not holding cash in their funds, even in falling markets, because equity funds are equity funds, not asset allocation funds, whose mandate is to reduce risk by mixing stocks, bonds, and cash. Investors who want their fund manager to move from stocks to cash should have a balanced fund or asset allocation fund with a mandate to adopt a more defensive asset mix in anticipation of a correction. But the experts are skeptical of anyone's ability to time the market accurately. Fund managers, observed the UBC business professor Paul Kedrosky in the *National Post*, "are poor market-timers; they are like soldiers who exit their bunkers before the barrage has ended, or stagger blinkingly from the jungle many years later."

Dave Picton is right that the TSE 300, as constituted in March 2000, was a dumb portfolio, and it would have been dumb to have all your money invested in it. But the historical record is clear: most of the time, index funds produce better returns than actively managed ones. Picton himself says it's unwise for a Canadian equity fund not to use the full 25% foreign content it's allowed because using the foreign content is a surefire way to boost returns. The same argument can be applied to indexing: index investments are a surefire way to boost the returns of a mutual fund portfolio, not least because they make no attempt to predict the unpredictable. In 1999, for example, the index, because it is dumb, didn't know that resource stocks were bound to go up (which most of them didn't, even though they should have), and so it overdosed on Nortel and JDS Uniphase, a boneheaded move, as it were, that paid off. The beauty of an index fund is that it goes up when the market goes up even when the market is behaving in ways that make it difficult for active managers to pick the stocks that are making the market go up. And in years when the market goes down, the index fund doesn't go down much more than most actively managed funds. The advantages of holding index funds in the good years, in other words, offset the disadvantages of holding them in the bad years.

While it would be imprudent not to include any index funds or IPUs in a mutual fund portfolio, it would be just as imprudent not to include any actively managed funds. It would also be boring, because investors would deprive themselves of the fun of picking a huge winner. Huge winners are almost always actively managed funds, not index funds. Smaller companies, for example, are not well represented in the indexes that most index funds and IPUs track, and there are vast numbers of them, which gives a good small-cap manager lots of scope to outperform. Active management also shines in specialized sectors such as emerging markets, technology, biotechnology, communications, and health care. For all Bogle's and Cadsby's talk of how hard it is to beat the index, someone out there is always beating it. Steven Kahn, for example, searches the world for promising technology stocks that the amateur investor is unlikely either to discover for himself or to gain access to through an index fund. Kahn's Talvest Global Science and Technology Fund returned 172% in 1999 after being up 54% the year before. And if you had the foresight in 1999 to buy YMG Emerging Companies, a Canadian small-cap fund, your investment would have improved by 120%.

That's the good part. The bad part is that if you bought YMG Emerging Companies in 1998, you lost 18%, and if you had Talvest Global Science and Technology in 1997, you made only 22%, which probably wasn't enough on a risk-adjusted basis. So is picking the right fund really just a lucky coin toss? Not entirely. Research shows that managers who follow a proven investment discipline consistently tend to do best over the long run. The sad part is that such managers, people like David Picton and Michael Lee-Chin, are a minority. Partly because the Canadian mutual fund industry has grown so big, there is huge pressure on managers to be average. "A lot of funds don't want their portfolio manager to get blown up by taking active bets," Picton says. "If you are doing adequately and not making any headlines for being bad, the money still comes in and your portfolio gets huge. So to protect your business you don't really try to put up good numbers because you've already got the assets and you want to protect them."

Size, therefore, is a major cause of closet indexing. So is the marketing of mutual funds as products. Most people who buy a product, be it a TV set, a package of gum, or a mutual fund, are delighted if it turns out to be the best product of its kind they've ever had. If it's just average, they won't be delighted – but they won't be upset enough to take it back to the store. That only happens if the product's performance is way below average. The difference between mutual funds and other products is that the maker of, say, TV sets has nothing to lose by trying to be the best. If he fails, his TV sets will be only good instead of excellent. But trying to make the best mutual fund is dangerous because it requires ignoring the index and therefore running the risk of underperforming it, of producing a product that the customer takes back to the mutual fund store to exchange for something else.

Does this mean the triumph of the closet indexer is at hand? I don't think so. The reason is the rise of index funds and index participation units. John Bogle, who created the first index funds for the public, was driven by the desire to give ordinary investors a better deal, and he succeeded. Before the decade is out, the debate about the so-called dangers of indexing and whether it is better or worse than active management will be forgotten. The facts could not be more clear: most index funds do better than most actively managed funds, but the best actively managed funds do better than all index funds.

As of early 2000, index funds accounted for only about 5% of Canadian mutual fund assets, but big things have small beginnings. Index funds are already huge in the United States and they are going to be huge in Canada. That's good for consumers, as Bogle said it would be, because real index funds will give them better returns at lower cost than closet index funds. The rise of index funds, paradoxically, is also good news for active managers like David Picton who can clearly articulate and implement an investment discipline. The same knowledgeable investors who buy index funds will also buy actively managed funds, but they will insist on ones with personality, run by managers who aren't afraid to take a chance at being different from the index in order to leave the index in the dust.

As a result of this process, the closet indexers will be left out in the cold. There will be declining demand for closet index funds. In this way, the rise of indexing is linked to the wave of consolidation likely to transform the industry in the years ahead. By 2000, Altamira and Atlas Funds were the only non-bank fund companies offering index funds. Indexing is a painful step for the independents because they have always proclaimed the virtues of active management. But Fidelity sells index funds in the United States because its customers insist on it and will do so here when necessary to protect its market share. If Altamira and Fidelity can do it, so can the other fund companies. But the dominant indexers will be the banks and, perhaps, a Canadian branch of Vanguard. Me-too companies offering bland closet index funds with average performance will fall by the wayside, but there will be plenty of room for niche players like Synergy who have something distinctive to offer investors looking to fill the index-beating part of their portfolios.

Normally, consolidation is bad for the consumer. The mutual fund industry is an exception. At the moment too many companies offer too many funds – twice as many, per capita, as in the U.S. This overabundance of funds confuses the consumer and magnifies the importance of intermediaries, since the typical consumer can't find her way through the maze unaided. The need for intermediaries, in turn, makes funds more expensive, and returns lower, than they should be. The rise of index funds, most of which are sold direct rather than through expensive middlemen, is putting welcome downward pressure on prices. Much as the active managers hate to admit it, the indexing phenomenon is helping to make the mutual fund industry a better place for consumers.

CHAPTER SIX

WHAT TO DO WITH MY MONEY?

As 1999 began, I had a problem. I owned a fund, MD U.S. Equity, that had returned 56.3% the previous year, twice as much as its benchmark index, the S&P 500. Such a return was all the more impressive because only 14% of American equity funds had beaten the S&P 500 that year. So why was MD U.S. Equity's success a cause for worry? Because doing well in the past may augur badly for the future. Smith Barney, an American brokerage house, did a study to find out if fund managers could consistently turn in high performance. It analyzed 72 managers over various time periods and found that the best performers over two years were more likely to goof up over the next two years than to repeat their good performance. The performance of funds that were in the top quartile for two years declined by almost 10% over the next two years. On the other hand, funds in the bottom quartile improved by almost 11% over the next two-year period. This was scary because MD U.S. Equity had not only been great in 1998, it had been great in 1997 as well, returning a sterling 42.3%. In fact, it had been an above-average performer since it was launched in 1993. Clearly I was in deep trouble.

The implications of the Smith Barney report were obvious. MD U.S. Equity (whose name changed in 2000 to MD U.S. Large Cap Growth Fund) was too good a fund to keep. I should dump it and replace it with something really bad. Fortunately, there was an embarrassment of riches from which to choose. Among American funds, Co-operators U.S. Equity looked good (it had lost 12.2% in 1998). Then again, perhaps I needed a fund that owned crummy stocks in a whole bunch of foreign countries instead of just one. In that case, Canada Trust Emerging Markets (–33.5%) might be a wise choice. Alternatively, I could be patriotic and buy a Canadian underachiever, such as O'Donnell Canadian Emerging Growth (–33.8%) or Cambridge Resource (–52.4%). Even more enticing for a fund-picker with a Smith Barney approach was the AGF 20/20 Managed Futures Value Fund. Somehow it managed to lose 65.7% of its value in 1998.

Which of these stinkers should I entrust with my money? That was not an easy question to answer, even though I owned a pile of guide-books to Canadian mutual funds. The books weren't much help because their authors didn't seem to understand that it's smart to buy bad funds. Instead, they chose funds that had done well in the past and recommended that their readers buy those. Still seeking guidance, I called John Caspar in Vancouver. He told me not to believe everything Smith Barney says. "The process of investing is a kind of black art, and to simplify it with hard and fast rules is very dangerous," he said. I checked in with Ted Cadsby, who contemplated my dilemma for approximately one and a half seconds and concluded that the most judicious course would be to sell MD U.S. Equity and buy an index fund instead. One possible choice, he suggested, was the CIBC U.S. Equity Index Fund, which was bound to produce more consistent returns than an actively managed fund like MD U.S. Equity.

Still confused, I sought out the guru of mutual funds, Gordon Pape. This is a man who knows as much about investing as anyone in the country even though, as a journalist who writes on financial matters, he is a member of the group described by the seminar speaker Jerry White as "penniless bumpkin bozos who work in base-ments." I went to visit Pape at his spacious house in a suburban part of Toronto. He ushered me into the basement where he works, a well-equipped office lined with bookshelves containing Pape's collected works, including three novels co-authored with the wine expert

Tony Aspler, 10 years of annual guides to RRSPs, and 10 years of annual guides to mutual funds.

Gordon Pape has achieved something other writers can only fantasize about: he has created a market for disposable books. For a freelance writer, it can be more profitable to write books than magazine or newspaper articles because the writer gets only a one-time fee for an article but gets paid a percentage of the cover price for every copy of a book his publisher sells. Normally a writer produces a book, some are sold, and the book goes out of print. Not Pape's books. He writes the 1999 mutual fund guide, people buy it for a few months, then it gets stale. So he writes the 2000 mutual fund guide, and the same people buy it again. Same with the RRSP guide. And as if rewriting and reselling essentially the same book every year weren't enough to keep him busy, he also does speaking engagements and radio appearances, runs an on-line mutual fund database available only by subscription, publishes a monthly mutual fund newsletter that sells for $10 a copy, consults for a bank, and writes for an investment newsletter. And it all started because Pape lost his job.

Pape had started his career in journalism in 1962 as a reporter for the Montreal *Gazette*. He held a variety of jobs at Southam before becoming publisher of *Today*, a national weekly magazine distributed with major newspapers. In 1982 the magazine folded, and one of the perks he got with his $100,000 settlement was free investment counselling. His counsellor advised him to put half the money into high-interest deposits at two trust companies, Greymac Trust and Seaway Trust. Shortly thereafter, these two companies went broke. Deposit insurance at the time would have covered only $40,000 of his $50,000 loss had the federal government not stepped in and raised it.

This episode started Pape thinking about investment. It occurred to him that the reason the trust companies had been able to pay him a high rate of interest was that they were charging their borrowers an even higher rate of interest. They could do so only because their borrowers were bad risks who didn't qualify for loans at normal rates from larger financial institutions. Because the borrowers were bad risks, some of them couldn't pay their loans back, which is why the trust companies went broke. So Pape had unwittingly done something out of character – made a risky investment. And his counsellor hadn't warned him. "I was a babe in the woods," he recalls. "I didn't think there was any danger because these were trust companies, and you can trust a trust company." The time had come, he decided, to learn about investing for himself.

He began by reading books, studying the business pages of the newspapers, and picking the brains of people who knew something about the subject. Then he got a regular gig talking about financial affairs on a morning radio show. After that, he took a job with Hume Publishing as publisher of the *Money Letter*. Now the babe in the woods was consorting with shrewd investors like Morty Shulman, Andy Sarlos, and Trevor Eyton, members of Hume's advisory board. "Hume was a very successful company and we would take members of the advisory board on wonderful trips. We went to places like Palm Springs and Jamaica. We would have meetings in the morning where we listened to the experts, and we as the executives would take it all down and talk about ideas for the *Money Letter*. Then in the afternoon we would take off and play golf. It was not only a fascinating business, it was a great lifestyle too, and I was learning a lot." It was at Hume that Pape was introduced to mutual funds because Hume was running its own funds. These funds were, he recalls, "a disaster. The problem was that the advisers were all pulling in different directions. They could never agree on anything. The funds ended up losing a bundle. But they had compiled a large list of clients and a good asset base. So when they sold them, they became Altamira's launching pad."

Pape's personal launching pad was finding himself downsized out of his *Money Letter* job in 1987. Hume promptly hired him back on contract (he still works for them), but, no longer having executive responsibilities, he had time to write a guidebook to RRSPs called *Building Wealth*. He tried to distinguish his book from existing guides by focusing on practical information the reader could put to use. Then he decided to do a guidebook to mutual funds, the first in Canada, which came out in 1991. The timing was perfect because mutual funds were exploding in popularity as the leading edge of the baby boom generation shifted from its spending to its saving years.

The 1991 edition of *Gordon Pape's Buyer's Guide to Mutual Funds* was 120 pages long; the 2000 edition has 868 pages. Fund guides have proliferated since, but Pape's is still the only one that rates all funds that have a three-year track record and are available to the general public. It's also the most popular, selling about 70,000 copies a year. Before the other guides came out, Pape's book sometimes topped 100,000 in annual sales; the mutual fund and RRSP books combined still exceed that total.

What with his publishing and his own investments, which have had an average compound return of 15%, Pape has done so well that he can proudly proclaim himself a multimillionaire when he promotes home investment courses for Hume Publishing. "My best salary before I got downsized was maybe $75,000 a year before taxes," he wrote in a 1999 promotion. "Now I often make $75,000 in a single month." Yet he does have his critics. Eyebrows were raised in 1997 when he agreed to be an adviser to the CIBC Choice Funds Program, which recommends a mutual fund portfolio, chosen from all available mutual funds, to CIBC customers. "All I'm doing for them is what I'm doing in my books," he explains. "Helping them select the best mutual funds from the universe that's out there. It's an extension of what I'm doing, which is why I had no problem doing it." Would Pape upgrade his recommendation on a CIBC fund because of his commercial relationship with CIBC? Of course not. But I couldn't help wondering what he'd have done if he were still a publisher and the freelance mutual fund columnist for his magazine signed on as an adviser to one of the fund companies.

More important are the criticisms of the methodology and the reliability of the ratings in Pape's guide and the others. In Chapter Five, we noted the awful record of a group of six experts who offered *Globe and Mail* readers their top fund picks for 1999. Of 36 selections, half wound up at the bottom of the heap. The guide writers don't do much better. Kelly Rodgers, president of Rodgers Investment Counselling, a Toronto consulting firm, analyzed four years' worth of picks by four guide writers: Pape, Jonathan Chevreau, Riley Moynes, and Ranga Chand. She discovered that most of the gurus' top picks performed worse than the median fund in their category. "Overall, our experts did worse than you would probably do if you simply threw darts at a list of mutual funds and bought the ones you happened to hit," she wrote in *MoneySense* magazine. "If you had written down their top recommendations and resolved to steer clear of them at all costs, you would have done yourself a favour." Many people in the industry, especially those whose funds don't always get good ratings, don't like the fund guides either. Wayne Deans calls such guides "a terrible disservice to the public. All [Pape] does is check the funds that had the best rate of return last year, and those are his picks for the next year."

Deans's comment raises the critical issue when choosing funds, the one that had brought me to see Pape in the first place: what's the relationship between past performance and future performance? Smith Barney's research shows that good performance is an indicator of bad performance to come. Yet, while Deans exaggerates, good past performance is the major factor that Pape and the other writers of fund guides use in making their recommendations. In this, they are following what seems like common sense. We make decisions every day based on past performance. It's the major criterion we use, for example, when we buy one brand of appliance over another. Appliances are products and mutual funds are said to be products too, so why shouldn't past performance determine our choice of fund?

For one thing, a style of managing might work well one year and not the next. If a fund's mandate is to buy undervalued stocks, and undervalued stocks are out of favour, the manager won't do well even though she may have shot out the lights in years past. If the fund has ballooned in size, the same manager will find it harder to make the same percentage returns. If the manager's mandate is to invest in Japan, and Japan is in an economic slump, there isn't much the manager can do to repeat the 50% return he had when Japan was booming. That's why John Bogle of Vanguard was astute to fine employees who referred to mutual funds as "products." Many things qualify as products, but a key characteristic of most of them is that their performance is stable and predictable. When you invest in a mutual fund you're not really buying a product, you're hiring a professional to manage some of your money. Her ability to safeguard that money and make it grow is going to vary dramatically from one year to the next.

We may understand intellectually that it's futile to chase yesterday's winners but, as Peter Lynch wrote in *Beating the Street*, "hope springs eternal . . . and investors are not about to stop sifting through the fund lists, looking for a fund that can consistently beat the averages." Studying mutual fund past performance is a "national pastime," writes Lynch. "Thousands of hours are devoted to it. Books and articles are written about it. Yet, with few exceptions, this turns out to be a waste of time." Lynch's skeptical attitude to fund guidebooks is widespread among those who do not write fund guidebooks. At the same seminar at which I heard Jerry White express his opinion on journalists, he also said that "mutual fund handbooks are worse than the *Racing Form* in total uselessness."

With that statement, White demonstrated that he knows even less about horse racing than he does about journalists. The *Racing Form* is one of the most useful publications in the world. It is a cornucopia of facts: who did the horse run against and when, does he come from behind or go to the lead, does he prefer long distances or short ones, does he run well on a wet course, and so on. Does this information guarantee that bettors will be able to pick winners every time? Of course not. But those who know how to use it have an edge over those who don't. And that's all Pape is claiming for his guidebook to mutual funds. "When I give a fund a good rating, it doesn't necessarily mean it's going to do well the next year," he says. "We do the best we can in an imperfect business. All I can say is, you look at the funds, you look at the manager, you look at what they've done, you look at what they're likely to do. Then you place your bets and you hope."

Since Pape's books rely so heavily on past performance, I thought my Smith Barney data might come as a bit of a shock to him. I was wrong. He calmly accepted the idea that some of the best funds to buy might be found among the worst recent performers. "If you think about it, what are the worst funds in a given year? They're the areas that have been the most badly hit – right now the Far East, resource sector, and so on. Historically what happens is that when an area has been badly beaten down, the prices of those securities become very much undervalued, and then when the markets rebound they rebound explosively." (A year after he told me this, the average Far East fund was up 81%, definitely explosive, and the average resource fund was up 18%, not bad either.)

"If you project out five years," Pape continued, "probably the best performers, based on percentage increase, are going to be Far East funds, resource funds, and emerging markets funds because they are now starting off from such a low that when they come back they're going to come back disproportionately strongly."

The time had come to deal with my problem. "From what you've just said, it seems pretty obvious that I should sell MD U.S. Equity and buy Cambridge Resource," I said. MD U.S. Equity isn't in Pape's book because it is restricted to doctors and their close relatives (my father is a retired doctor), but that didn't stop him from having an opinion. "I wouldn't dump it right now and buy a resource fund because I'm looking one year ahead, and one year ahead is it likely the Canadian resource funds are going to come back? Until I see some recovery in the Far East [it hadn't yet happened], my answer is no, because commodities aren't going to come back. Also, the New York market is likely to outperform the Canadian market in 1999, which would be another reason to keep MD U.S. for now. But if I were looking five years down the road, I would say the time is coming to dump it and replace it with AGF Japan or something. But the timing is the key. If you switch to a resource fund now, you could end up in a situation where you sold the thing and resources went down even further, and the gap between the two funds actually widened."

This, it seems to me, is an intelligent and nuanced response. Clearly, there's more to Pape's approach than just buying the top performers. But buying the worst performers is too simple-minded an approach as well because, as Pape points out, when you buy can be as important as what you buy. John Caspar was right when he said there are no hard and fast rules. And because the subject is so important and so confusing, experts like Pape are able to make a lot of money explaining it to people.

Writing guidebooks or other financial advice books is a good way to get onto the advice circuit. Successful authors such as David

Chilton and Garth Turner travel the country speaking about investment. Pape used to do as many as 100 speeches a year, but he's cut that down to a handful. The problem with the speaking circuit, in the eyes of its critics, is that the sponsors, who stage the events and pay handsome fees to the speakers, are usually companies in the business of selling mutual funds and other investments. "Because of their high public profile," wrote Rod McQueen in the *National Post*, "the gurus are like beaters on a grouse hunt, able to drive birds toward the guns."

The consumer advocate Joe Killoran calls the seminar speakers "shills," which *Webster's* defines as persons "employed by an amusement enterprise (as a circus or carnival) to get the sale of tickets started after the barker has finished his spiel." This insult found its way into a decision by the Ontario Securities Commission (OSC) in the case of the mutual fund dealer from hell, Dino DeLellis, whose main marketing method was to hold seminars featuring such speakers as Jerry White and Brian Costello. DeLellis was banned in 1998 from selling securities for his activities when he worked for AIC Investment Planning Ltd. (That's Michael Lee-Chin's sales branch, the one later renamed Berkshire Investment Group Inc. AIC fired DeLellis in 1995.)

DeLellis sold units in a series of limited partnerships set up to import cattle embryos from Italy, the object being to produce a herd of low-fat cattle in Canada. Some 138 investors bought the units, which cost around $20,000 each, money DeLellis had urged them to borrow. But the partnerships wound up with few cattle and hardly any cash while DeLellis got $98,000 in payments and $280,000 in commissions (which he paid back) and some trips and an all-terrain vehicle and a hot tub and $100 for every client he referred to National Trust to take out a loan.

The OSC ruling is instructive in its description of DeLellis's marketing methods. About 40,000 mutual fund dealers and financial planners ply their trade in Canada. Most are honest but, the laws of probability being what they are, some aren't. The ruling did not name any speakers engaged by DeLellis. It did say, however: "It would appear that DeLellis' principal method of obtaining new clients was by means of 'educational' seminars, widely advertised and paid for in part by mutual fund management companies, at which 'name' speakers would be used to attract a large audience, and at which DeLellis would speak as well. In effect, these speakers served as 'shills' for DeLellis, recommending him at the seminars as an expert financial adviser on whom reliance could be placed for expert advice. Persons attending the seminars would be asked to give their names etc., so that follow-up calls could be made to them by DeLellis' staff, in order to arrange appointments for those persons with DeLellis, at which DeLellis could make his sales presentation to them. DeLellis had a standard sales patter, which emphasized his expertise, that the investor should rely on him as the expert adviser, that the investor should leverage to the full extent possible, so as to make use of 'other people's money,' and that the investor should make tax advantaged investments. In this regard, DeLellis did not seem to pay much attention to whether the investor's tax position enabled him or her to obtain the tax benefit. Nor did he seem to pay any particular attention to whether the investor's income and cash flow would enable the investor to service the indebtedness to be incurred as a result of the leveraging, which DeLellis suggested be obtained by mortgaging whatever equity the investor had in his or her home ... After the initial couple of meetings with an investor, DeLellis would make his recommendations, usually consisting of a mix of mutual fund units being marketed by DeLellis and limited partnerships being marketed by him, and the investor would be handed off to one of DeLellis' assistants, to be thereafter normally dealt with personally by DeLellis only when he wanted to market further products to them."

This passage from the OSC decision should be studied by all investors as a guide in how not to invest. Just about everything you shouldn't do is in there. Don't make investments that you can't afford to make. Don't borrow money to invest in cattle embryos, mutual funds, or anything else. Don't make the mistake Gordon Pape made when he entrusted his money to Seaway Trust: if the returns being offered are unreasonably high, something is probably wrong. Don't sign on with a financial adviser unless that person comes highly recommended by someone whose judgment you trust. Finally, don't invest money solely on the basis of information given you by sellers of financial products. Do your own independent research. Some "financial planner" says you can make a ton of money and save taxes by making a certain investment? Don't believe everything you hear and don't forget that anyone, qualified or not, can call himself a financial planner. Talk to a lawyer and an accountant before you sign a cheque. DeLellis's seminars were marketing events, and marketers don't usually tell both sides of the story. The same is true, obviously, of the mutual fund ad campaigns every RRSP season. Randy Van Der Starren, AGF's vice-president of marketing, is one of the people responsible for those campaigns, and even he doesn't think you should invest on that basis. "If anyone buys a fund based on a commercial, then they're insane," he told a magazine interviewer.

That's how not to invest. What about how to invest? And what about my MD U.S. Equity, which, Smith Barney suggests, may take a dive at any moment while I'm dithering about what to do? I had one more stop to make before deciding. In the meantime, I reviewed all the information I'd collected from the industry players and experts I'd interviewed, the gurus I had heard, and the tons of material I'd pored over. I boiled it all down to the following essentials.

Buy and hold or buy and sell?

The S&P 500 had an annual average return of 21% from 1992 to 1998. That's about what you'd have made per year if you'd put your money in an index fund based on the S&P 500 and not touched it. But if you'd decided to move in and out of the market and picked the wrong times to be out, those returns would have been slashed. Investors who missed the 30 best days out of almost 4,400 trading days from 1992 to 1998 would have gained an average of only 9% a year instead of 21%. That's the evidence behind the strategy of "buy and hold," every mutual fund company's three favourite words.

There is much to be said for a Rip Van Winkle kind of portfolio, the kind you can hold while you snooze for the next 30 years. What would such a portfolio look like for a Canadian investor? It might have some index participation units, index funds, or low-MER actively managed funds invested in the Canadian and American markets; a government bond or two or a low-MER bond fund; a diversified global equity fund, like Templeton Growth, Fidelity International, or the Trimark Fund; and, for 5% or at most 10% of the total, a science and technology fund. (There's an argument that the American, global, and Canadian funds will have all the science and technology you need, but a specialized fund, although it will bounce around, will give you additional exposure to the fastest-growing sector. Since it's a small portion of the portfolio it shouldn't disturb your slumber.)

As for the diversified global fund, it's the epitome of what buy-and-hold investing is all about. At the end of 1999, Templeton Growth, the first fund mentioned in this book and the largest in Canada, had investments in 25 countries across all major industrial sectors. It has good years (up 36.3% in 1993) and bad ones (down 13.6% in 1990), but if you'd bought it 30 years ago you would have enjoyed an annual compounded rate of return of 16.5%. And it has achieved this solid return by adhering to a low-risk, value style of investing based on buying profitable, well-managed companies when they are underappreciated by the market.

Buy and hold still makes sense, as it always has, for a diversified fund, assuming that it's a good one. But the advent of highly volatile specialty funds has made the buy-and-hold philosophy less compelling than in the past. "Put your money in a precious metals fund for the long term?" exclaims Gordon Pape. "You'd have to be out of your mind." Precious metals funds are an example of what Pape calls "opportunity funds," ones that have explosive gains and terrifying falls. If you're going to dabble in these things, you need to keep on top of the news and be prepared to trade actively. The object, much easier said than done, is to buy them when they are in the pits and sell them after they explode.

Green Line Precious Metals is a case in point. It exploded to the tune of 70.1% in 1996. If you didn't sell it then, you sat and watched most of your gains evaporate as it lost 41% the next year and 11.2% the year after that. It gained all of 0.4% in 1999, and even that was above average in its beaten-down category. Many funds specializing in individual countries are also unsuited for buying and holding.

Japan, despite its huge and powerful economy, is a case in point. The average Japan equity fund sold in Canada made 77.7% in 1999. That was terrific if you bought at the start of 1999. But if you had owned the average Japan equity fund for 10 years, you made an annual compounded return of 3.2%, even after the glories of 1999. You'd have been better off with a no-risk money market fund.

There's just one problem with dropping the buy-and-hold policy. Most people aren't good at knowing when Japan is going to plunge or precious metals are going to soar. Moreover, amateur investors are incapable of selling high, because they're sure the fund they so brilliantly picked will go higher, or of buying low, because they're petrified the fund they are considering will go lower. A study by Dalbar Inc., a consulting firm, found that Canadian investors, because of their deeply ingrained habit of buying high and selling low, get much lower annual returns than the funds they own.

My solution, based on personal experience and expert advice, is to simplify your life. Don't worry about timing the market. If you want to invest in Japan – and you should – do it through a diversified global fund. Let the fund manager worry about Japan while you're resting on the beach. As for precious metals and other resources, a diversified Canadian fund or one based on the TSE 300 index will cover that. You don't need a Japan fund or a precious metals fund. In mutual fund investing, less is more.

There's one last point about buying funds: if you're investing in a non-RRSP account, don't put money in a mutual fund towards the end of the year because capital gains and income are usually distributed to the unitholder in December. If you bought a fund that doesn't turn over its portfolio much, capital gains won't be a problem immediately. But if you bought one that sold a lot of stocks for a profit during the year, you have to pay the taxes even if you didn't own the thing when the gains were made, and even if it's gone down in value since you bought it. Nor does waiting until January always protect you from paying taxes on other people's gains. If you bought a fund that sells stocks it has held for a long time, you get hit with the taxes even though you weren't there when the gains were made. If fund companies didn't distribute these tax liabilities among all unitholders, the fund itself would be taxed so that all investors would effectively be paying the highest marginal rate. Still, it's outrageously unfair to those who get taxed on gains they didn't make. And it's one reason some investors won't go near mutual funds.

Front load, rear load, or no load?

No load is best. A low front load, which is negotiable between the investor and the salesperson, may be acceptable, if you need an adviser's guidance. Rear load, also known as back-end load, is always unacceptable. Many funds now let investors choose between front load and rear load. Never choose the rear-load option. Your adviser, if you have one, may insist on it, but in that case the adviser has done you a favour. By urging you to buy a rear-load fund, she's in effect telling you that you need a new adviser.

About 80% of mutual funds are sold with rear loads, also known as deferred sales charges (DSC), "deferred" because you have to pay them only if you cash in the investment within six or seven years. Advisers love the DSC because they make a 5% commission on it, a commission most customers don't know about although they're the ones who pay for it through higher management fees. Most brokers and planners tell you this is the best way to buy funds because the absence of an upfront commission means that "all your money goes to work for you right away." In fact, most people do wind up paying commissions because the average period for holding a fund is about four years. And staying put to avoid the DSC can be worse than paying it, because you may be trapped in some third-rate closet index fund whose mediocre performance is compromising your financial future. The dominance of the detestable DSC probably explains why Canada has twice as many mutual funds per capita as the United States; without it, many untalented portfolio managers and unqualified advisers would be out of business.

Defenders of the DSC have one good argument: it deters costly and ill-timed switches. Jumping in and out of funds at what usually turns out to be the wrong time is why the annual returns of investors are worse than those of the funds they own. Excessive switching also increases the administrative costs of the fund, so it's fair that those who trigger those costs should foot the bill for them via the DSC. But the DSC isn't the only way to handle this problem: no-load funds deter excessive switching by imposing a fee on those who redeem after only a short period. Perhaps the biggest problem with the DSC is that not all advisers have the best interests of their clients at heart, and for them it's an irresistible temptation to churn. They take the client out of one rear-load fund, the fund company subtracts the DSC from the departing account, then the adviser puts the money in another rear-load fund and collects a 5% commission from the new fund company.

This can cost unsuspecting clients a lot of money. A retired investor who had entrusted his savings to Mark Fridgant, a Toronto broker for BMO Nesbitt Burns Inc., paid out $26,595 in deferred sales charges in a registered retired income fund (RRIF) that initially had $113,214 in it. All the DSC mutual fund units in the account were sold within a year, so the investor had to pay the highest fees. By the time the account was closed in 1996, it was worth $17,211 less than when it came to Burns Fry (predecessor to Nesbitt Burns) in 1992. Nesbitt Burns, which compensated the client, was fined $25,000 by the Investment Dealers Association of Canada for not adequately supervising its employee (who no longer works there).

This was an egregious case but not an isolated one. Glorianne Stromberg, a former member of the Ontario Securities Commission, in her second exhaustive study of the mutual fund industry, concluded that a lot of churning goes on because churning makes money for advisers. The load fund companies and the distributors are in bed with each other, so they pretend it isn't happening, although a fund company could program its computers to spot churning. But why should they worry? The money comes out of the customers' pockets, not theirs.

Sellers of DSC funds will also point out that in most cases the MER is the same whether you choose the front-end or rear-end load option (Trimark, which has lower MERs for some of its front-end-load funds, is a rare exception). So why pay the front-end load, they will argue, when you can get the same fund with the same MER without paying any sales commission? Part of the answer is that you should be able to make a change in your portfolio as part of a rational investment strategy and not remain stuck in a fund that no longer serves your purposes just because you want to avoid paying the rear-end load. The rest of the answer is that the prevalence of the DSC inflates MERs for everybody who buys load funds, because the fund company has to pay for all those 5% DSC commissions somehow. If more investors sought alternatives to the DSC, the companies would have no excuse to maintain bloated MERs that eat away at investors' returns.

The good news is that there is no need for anyone to pay commissions to buy mutual funds. Sixteen independent companies sell mutual funds with neither front-end nor rear-end commissions. As well, there are affinity organizations that offer no-load mutual funds to various occupational groups and their families. Millions of Canadians have access to these funds. Finally, there are the banks, all of which offer families of no-load funds.

A big advantage of buying no-load funds is that, on average, they have lower MERs than load funds. This is important because, over the long term, fees are a bigger drag on returns than commissions. What is a low MER? Phillips, Hager & North sets the standard for mutual funds available to the public. The MER on its Canadian Equity Fund is 1.07%, on its Bond Fund 0.54%, and on its Money Market Fund 0.45%. So investors should look for equity funds with MERs below 2% and fixed-income funds in the 0.5% range. Most of the no-load and affinity fund families are in this ballpark, but not the banks (except for their index funds), and not the Altamira and Ethical fund groups, which have high MERs.

Companies with high MERs, naturally, downplay their importance, pointing out that a difference of 1.18% (the gap between the MER on PH&N's Canadian Equity Fund and that of the average fund in that category) is minuscule. But it only looks minuscule when expressed as a percentage of the total assets in the fund. Expressed as a percentage of the return, it starts to look big. So if the Average Fund earns a before-MER return of 10% and has an MER of 2.25%, the

MER actually consumed 22.5% of its return, compared with 10.7% taken by the PH&N fund. That's a big difference, and it will loom larger in people's minds when equity returns are in the 10% or lower range. Even if the American economy keeps charging ever upward, I know that MD U.S. Equity will not earn 56.3% every year. Such a result is abnormal and unsustainable. So if I keep it and it makes only 10% or less, I'll be happy that its MER is a reasonable 1.27% compared with the fatter numbers on the contenders to replace it, such as Co-operators U.S. Equity's 2.09%.

If you buy a no-load fund, you're usually better off buying direct from the fund company than through a broker, discount or otherwise. The no-load companies with the lowest MERs don't pay trailer fees (that's why they have the lowest MERs), so the dealer has to charge you a commission – even though it's supposed to be a no-load fund – to make anything at all on the transaction. But if you're a good customer who owns some fee-producing funds as well, the adviser might get you the no-load fund for free to keep you happy.

Is no load with low fees a guarantee of good performance? Definitely not. The no-load companies have their share of erratic and underperforming funds. And they have their bad years too. PH&N, often praised for its low-fee, no-hype approach to mutual funds, had an abysmal 1999. Owners of its U.S. Equity Fund, which delivered a wretched 4.2% return, would have been better off in just about any high-MER American equity fund. In the technology-driven frenzy of 1999, PH&N's cautious investment style was as out of place as a boy scout at a rave.

But 1999 wasn't typical, for the stock market or for PH&N. It stands to reason that, over longer periods, you'll do better if you don't pay commissions and if your funds carry low MERs. When that happens, more of your investment stays in your account and less is diverted to the revenue stream of fund companies and distributors. The only valid counter-argument to this proposition would be that load companies consistently outperform no-load companies, but they don't. In 1999, an analysis of the three-year results of 10 major Canadian no-load companies and 15 major Canadian load companies found that the no-load companies had better returns. That might not happen in all three-year periods but it will in most because, just as hardly anyone flips heads 11 times in a row, fund results tend to average out. When that happens, the ones with the lower fees have an edge.

The downside of restricting yourself to no-load companies is that you're excluded from investing in some of the more interesting funds and from profiting from the talents of some of the most talented managers. Synergy, the young company described in Chapter Five, had better returns in 1999 than any of its no-load competitors despite some of the highest MERs in the business. And those investors who want to buy funds specializing in the hottest areas of the new economy – biotechnology, the Internet, health, telecommunications – will find that most of the best ones are offered by load companies. Technology has at least a partial answer to that problem. Via the Internet, you can set up an on-line account with a discount broker who will sell most front-load funds without charging you the front load. You'll still be paying the higher MERs that most load funds have, including trailer fees for advice you neither asked for nor received, but you can buy the fund you want without a sales charge.

What about investors who feel they need support and advice and want to work with a broker or planner? Insist on paying a front load, not a rear load. And remember that front-end sales charges are imposed by the seller, not the fund company, although the company usually sets a maximum of 5% (in some cases, as high as 9%). If the seller wants to waive or lower the sales charge, that's his business. You can negotiate. And don't let the broker tell you he must get the full 5% to make a living. Front-load funds usually pay a 1% trailer fee (as opposed to 0.5% for rear-load funds), so the broker will be collecting $100 a year on each $10,000 you've invested with him. That's enough for Chris Tidd, the veteran Vancouver broker for Odlum Brown who specializes in mutual funds and hates the DSC. He charges a 1% front load and makes a good living out of that and his trailer fees. And he has the satisfaction of knowing that he and his client can decide together to make a portfolio change without the client having to pay for the privilege. If Tidd can operate without the DSC, other brokers and planners can too.

Do I need bond funds or balanced funds as well as stock funds?

Is it worth paying an expert to run a bond portfolio for you (either in a stand-alone bond fund or in a balanced fund that mixes stocks and bonds), or should you buy bonds directly? Should you own bonds at all? The answer to the last question depends on how risk-averse an investor you are and what your time horizon is. When you buy a bond, you're loaning money to a government or a corporation, so whether the investment is safe depends on how creditworthy the borrower is. As with stocks, the value of a bond goes up and down (if interest rates go up, bond prices go down), but that's a factor only if you want to sell it before its maturity date. Unlike a stock, a bond has an intrinsic face value, and the issuer will redeem it for that amount when it matures. In the meantime, the borrower pays you regular interest. So bonds add stability to an investment portfolio, and stability is good to have when stocks are bouncing around like corn in a popper. If you're a Rip Van Winkle investor, you needn't give a thought to the fluctuations in value. Just keep the bond until maturity and then buy another one.

Most people think of bonds as less risky than stocks because they're guaranteed eventually to be worth their face value. But whether they really are less risky depends on how you look at risk. It's true there's no risk of losing the principal when you buy a high-quality bond, but what will that principal be worth when you get it back? Charles Ellis, author of the book *Investment Policy*, found that stocks in the United States were less risky than bonds when the two were analyzed in terms of real returns ("real" meaning adjusted for inflation). This relationship was especially pronounced over the longer term. In the worst-case scenario over 10 years, bonds lost 5.2% while stocks lost only 3.5%. In the best-case scenario over 10 years, bonds made 11.9% and stocks 17.7%. So stocks were both more rewarding and less risky.

Moshe Milevsky, an expert on risk management who teaches in the business faculty at York University in Toronto, did a study that concluded investing in stocks is prudent even for seniors. He took the example of a 65-year-old who had $100,000 saved up and who wanted to make that capital grow so she could get $7,500 (after inflation) out of it each year and not die before it was all spent. He and his colleagues created a computer program that generated millions of different scenarios, involving bull markets, bear markets, and different lifespans for the hypothetical retiree. They found that a 65-year-old woman who allocated none of the $100,000 to stocks had only a 29% chance of getting the $7,500 each year until death. The chances increased with the amount allocated to equities, rising to 68% with a 100% allocation. So the case for stocks is a powerful one, and a young investor with a long time horizon who doesn't feel a need for the stability that bonds add to a portfolio may choose to dispense with them. But it shouldn't be done in the belief that bonds are always duds. During a period of falling interest rates, they can outperform stocks. That's exactly what happened in Canada through much of the 1990s when the average bond fund did better than the average equity fund.

Bonds or bond funds? Actually, they are two different investments. A bond offers a guaranteed amount of income and a guaranteed payment when it matures. A fund offers no guarantees. The units of the bond fund could go down in value. If you stay in the fund long enough, you'll probably at least recoup your investment, but that's not guaranteed as it is with an individual bond. That said, long-term investors in some of the more reliable bond funds in Canada, including those of Altamira, Trimark, and PH&N, have reason to be happy. A skilled manager makes educated guesses about interest rate movements to buy and sell bonds for capital gains. And she can juice her returns by taking calculated risks on high-yielding but dodgy issues that amateurs shouldn't touch. Moreover, a fund, because it is a high-volume buyer, gets its bonds cheaper than the average small investor can. But, as always, professional management costs money, and a high MER will easily gobble up all the added value the manager has delivered. Don't even consider a bond fund with an MER above 1.5%.

The same advice goes for balanced funds, which usually have from 30% to 50% of their assets in bonds. Take a look at the monthly mutual fund supplement in the *Globe and Mail*, which gives the MER for every mutual fund. You'll see that most balanced funds have MERs above 2%. Then take a look at the annual report of any fund company and check the list of bonds in its balanced fund. You'll see that most bonds these days have yields in the 5.5% to 7% range. It makes no sense to pay 2% to get a 6% return, which leaves you with 4%, when you can have the whole 6% for yourself by buying a government bond directly. The clincher in this argument is that with bonds, unlike stocks, you don't need the additional safety that comes from holding a diversified portfolio because bonds are guaranteed.

Should I buy individual stocks as well as, or instead of, mutual funds?

If you've read this far, you've probably figured this out for yourself. Do you have enough money to buy at least 100 shares (you can buy less but it's uneconomical) of the stocks you want to own? Do you have the time and interest to research and monitor an investment portfolio? If the answers to these questions are no, you're among the millions for whom mutual funds were invented. If the answers are yes, you may be among the growing numbers of investors who are gravitating from funds to stocks. This can be viewed as part of the process of growing up. Just as our taste in music, food, and wine becomes more sophisticated, so investing habits tend to evolve – from bank deposits to GICs to savings bonds to mutual funds and on to individual stocks.

Mutual funds offer the small investor diversification, and the mitigation of risk that comes with it. Moshe Milevsky has said an investor in the Canadian market needs about 20 to 30 stocks to be adequately diversified. That's more than most of us can afford, at least all at once, but you don't have to wait until you win the lottery before venturing into the stock market without a fund manager holding your hand.

If you own mutual funds or index participation units, you already have diversification. Now you can gradually add some stocks to your portfolio. What are the advantages? For one, there are no management fees to drag down the results. And fees aren't the only drag on mutual fund returns. Remember how Wayne Deans complained in Chapter One about investors who bailed out of his small-cap fund at exactly the wrong time? As a result, he couldn't buy up some of the bargains he saw on the market. The unitholders who didn't bail out were hurt by the actions of those who did.

A mutual fund is a share-owning co-operative, and as a member of the co-operative, you are affected by the actions of the other members. Sometimes the irrational acts of the other unitholders can force the manager into doing just what a professional should never do: buy high and sell low. New money pours in when stocks are doing well; managers aren't supposed to sit on cash, so they have no choice but to buy high. The opposite happens when stock prices are diving and investors sell, forcing the manager to sell low in order to meet the redemptions. When you buy shares as an individual rather than as part of a group, the only decisions that matter are your own. You can be patient because, unlike a fund manager, you don't have to worry about short-term performance. In short, you can invest like a pro.

There's a good reason why people buy stocks close to home. Millions of Canadians have experienced for themselves the operations of such companies as Canadian Tire, the Bank of Montreal, and Telus. Obviously they know a lot more about these companies than about the American, French, or Australian equivalents. And just as technology, through the development of on-line brokerage services, is putting downward pressure on the price of funds, so it has reduced the commissions charged for selling and buying stocks. Moreover, a vast amount of investment research, much of it once accessible only to pros, is available on the Internet.

As these resources grow more efficient and available, and as boomers, nearing or entering retirement, have more time to manage their own investment portfolios, it's certain that many of them will decide they don't need to pay somebody to buy shares in Canadian Tire and Bank of Montreal for them. On the other hand, they will still need professional help to find the right investments in foreign markets and in such specialty areas as small-cap companies and technology. For those important niches of the stock market, even sophisticated investors will continue to use mutual funds.

What is a clone fund and do I need one?

Suppose you were convinced, as some smart people are, that biotechnology stocks are the next big thing. You have a problem. If you're like most people, you don't have a lot of money for investment left over after you have maxed out your RRSP, so you have to make your biotechnology investment within your RRSP. But the Canadian government, in its wisdom, decrees that only 25% of the investments in your RRSP can be in foreign securities. Canada has biotechnology companies, to be sure, but much of the growth in this exciting field is taking place elsewhere. What to do? You could invest in a fund, such as C.I. Global Biotechnology, but that fund is foreign content so it can be only 25% of the book value (original cost) of your RRSP. As any competent financial adviser will tell you, 25% is more than enough of your retirement nest egg to put into a fund that is guaranteed to be as volatile as a jar of nitroglycerin. But you're an aggressive investor and you know more about biotechnology than a financial adviser does, so you want more. Luckily for you, the fund industry has an answer. You can buy the C.I. Global Biotechnology RRSP fund, which is a clone of the other one and will have almost the same returns, and which, through the marvels of modern financial engineering, passes as Canadian content. If your enthusiasm for the future of biotechnology has brought you to the brink of insanity, you can even invest every penny of your RRSP in the C.I. Global Biotechnology RRSP Fund. Revenue Canada won't mind at all.

Clone funds illustrate the ingenuity of the industry. Of course, it was the industry itself that created the demand for them by loudly complaining that, because Canadian stocks were chronic losers, the foreign investment restrictions were compromising the financial futures of Canadians saving for their retirement. Why should Canadians be forced to cram 75% of their savings into just 2% of the world's stock market capitalization? A reasonable question, and the industry's answer was to invent Canadian funds that used derivatives to enable them to behave like foreign funds. A derivative is a financial instrument that derives its value from something else. A clone fund is not really a foreign fund, but it can behave like one by entering into forward contracts that derive their value from a foreign fund. Most mutual fund investors have no idea how this works, but that didn't deter them from making clone funds the hottest products in the mutual fund marketplace in 1999. Clone funds have been around since 1983 but the major companies didn't offer them until May 1999. From then until the end of the year, Canadians poured $6.3 billion into clone funds. One of the first major clones, Mackenzie's Universal RSP Select Manager's Fund, hit the $2-billion mark by the end of 1999.

How do they work? Say you invest $10,000 in the RRSP-eligible clone of your favourite foreign fund. Just like a Canadian person's RRSP account, a Canadian equity fund is allowed to have 25% foreign content (as of 2000), so the fund invests $2,500 of your money in the underlying foreign fund. It invests the other $7,500 in Canadian treasury bills, thereby making itself into a Canadian fund.

That's the first step. The fund then gets a bank to put $7,500 of its money (with your $7,500 worth of T-bills as collateral) into the foreign fund. Here's where the derivative part comes in. The fund and the bank make a deal. If the underlying foreign fund goes up during the day, the bank pays the gain on the $7,500 investment to the clone fund. If it goes down, the clone fund reimburses the bank. The clone fund, therefore, can win or lose, depending on what happens to the underlying fund. The bank (called the "counter-party" in this kind of deal) takes no risk and gets a fee for its trouble. The deal is a forward contract; the contract is a derivative because it derives its value from the underlying foreign fund. By this financial magic, the Canadian clone fund could turn in the same result as the actual foreign fund. It could, but it doesn't because the MER on it is as much as 0.75% higher than that of the underlying fund, the cost – so the fund companies claim – of paying the bank for doing the forward contracts.

Even if we understand clone funds, do we want them? We've heard how a rogue derivatives trader destroyed Barings, a venerable

British bank. Aren't these things dangerous? Actually, derivatives have been used for decades and most of the time they aren't dangerous at all. In the case of clone funds, however, complexity does add extra risk. If the fund is issued by a major fund company and the counter-party is a major bank, there's nothing to worry about. But if it was a smaller fund company that got into financial difficulty (because of a rush of redemptions, for example), it might not be able to renew the forward contract one day, in which case the clone fund would not be able to track the underlying fund. The same thing would happen if the counter-party had a cash squeeze and couldn't make the payments due to the clone fund. If you remember the lesson Gordon Pape learned after he deposited money with Seaway Trust, you'll make sure the fund company is solvent before you entrust your money to it.

Clone funds are expensive. Are they worth it? Some of them might be, some of the time. Rudy Luukko and June Yee, researchers in Toronto, compared the returns of Canadian equity funds and three categories of foreign funds for the decade ending August 1999. They factored in an additional MER of 0.50% that the foreign funds would have carried had they been clones. And they found that for most of that period, the clones of foreign funds would have outperformed Canadian ones.

Still, there's no good reason to put your whole RRSP into foreign clones. For one thing, the Canadian market doesn't always underperform foreign ones. For another, the Canadian dollar has sunk to new lows over the past decade, which increased the value of funds denominated in foreign currencies. If the dollar recovers, that will hurt the value of foreign funds sold in Canada, so investors should avoid overdosing on foreign equities at the wrong time. Also, there are cheaper ways to get foreign content into an RRSP. As explained in Chapter Five, by 2001, when the allowable foreign content is raised to 30%, a combination of 30% real foreign funds plus 70% Canadian funds using full foreign content will result in an RRSP that is 51% foreign, and that's probably enough. If you want to bring it higher still, index clone funds are available with MERs of only 0.50%. Assuming similar returns, the lower MERs will leave thousands of extra dollars in your RRSP by the time you're ready to cash in your chips.

Like most investment decisions, mine about MD U.S. Equity turned on the issue of risk. The fund had gone up more than could reasonably have been expected. That meant that the risk of its going down, according to the Smith Barney data, had also increased. I'd discussed the matter with the guru of mutual funds. Now it was time to check in with Ron Dembo, the guru of risk, a lanky, laid-back South African émigré who spends much of his time in the air, travelling to the corners of the globe to teach large banks how to avoid the fate of Barings. (Let it be said, in the interests of full disclosure, that Dembo is a friend of mine, but I probably would have found my way to him anyway because his pioneering work has captured a lot of attention in the investment industry.)

Dembo's company, Algorithmics Inc., started in 1989 in a second-floor walk-up on College Street near the University of Toronto, where he used to teach mathematics. It now occupies five floors in the heart of Toronto's pulsating Chinatown in a building that once was a garment factory and now sports sandblasted walls, a dramatic circular staircase, and a roof garden. These stylish quarters are where 200 casually dressed financial engineers and other computer nerds labour at their monitors in search of ways to make risk more manageable. Another 200 employees work at Algorithmics offices in London, New York, Frankfurt, Tokyo, Singapore, Mexico City, Rio de Janeiro, and Johannesburg.

Algorithmics is based on a simple idea: we should be able to insure our investments, just as we insure our house and our car. An insurance policy is a piece of paper that has value only when something else loses value. If somebody steals your car, suddenly that piece of paper is worth the replacement value of your car. If the policy expires with your car still in your garage, the piece of paper is worth nothing. It's the same with investments. I can buy a piece of paper called a "put" option that will pay off if a stock goes down in value. That option is a derivative: it derives its value from something else, namely the stock. If I own a lot of that stock, it makes sense to insure it, just as I insure my house. In both cases, I hope these pieces of paper – the put option and the home insurance policy – will turn out to be worthless even though I paid good money for them. The peace of mind I had in knowing the risk was covered was worth the expense. (Some people buy options without owning the underlying stock; that's speculation, not insurance, and it's the reason derivatives have a bad name.)

Using derivatives as investment insurance has heretofore been the preserve of the rich and sophisticated. Just as Edward Leffler, the Boston broker who created the first modern mutual fund, revolutionized the investment industry by making a diversified portfolio of stocks available to small investors, Dembo wants to democratize investment insurance. Anyone, he says, should be able to go onto the Internet, input his portfolio at a site selling investment insurance, and buy, at a reasonable price, a customized package of derivatives that insures his particular portfolio against catastrophic loss.

Although options have been around almost as long as stocks have been traded, the advance of computer technology has allowed the creation of an almost limitless variety of customized derivatives. Long before the computer age, you could insure a single stock by buying options. But insuring an entire portfolio, including mutual funds containing dozens of different stocks, is another matter. Something like portfolio insurance for the masses would never have been possible without powerful computers to create and recreate the necessary financial instruments continuously as market conditions evolve. How this is done is too complex to explain here; Dembo has found that even senior bank executives look mystified when he tries to explain how the Algorithmics software works. But if you understand insurance, you understand the basic principle. You'll be able to buy a financial instrument that goes up when your other investments go down or, as Dembo puts it, "you insure part of the downside. But you can't insure all of the downside, just as it would be too expensive to insure your car to the last scratch. In an efficient market, if you insure all of the downside, you won't be able to achieve any upside."

Once such a system is in place, investors will have a clearer picture of where they stand. The hypothetical individual who put his entire RRSP into a biotechnology clone fund, for example, may find that the cost of insurance is more than he can afford. Perhaps that will persuade him, where his financial adviser couldn't, that a bit of diversification is in order.

In 1998 Dembo wrote a book, *Seeing Tomorrow*, to explain risk to the average, non-mathematical person. The idea was to get people thinking in new ways about the future – positing different scenarios, including the most unlikely ones, and thinking about how they would affect one's economic security. A key concept here is regret: how much regret would you feel if your investment in that hot biotech stock evaporated because the company's technology was superseded by something better? If it's a lot, then maybe you should sell the investment or at least find a way to hedge against a potential loss. It sounds obvious but hardly anyone thinks that way. Most people don't think about regret until they feel it.

Dembo's book was written clearly (with the assistance of a co-author, Andrew Freeman, a journalist for the *Economist*), and it sold well in several countries, including Japan, where it hit the best-seller list. But it turned out to be impossible to explain risk without going into quite a bit of mathematics, and when the average person – the book's target reader – sees mathematics she runs for cover. So many people didn't understand the book, and Dembo has since decided that they don't really need an in-depth understanding of risk in any case. Just as anyone can test drive a car without understanding how the engine works, anyone can take risk for a test drive on his computer. Algorithmics is working on software that, once you've got your portfolio input into an Internet risk management site, will allow you to see different future scenarios just by pointing your mouse. What happens to my RRSP if the latest forecast by Sherry Cooper, chief economist of Nesbitt Burns, turns out to be right? Click on the Cooper link and you'll see the damage instantly. What happens if oil prices soar? Click and look. What happens if inflation comes back? One click and there it is.

Dembo wants us, and especially the millions of us who have invested so massively in mutual funds, to start seeing tomorrow instead of only yesterday. He's in full accord with the critics of most established rating systems for mutual funds. Virtually all of them, in his opinion, are worthless because they are too focused on past performance. "Past performance is absolutely unreliable," he says. Suppose we're considering buying a fund that's just had a couple of great years. There isn't enough information in the guidebooks to allow us to evaluate how those results were attained and whether they're likely to be repeated.

"To achieve outstanding performance you had to have taken more risk. The information you don't have is the risk-adjusted value of the fund. If you did, you'd be able to make a better decision. Because maybe the manager's strategy was a good bet given the conditions in the market. So unless the structure of the market changes, he's still a good bet. But that analysis is not included in the guidebook. You know the upside, but you don't know the potential downside." Looking at the stocks in the portfolio is one way to assess the potential downside, but that information is published only once a year, in the fund company's annual report, by which time it may be out of date.

So what about the future of MD U.S. Equity? Well, first we have to know something about it. MD U.S. Equity is managed by Alliance Capital Management Canada Ltd., which gets its advice from Alliance Capital Management L.P. of Minneapolis and New York. The fund is managed according to the growth investment style and has recorded huge returns during a period when growth stocks have been thriving. It is not a technology fund but it has large positions in some big technology companies like Dell, Cisco, Sun, and Intel.

"The last few years have been a fantastic time to invest in technology," Dembo says, "so they made the right bet. But the risk could have been high. How many times have you heard that technology is going to crash? Also, MD U.S. is a managed fund, and I mistrust the managed funds. It doesn't mean you can't make more money with them. But you should realize that you're betting more heavily with them than with index funds. Think of the cost of managing the fund, and think of how much upside you have to make to offset that cost. The managers have to take on more risk just to get the same return as an index fund. And to outperform, they have to take still more risk."

So do I sell it? "Not necessarily," says Dembo. "But use it as a small part of your portfolio, the part you want to bet."

In pursuing investment insurance for the masses, Dembo could be on to something big. One of the surprises in the mutual fund industry in the last couple years was the sudden surge of popularity in segregated funds, which are mutual funds with insurance policies attached. The insurance promises that, if you hold on for 10 years, you will get your money back, even if the units of the fund have dropped in value. Of course, the insurance costs money, adding from 0.5% to 1% to the MER. That's a lot to pay to cover a minuscule risk – there is only a 1% chance of a stock fund losing money after 10 years – but a segregated fund may be worth the extra cost for someone who wants some other unique features, including creditor protection and direct portability to beneficiaries while bypassing probate fees.

Another kind of fund developed for the fearful is CIBC's Protected Funds. These are the same as CIBC's regular index funds, but they carry a guarantee that promises the investor will get all her money back after five years even if the market has gone down. This makes more sense than a segregated fund, because the chances of being a loser jump to 10% when an investment is held for only five years, and that's a genuine consideration for someone nearing retirement. However, the protected funds were closed to new money in 1998 because the cost of the guarantee went up so much that CIBC would have had to boost the MERs to unacceptable levels.

The success of these funds for nervous investors is a portent of things to come. The boomers have more than a decade to go before they hit 65, but some are already taking early retirement and others are thinking about it. Inevitably, they'll become more risk-averse as they grow older. If Dembo and others are successful in finding ways to insure their investments at reasonable cost, a lot of aging boomers will sleep more soundly in the years ahead.

Ted Cadsby thinks I should sell MD U.S. Equity and buy an index fund instead. Gordon Pape thinks I should keep it for now but get ready to buy a Japan fund when the time is right. Ron Dembo thinks there's no harm in keeping it as long as I don't get too dependent on it.

This is not an easy decision. Complicating matters is the fact that Smith Barney's analysts are not the only ones who have done research in these matters. John Caspar is a student of the subject, and he says the research he has seen indicates that "the durability of negative performance is higher than of positive performance." In other words, there is a better chance that a stinker will continue to stink than that a winner will continue to win. This would indicate that just switching MD U.S. for something truly rotten may not be a brilliant strategy. But keeping it is also risky. Maybe I should call the bank and see what interest rate Canada Savings Bonds are paying this year.

In the end, I weighed the pros and cons of keeping it and decided that the pros won. The cons were that MD U.S.'s growth style was bound to stop working eventually and that the odds of continued spectacular performance were poor. The pros were that the United States was still booming and that, as Pape had pointed out, the American economy is so large and diversified that a buy-and-hold strategy for a diversified American fund may make sense. Then there was the low MER, a major advantage. But the deciding factor was that the fund's manager is certain never to be named Fund Manager of the Year.

Because MD U.S. Equity is not available to the public, it is not even eligible for the award. So, whatever may happen to it in the future, at least it is immune to the jinx that has brought disaster to funds managed by previous Fund Managers of the Year. The most recent victim was Jerry Javasky, who won in 1998 for his excellent work on the Ivy Canadian Fund, the largest Canadian equity fund. Javasky won after posting successive returns of 25.2% and 17.6%. In 1998, Ivy Canadian earned 5.7%, and in 1999, it earned 3.1%, about a tenth of the TSE 300 index's return. In the 12 months ending February 2000, investors pulled $1.6 billion out of the fund, which is more money than most mutual funds have ever had.

Did MD U.S. Equity repeat its brilliant performance after I decided at the beginning of 1999 to keep it? That depends on how you define brilliant. It returned 18.1%, above average for the category but way below the results for YMG Enterprise, another American fund I would have bought had I known it would return 119.7%. As for the stinkers I'd been considering, Co-operators U.S. Equity, which had lost 12.2% in 1998, dropped another 6% in 1999. On the other hand, Canada Trust Emerging Markets, which had lost 33.5%, soared to a gain of 52.7%. O'Donnell Canadian Emerging Growth went from a loss of 33.8% to a gain of 35.3%. Cambridge Resource, which had lost 52.4% in 1998, was down another 25.6% in 1999. And the AGF 20/20 Managed Futures Value Fund, which had suffered a spectacular 65.7% nosedive in 1998, turned around and gained 37.6%.

All of which proves that there's definitely something to be said for picking losers – as long as you pick the right ones. And that there are no easy answers in the black art of investing.

CHAPTER SEVEN

THE MONEY MACHINE IN THE 21ST CENTURY

As if Trimark didn't have enough problems in 1999 and into 2000, with billions of dollars floating out the door and value investing looking as if it were dead and buried, Joe Killoran was on its case again. Killoran is a former stockbroker – a very knowledgeable one, with an MBA – who has made almost a full-time occupation out of hounding the mutual fund industry for its sins against the oppressed folk he refers to, in angry e-mails he sends off in all directions, as "consumer/investors."

Killoran believes the industry exploits the ignorance of investors. Investors are ignorant because they didn't learn anything about investing in school and because the industry doesn't tell them enough and because salespersons and seminar speakers fill their heads with misinformation. Killoran wages a lonely crusade and seems convinced he isn't getting anywhere. In fact, he's more influential and successful than he knows.

I talked with him over lunch in a noisy Thai restaurant on Bloor Street in Toronto. He's 49, a stocky man with grey hair and an impish grin. He was wearing a green sweatshirt bearing the emblem of the Ivey School of Business at the University of Western Ontario, his alma mater. "I haven't had a cent of income this year," he tells me. As this is December 17, it's not looking like a big year, income-wise. But the year has been eventful in other ways. The highlight was getting booed off the floor at the Trimark annual general meeting.

Killoran thinks it's his duty to harass Trimark more than other companies because he's the cousin of the company's co-founder, Arthur Labatt. If he pestered Mackenzie or Fidelity more than Trimark, that might be construed as showing favouritism to Trimark because he has warm, cousinly feelings for Labatt. That would be unethical, and Killoran is uncompromising on ethics.

He's been on Trimark's case for a long time. His major issue is the same one he has with all the other fund companies: Why won't they adopt his one-page disclosure document, which should be completed by salespersons and approved by all investors before they invest a penny in a mutual fund? This document would tell investors, among other things, exactly how much money the fund company proposes to extract from their investment, how much of that money will be wending its way into the pockets of their financial adviser, and what they'll have to pay to get out. It would also ensure that they understand the asset mix and volatility of the fund.

"Sunshine is the greatest disinfectant" is Killoran's favourite saying. The document is his way of expressing that idea. Most people don't understand that the Canadian mutual fund industry is organized more for the benefit of salespersons than for that of investors, and that the result is inflated MERs that eat away at their retirement savings. Even relatively well-informed people have never heard of trailer fees and don't know that the adviser will be getting paid (out of investors' money) every year he keeps the account. People think that when they buy a mutual fund they're paying mainly for professional money management; they're surprised to learn that they're paying as much every year to the person who sold them the fund as to the one who's actually managing it. Nor do they know that, in addition to the trailer fees he collects, the adviser also gets a 5% commission when he sells them a DSC (rear-load) fund and that this is probably more than he'd get by selling a front-load fund; most investors assume the adviser is doing them a favour by pointing them towards an option that allows them to avoid paying a sales charge up front.

If every adviser had to sit down with every customer and fill out a document like Killoran's, the adviser would be forced to educate the customer on these matters. Killoran believes, and it's hard to disagree, that such a document would be a powerful force for reform. Some customers would react like Sarah, whom we met in Chapter Three; she thinks her adviser's compensation is more than justified by all the work he does on her behalf. Others would decide they want either more service or lower prices. Still others, once they understood the cost of buying retail, would buy wholesale instead and invest directly with no-load, low-MER companies. Or they'd dispense with mutual funds entirely and buy stocks or index participation units for themselves.

Glorianne Stromberg, the former Ontario Securities Commissioner who has conducted two investigations of the industry, endorsed Killoran's document in one of her reports. But so far the 40,000 or so Canadians who sell mutual funds have managed to restrain their enthusiasm. Only a handful of financial planners dotted across the country are using it.

Killoran believes advisers can provide an important service because many consumers don't have the knowledge to make wise decisions about their investments. But he thinks they should be rewarded as professionals for the services they perform, not as salespersons for how much they sell. "The doctor doesn't get paid according to what drug he prescribes, how much he prescribes, or how long he keeps you on it. But in the financial arena, sales reps get paid to sell the things that put the most money in their own pockets."

One reason so many billions of dollars flowed into mutual funds during the 1990s was that thousands of aggressive salespeople were pushing mutual funds. And because of the compensation structure, these "advisers" are unlikely ever to advise their clients to switch to other, more cost-efficient investments. "The brokers are not going to say, 'Get out of funds because of the hidden trailer fee,'" Killoran says. "They count on that distribution from the fund companies. When are the regulators going to require that the fund company tell you how much MER they deducted in the quarter and how much of that they paid in trailer commissions and to whom? There are people who bought a mutual fund 10 or 20 years ago that don't know they're paying a trailer fee to somebody they haven't talked to in years."

The industry's response is that it's all there in the prospectus, so what's Killoran complaining about? But until recently prospectuses have been virtually unreadable and thus unread. Killoran thinks consumers untutored in the ways of the industry deserve to be told about MERs, loads, and trailers directly by the salesperson. Some companies, including Trimark and Fidelity, now publish clear and informative prospectuses, but often they arrive in the mail after the client has plunked down her money. "That's like trying to practise safe sex seven days later, when the blood test is in the mail."

In addition to a point-of-sale document, there should also be a document to be filled out when an adviser gets a client to cash in one fund in order to buy another. Killoran has produced one of those as well, to resounding silence from the industry. He uses the example of an adviser wanting to switch somebody out of the Trimark Canadian Fund, a low-MER, front-load fund that pays a trailer fee of only 0.3% (most front-end funds pay trailers of 1%). There might be a good reason, such as chronic underperformance, why the adviser wants his client to make the switch, but the client deserves to know if the new fund pays the adviser more and extracts a higher MER. If Killoran's document had to be completed, the client would know. "People who need advice should be able to get it without being churned and taken advantage of. You do that through disclosure. If people know what they're paying, over time the costs will get in line."

Killoran's documents are so obviously necessary to the public interest that they, or something like them, are bound to be introduced sooner or later. But because they threaten the profitability of the industry, Killoran is persona non grata. He survives on his wife's salary and occasional work as a substitute teacher in elementary schools in Oshawa, where he lives. Killoran is emotional, relentless, and combative, traits that probably were an advantage when he played defence for the UWO Mustangs hockey team but that kept getting him into trouble during his 10-year career in the financial industry. He believes he's been blackballed for such actions as reporting insider trading. "Your employer is a member of a club, the Investment Dealers Association. If you step outside and start talking about improprieties among club members, you're going to be gone. No club member is going to hire you."

At every Trimark annual general meeting since 1997, Killoran has tried to present proposals for reform. These would require that Trimark disclose how it votes the stock it owns, rebate some of the fees it charges on DSC funds, appoint one of its directors as an ombudsman to whom whistle-blowers could report misdeeds, implement steps to deter substance abuse among fund salespersons, and not sponsor seminars featuring shills. When he demanded to present them again in 2000, Trimark declined, saying its shareholders had already indicated they are not interested and that the proposals should be considered by an industry-wide organization rather than just one fund company.

Killoran is angry, and not without reason. Most Canadians accept paying higher taxes than Americans to get a higher level of public services such as medicare. But why should they have to pay more than Americans to buy mutual funds? Many people wrongly assume their broker or dealer is an impartial adviser who'll select just the right fund for them at a fair price from the vast array laid out in Gordon Pape's guidebook. Not so. Just as a shoe store has room on its shelves for only three or four brands of shoes, so a brokerage or financial planning company has "shelf space" for only a handful of fund brands. The broker will sell you a fund that's not on her shelf if you ask for it, but people use brokers and planners because they need advice, so what mainly moves out the door is the funds on the shelf.

Dozens of fund companies compete for this precious shelf space, and one way they do so is through trailer fees. Glorianne Stromberg, in the first of her two reports on the industry, was harshly critical of this system. If one fund company doesn't match another's trailer fees, she wrote, the sales rep will switch to the higher payer "regardless of whether this benefits the client or has tax consequences for the client." And rather than make a switch that would be best for the client, an adviser will stick with the highest-paying funds. Stromberg approvingly quotes sources in the industry who call trailer fees "bribes."

Who pays for these bribes? The investor, of course. Canadian MERs, on average, are more than 1% higher than those in the United States, according to Cerulli Associates, a Boston research company that examined the Canadian fund industry in 1998. The result? On a $10,000 investment, "the Canadian investor would earn between $1,500 and $1,900 less than the typical U.S. investor over a ten-year period," Cerulli concluded. One reason Canadian MERs are higher is that salespersons get more. If an American fund salesman sells a DSC fund, he gets a 4% commission and an ongoing trailer fee of 0.25% while his Canadian counterpart usually gets a 5% commission (Spectrum United pays 6%) and a trailer of 0.5%. The other reason for the higher costs in Canada, said the Cerulli report, is that Canadian fund companies charge more for investment management. The fund companies say they have to do this because they lack the economies of scale of large American fund companies, operating in the much larger American market. This is a flimsy excuse. Many Canadian funds are large enough to enjoy considerable economies of scale and yet MERs, even on the biggest funds, remain stubbornly higher than those in the United States.

The mutual fund industry is not consumer-friendly. Joe Killoran is right: it needs reform. Outlawing trailer fees and the DSC would be a good first step. Still, the situation is not as dark as Killoran thinks it is. Many others have picked up the torch for change that he helped to light. His views were reflected in Stromberg's reports, and they are also reflected in the increasingly critical tone that writers in newspapers and business magazines have adopted towards the fund business. He has succeeded in attaching the "shills" label to seminar speakers who tout fund dealers' products. The result, even in the absence of a point-of-sale document, is a more discerning investing public.

During my talk with Gordon Pape, I mentioned a survey that revealed only 72% of people who had mutual funds in their RRSPs knew what an MER was. He smiled. "You've got to put that in perspective," he said. "A decade ago, 72% of people who had RRSPs wouldn't have known what a mutual fund was. I can still remember a staff meeting at Hume in the mid-1980s. There were about 100 people there. I got up and asked, given that we were putting out all this stuff on finance, how many people in this room were not really quite sure what a mutual fund is. Almost every hand went up. This was a company that was in the financial information business! The knowledge that people generally have in investing and money today is light-years ahead of where it was a decade ago. This is pretty sophisticated stuff when you start getting into MERs. It's a whole different level of expertise from where it was when I got into this business."

An important reason why there's more expertise is that mutual funds, once the preserve of a relatively sophisticated minority, have become the standard investment vehicle of the Canadian middle class. More people than ever have mutual funds, and many have had them for a decade or more, so it's natural that they'd become better informed with experience. That trend will continue; meanwhile, other trends are emerging that, in years ahead, will bring down prices, improve competition, and, in general, strengthen the position of consumers.

The simple fact that a growing number of people have been invested in funds for long periods gives those investors more power. This is because their portfolios, as a result of regular contributions and rising asset values, have swelled into the six figures. Investors with large portfolios are in a position to demand a better deal, and fund companies are responding, in some cases slicing MERs for clients with larger accounts. This trend will accelerate as more demanding investors indicate they are ready to move over to direct purchases of stocks if the fund companies don't stop gouging. The growing acceptance of indexed investments that are bought as commodities for the lowest price will put additional downward pressure on the cost of owning funds. Most important of all, the Internet revolution that threatens the position of intermediaries in every industry, from cars to books, will have a major impact on the mutual fund industry as well.

The industry has now passed through what the Toronto-based consultant Dan Richards calls the "hypergrowth stage" and has moved into the "maturation" stage. Hypergrowth is a good description for what happened in the 1990s. Mutual funds, as we've seen, had been around since the 1930s, but as recently as the early 1980s they were an insignificant part of the investment industry. It took 50 years, until the early 1980s, for the Canadian fund industry to reach $4 billion in assets. The 1980s were a pivotal decade because that was when the older baby boomers began investing in mutual funds and assets started to increase rapidly. But the 1980s were only a foretaste of what was to come, just as the increase in house prices in the 1970s was only a foretaste of the real estate explosion of the 1980s. It wasn't until the 1990s, when most of them were housed, that large numbers of boomers turned their attention towards investing for the future. When the boomers turn their attention to something, the impact is dramatic. By 1991, Canadian funds had $50 billion in assets; by 1993 that total had doubled to $100 billion; by 1996 it had reached $200 billion; and by the turn of the century, Canadians had $400 billion stashed away in mutual funds.

By then, however, the maturation stage was already under way. As the 1990s drew to a close, mutual fund sales were in decline, and it was starting to look as if maybe the party was over. It had been a great party while it lasted. In the 1980s and the first part of the 1990s, setting up a new fund business had required little capital, customers were eager to hand over their money, and most of them cared so little about price that they didn't even bother to find out what the price was. No wonder the fund dealer Richard Charlton called mutual funds "the ultimate business." But as the millennium celebrations approached, one fund dealer complained that "the fruit that was on the low branches is gone." Now companies could grow only by taking business from other companies.

In a mature industry, size matters. To position themselves for the future, companies have to fight for market share, and that takes financial strength. As Dan Richards points out, every new industry goes through the same thing; the auto industry, which had 200 manufacturers in 1920, is just one example. As 2000 began, it was obvious that not all the players in the Canadian fund industry would survive. The battle over Altamira in 1997 and 1998 had been the advance signal of an inevitable wave of consolidation. The May 2000 deal to bring together Trimark and AIM, if successfully concluded, would be the ninth merger since 1998. It was already clear that some of the companies that had dominated the industry through the 1990s would not endure as separate entities.

The industry in 2000 is far different from the industry of 1990. That of 2010 will look far different still. Let's consider how change is likely to affect the two halves of the industry – distribution and investment management.

Distribution

Most people in the mutual fund industry are confident of the durability of the current distribution system and convinced of the importance of the intermediaries, who, they seem to believe, play just as important a role as the investment managers. This attitude, it seems to me, reflects contempt for the people who buy mutual funds, a belief that ordinary Canadians are too dumb to make decisions for themselves and neither care nor understand that the cost of maintaining hordes of intermediaries is eating away at their retirement savings. I've given several examples of the damage high MERs can do. Here's one last example that gets the point across powerfully. It's from Malcolm Hamilton, a pension consultant and actuary, writing in the foreword to *The Wealthy Boomer*, a book of financial advice by the *National Post* columnist Jonathan Chevreau. Hamilton writes: "Low fees are particularly important to those saving for retirement, because retirement savings are invested for 20 to 25 years. Compare a member of the Ontario Teachers' Pension Plan to someone saving for retirement in a mutual fund. The Ontario Teachers' Pension Plan can manage a teacher's retirement savings for 0.15% per annum. The mutual fund investor pays over 2% per annum. Compounded over 25 years, the teacher will get 60% more for every dollar invested."

The teachers' pension plan charges low fees because it's a non-profit organization with minimal distribution costs. What can you do if you're investing outside a pension plan? Unless you have access to an affinity organization, you have to invest with a for-profit investment company. You can't get rid of the profit, but you can get rid of the distribution costs. You can do that by buying direct from a no-load, low-MER fund company. Or by buying low-cost index funds, such as the TD eFunds, whose 0.25% MER is close to that of the teachers' pension plan. Or you could buy i60 index participation units that track 60 stocks on the Toronto Stock Exchange and have a management fee of 0.17%, which is closer still to that of the teachers' pension plan. Or perhaps there's a mutual fund whose style you admire, but it isn't available at a reasonable cost. (Remember that even if you buy a front-load fund but pay no load because you're buying from a discount broker, you still pay for distribution in the form of annual trailer fees that typically swell the MER to more than 2%.) You can find out, either from the fund company's annual or quarterly report or from one of the mutual fund Web sites, what stocks the fund holds. Then you can buy some of its top holdings directly and pay no management fee at all.

It takes a while for numbers like Hamilton's to sink into the public consciousness. But sink in they will: inevitably Canadians are going to demand a better deal. Fund companies are going to have to cut the fat out of their fees, and the distribution costs are the fat. The success of Vanguard in the United States is proof that vast numbers of people will invest with a fund company that delivers performance at a low price, and they will do so even if that company does not use intermediaries, does not advertise, and puts no effort into turning itself into a "brand." This goes against the conventional wisdom in the Canadian fund industry, which prefers to ignore the Vanguard example as if it were some inexplicable aberration. Paul Starita, who ran the mutual fund operations for Royal Trust and CIBC, now observes the industry from outside and he knows otherwise. The overnight success of Wal-Mart in Canada should be a lesson to the fund industry, he says. "You're telling me the consumer says, 'I'm going to buy my household products on the basis of price, and I'm going to use some other basis to buy my financial services'? Hello? Guys, you're kidding. You're absolutely crazy."

It's human nature to assume the future will be like the present. But shifting demographics and technological change ensure that the future of the mutual fund industry will be different. The demographic shift, of course, is the aging of the boomers. As they get older, they become richer and wiser and have more time on their hands to do their own investment research and make their own decisions. That they will be able to insure the portfolios they assemble themselves will only add to their confidence about making their own investment decisions. And consolidation of the industry will mean fewer funds and less need for advisers to provide a sorting mechanism. The fund industry is going to find 60-year-old boomers much tougher customers than the 40-year-olds who were uninformed about investment and too busy to learn.

As for technology, it's transforming the entire investment industry, as it is so many areas of our lives. As this book was going to press, an American company was about to launch an Internet trading system in which share owners could trade directly with one another without going through any intermediaries or using a stock exchange. In a typical trade on an exchange, several intermediaries are involved, all of whom capture a fraction of the investor's capital. Cutting them out both empowers and enriches the consumer. This is just one example of the Internet's ability to sweep aside transaction costs. As we've seen, this trend is already affecting the fund industry to the consumer's benefit. The TD eFunds, mentioned above, are available only to on-line buyers, as are the 0% front loads offered by discount brokerages.

The dealers who think they are an important part of the investment industry are in for a rude shock. The example of the newspaper industry is instructive. There was a time, not long ago, when newspaper proprietors thought they were in the printing and delivery businesses as well as the information business. Now it has dawned on them that they are in one business only, the information business. Printing and delivery are just overhead costs, and some papers have contracted these operations out. And all major newspapers now offer on-line editions, thereby eliminating printing and most distribution costs. A dealer who does nothing but distribute mutual funds will soon discover that he is no more important to the investment industry than a delivery-truck driver is to the newspaper industry.

The advisers who stay in business will be genuine financial planners. That means advising on the whole spectrum of investments, not just mutual funds, as well as assisting in tax planning and estate planning. If advisers want to be respected as professionals they will have to stop clinging to a compensation system, based on commissions and trailer fees, that's unworthy of a professional and that promotes unprofessional behaviour. Reform of the fund industry, therefore, requires the unbundling of dealer compensation from management fees. This will have the salutary effect of liberating the mutual fund companies from the undue power of intermediaries and liberating the intermediaries from the undue power of the companies. As Trimark found to its chagrin, overdependence on dealers is a double-edged sword, because the dealers will turn on you when it suits them. As for the dealers, once they're paid directly by the client, rather than indirectly through money the fund company skims from the client's account, they'll be free to act as true financial planners instead of fund peddlers. The decision to use mutual funds, or not to use them, will be purely an investment decision; the adviser's income will not be affected either way.

Unbundling is already under way. ASL Direct.com, an on-line discount broker, rebates all trailer fees and reinvests them in more mutual fund units for its customers. It also charges no sales commissions. It makes a profit by charging the customer a fixed monthly fee of $29.95 that includes one free transaction. Additional transactions, regardless of their value, cost $9.95. The ASL site features a trailer fee calculator so you can figure out how much you are saving. It won't be much, if anything, on a small account, but it could be huge on a large account maintained for a long time. Sure, ASL is expensive – so were cellphones and CD players when they first came out. New technologies are always expensive at first, but after they catch on and new competitors emerge, the price drops.

While price-cutting competitors like ASL mean trouble for middlemen who don't add value, the fund companies should have no trouble adapting because they already use different pricing for different customers. Several offer pooled funds, which are mutual funds for people with a lot of money to invest that charge lower fees than regular funds. When I interviewed Joe Canavan, the president of Synergy, I offered the opinion that an investor who buys any fund without the aid of an adviser should not have to pay trailer fees.

Canavan agreed. "That's where I think the next point of differentiation will be," he said. "Suppose Schwab [Charles Schwab, a discount brokerage] came to us and said, 'We want you to be one of three or five fund groups, but we want our clients to be Schwab clients, so we don't want a trailer fee. We want it stripped out. Can you tailor something?' I think that's the wave of the future."

A taste of the future that's already here is a fund company called Opus 2 Direct.com, which eliminates intermediaries from the investment process as effectively as an on-line newspaper eliminates the printing press and delivery trucks. Opus 2 is an on-line investment company that offers managed portfolios known as wrap accounts. Most wrap accounts require a high minimum investment, usually at least $50,000. For an all-inclusive fee, a manager provides a mix of stocks, bonds, and cash tailored to the client's risk-reward profile. Until now, sensible investors have avoided wrap accounts because, like segregated funds, they are notoriously overpriced. Opus 2 is the first consumer-friendly wrap account. The minimum investment is only $10,000. The investor can choose among seven portfolios, from ultra-conservative to aggressive. The different components of the portfolios are run by outside specialists in each asset class. There are no loads of any kind and the only fee is an MER of 1.85%, about 30% lower than that of other wraps and well below the average conventional mutual fund's MER as well. A sign that Opus 2 is aimed at cost-conscious investors is that its Web site features an MER calculator.

While Opus 2 Direct keeps its costs down by operating on-line, clients are encouraged to call and talk to live advisers should they feel the need. A service like this is made to order for the investor who operates independently, or the one who uses the advice of a financial planner on a fee-for-service basis. (In the United States, several fund companies have lower-priced versions of funds to accommodate fee-for-service planners.) This poses no threat to mutual fund companies because they have the money management expertise that Opus 2 needs and that will always be fundamental to the investment industry. Left out in the cold are brokers and planners who survive on payments from fund companies because Opus 2 doesn't make them. That's what e-commerce is all about: cutting prices by cutting out the middleman. Opus 2 Direct and ASL Direct are both small operations, but so was Amazon.com when it opened for business. They or others like them will be big operations before the decade is out. They'll change the way mutual funds are distributed, and the consumer will be the beneficiary.

Investment management

Mutual funds weren't always bought and sold on the basis of performance. There was a time when prudence was more important than performance. That changed in the 1960s for two reasons. One was the emergence of high-flying new technology companies like Xerox, Polaroid, and IBM. Their stocks were shooting up and aggressive fund managers like Gerald Tsai, whom we met in Chapter Two, decided to load up on them and aim for big numbers. The other factor was inflation. The idea behind prudence was preservation of capital, but if inflation was outpacing your investment return, then your capital wasn't being preserved; in that case, even if preservation rather than big returns was your goal, you required a more aggressive investment style. That, in turn, meant a greater emphasis on performance.

Now inflation has all but vanished. Does that mean the cult of performance will vanish as well and mutual fund managers will go back to the old cautious ways? Definitely not. Since Mackenzie stuck its logo on a racing car back in the 1980s, the Canadian fund industry has embraced performance, and there is no turning back. A racing car is a high-performance machine and the fund industry wants you to believe that it is too. That's why most of its advertising stresses double-digit, sometimes even triple-digit performance numbers. These figures are usually misleading in two ways. One is that spectacular recent returns frequently mask previous lousy ones. The other is the false implication that good past performance assures good future performance. But the advertising has been effective – it has trained investors to seek spectacular performance. The dazzling stock market gains of new technology companies only add to the frenzy.

In this environment, savvy investors will distinguish between core holdings, such as a Canadian or American index fund or a diversified global fund, and what could be called "performance funds" or, to use Gordon Pape's term, opportunity funds. The core holdings, despite misleading fund company advertising, are not high-performance vehicles and should not be expected to return much more, on average, than 10% a year. As the returns are modest and the funds are owned for the long term, low fees are essential.

Performance funds are another matter. These are traded actively, just as volatile stocks are traded on ups and downs. In 1999, three mutual funds sold in Canada had returns in excess of 200%. The previous record high was 146.9%. And a total of 28 funds were up more than 100% in 1999, compared with the previous high of seven. Anybody who thinks mutual funds are boring investments didn't own one of these supercharged performers, all of which were invested in technology or in Asia. One was the Excel India Fund, which rose 202.4%. The Excel India Fund is not a buy-and-hold investment, nor is it suitable for more than a small fraction of a serious investor's portfolio. It's a roll of the dice that India is going to have a great year. These kinds of funds will play an increasingly important part in the mutual fund industry as technological advance and globalization continue to transform economic life. The demise of sales commissions will make it cheaper to trade such funds frequently. And the investor needn't give a thought to MERs because she's looking for a big win and is not going to hold on long enough for the MER to make a difference.

The earliest fund managers were anonymous. Then the celebrity manager arrived in the 1960s and stayed on the scene for a couple of decades. In the 1990s, the celebrities faded away as fund companies got bigger and began to see celebrities as a business risk. In the coming decade, however, celebrities are poised for a comeback. The industry will be dominated by a small number of huge companies, most of them global players like Fidelity and small, innovative companies occupying specialized niches. In parallel, a typical portfolio will be divided among faceless giant funds, along the lines of the Vanguard 500, and small funds that are the expression of a particular manager's style. When you buy the big fund, you're investing in the market. When you buy the small one, you're hiring a particular manager to invest some of your money in a specialized area, such as global telecommunications or Canadian small caps or emerging markets. Or maybe it's a manager who has a unique way of approaching the entire Canadian market, an idiosyncratic investment style that is not remotely related to the TSE 300 index. The best of these managers will become celebrities.

The most interesting change on the horizon is the prospect of a shift of power to individuals, not just on the distribution side (by cutting out the middleman) but on the investment side as well. Just as computer power makes it possible to create a basket of derivatives to insure every portfolio, so it will allow smaller investors to own a portfolio of investments more customized to their own needs than is currently possible with conventional mutual funds. A stockbroker might respond that he was doing just that long before the advent of computers. But mutual funds were invented because smaller investors couldn't get the diversification they needed by buying individual stocks and bonds.

An early example of the new wave in investing is an on-line investment company called Folio[fn], based in the United States. (The "fn" stands for financial innovation.) Investors can ask Folio to choose a basket of stocks (called a "folio") that is suitable for their risk tolerance and interests. If you wish to exclude certain industries for ethical reasons and focus on others because you think they're going to be hot, you can. It's like choosing your own stocks, but it's also like a mutual fund, in that you can invest specific dollar amounts and own fractional shares. In other words, you can own Nortel directly without having enough money to buy 100 shares of Nortel. Unlike a fund, however, it's your personal portfolio, not one you share with thousands of others, so your investment returns are not affected by, for example, a manager's need to sell shares to meet redemptions. Nor will you have to pay tax on someone else's capital gains. Investors pay commissions as well as a flat fee of $250; that's a better deal than a management fee that takes a percentage of assets.

It's early days, but this sounds pretty good, as if someone has combined the advantages of both individual stock ownership and mutual funds while removing the disadvantages of both. There will be other variations on this theme, but the future of mutual fund investing may well turn out to look a lot like what Folio is offering. And it would have been unthinkable without today's computing power and impossible to implement without the Internet. It's proof, if more were needed, that technology, not lobbying by reformers or critical reports, is the most powerful force for beneficial change in the mutual fund industry.

The mutual fund was a necessary invention. It plays an essential role in transferring the savings of the average investor into equity markets, once the preserve of the rich. In that sense, Bernie Cornfeld was right to call mutual funds "people's capitalism." They are a democratizing force because they allow millions of people to become owners rather than loaners, to become wealthier than they otherwise could have by owning a piece of an expanding economy.

If funds were a good thing for the average investor, they were a very good thing for the people who managed them and sold them. Mutual fund assets in Canada grew, as we've seen, by $350 billion in the 1990s. Taking an annual cut out of that vast pool of cash made a lot of people rich. Because the business is so lucrative, owning the stocks of mutual fund companies was a better investment during the last five years of the 1990s than owning the same companies' funds. For example, an investment of $1,000 in Mackenzie's flagship, the Ivy Canadian Fund, was worth $1,793 after five years; an investment of $1,000 in Mackenzie stock was worth $3,485. Stocks of Investors Group, Trimark, and AGF also outperformed those companies' flagship funds.

It might not be extraordinary if one major company's flagship fund lagged its own stock. But four? Could this mean that mutual fund companies are making too much money and investors not enough? Probably. Canadians pay too much to own mutual funds because too much of their money gets siphoned off to pay for advertising and sales commissions and profits. The advertising pulls in new assets, thereby inflating the size of some funds, including the four flagships just mentioned, making it harder for the manager to produce a decent return. But the fund companies are happy because the bigger the fund, the more management fees it spins off.

The massive outflow of money from underperforming funds in recent years indicates that investors are growing intolerant of mediocrity. The future is not bright for funds that do little but tread water, trailing the return of their benchmark index by the amount of their MERs. Because of more demanding consumers and growing competition, the industry as a whole will be less dominant in the decade ahead than it was during the 1980s and 1990s. The advent of individualized quasi-funds is one reason. So is the growing ease of trading stocks on-line. The aging of the boomer generation means that an increasing number of older, more experienced investors will be more confident about assembling their own portfolios. A portfolio that in 1995 contained a dozen different mutual funds may, in 2005, contain a basket of stocks, some index participation units, and two or three specialized mutual funds managed by high-profile managers.

The excessive numbers of companies and of funds are the marks of a young and immature industry. In the decade ahead, the fund industry will attain maturity. The many mid-size companies – Canada has 31 fund companies with assets over $1 billion – will consolidate into a few. The survivors will no longer be able to use a lack of economies of scale as an excuse to keep prices in Canada higher than in the United States. In this new environment, there will still be room for creative niche players to keep the industry lively.

The growth of the money machine has been phenomenal, and it's not over yet. Many younger Canadians, including some of the younger members of the large baby boom generation, are just beginning to save. For them, mutual funds are still the safest and most convenient way to get growth and diversification for an investment as small as a few hundred dollars. These new investors would be well advised not to hand over their money without asking some tough questions. Only when they understand exactly how the mutual fund industry works will they have the power to make it work for them.

GLOSSARY

Active manager
One who chooses investments based on his own research and investment philosophy.

Asset allocation fund
In an asset allocation fund, also known as a tactical asset allocation fund, the manager changes the weighting of equities, bonds, and cash as market conditions change. Such funds are similar to balanced funds but can be more aggressively managed – they can, for example, have a higher weighting in equities than is permitted to a balanced fund.

Bear market
A stock market in which share prices are falling.

Benchmark index
An index that is commonly used to assess the performance of an active manager. For example, the performance of a fund containing large American companies would be compared with that of the Standard and Poor's 500 index.

Blue-chip stock
The stock of a large, profitable, dividend-paying company whose products have wide distribution and a good reputation.

Bull market
A stock market in which share prices are rising.

Capitalization
Often shortened to "cap." The total value of all the shares in a company. A large-cap stock in Canada would have capitalization over $1 billion. A small-cap company would be less than $300 million. A mid-cap company would be in between.

Clone fund
A fund designed to circumvent the foreign content restrictions in RRSP accounts. It uses derivatives to mimic the performance of an underlying foreign fund while still qualifying as Canadian content.

Closed-end fund
A fund that has a fixed number of shares. These shares can be acquired only from someone who already owns them, and they trade as stocks, with the price set by supply and demand, rather than by the underlying value of the fund's holdings.

Closet indexer
A manager who claims to be active but is careful not to stray too far from his benchmark index in his stock selections.

Commission
Also known as sales charge. On a front-load fund, the amount of the commission, paid by the investor to the salesperson, is negotiable. On a rear-load (deferred sales charge) fund, it is non-negotiable and paid by the investor to the fund company; however, the seller of a rear-load fund also receives a commission directly from the fund company at the time of sale.

Deferred sales charge (DSC)

Also known as back-end load, rear load, or redemption fee. A charge, calculated as a percentage of the value of an investor's fund units, that the investor pays when selling the units. Depending on the fund family, the charge is based on either the original cost of the investment or the current market value. The charge may be 5% in the first year but declines each year the fund is held, eventually reaching zero in the sixth or seventh year. Although the investor doesn't have to pay a sales charge up front, the seller earns a 5% commission at the time of sale. This is paid by the fund company out of money it deducts from the assets under its management (*see* management expense ratio).

Derivative

A financial instrument that derives its value from some underlying asset such as a stock or a bond. An example is an option, which is the right to buy or sell a security or a commodity at an agreed price within a certain time.

Discount broker

A brokerage company that furnishes transaction services for a lower price than a full-service broker. It does not offer the personal attention and investment advice that a full-service broker provides.

Equities

Stocks.

Front-end load

Also known as front load, front-end commission, or sales charge. A fee, negotiable between the investor and the salesperson, calculated as a percentage of the total amount invested. It is paid by the investor at the time of acquisition of a mutual fund. Most discount brokers sell front-load funds for no charge (known as "0%"). Other sellers typically charge between 1% and 5%.

Growth investing
The growth investor likes to buy "growth stocks," those of companies with above-average earnings growth. These stocks tend to have a high price-earnings ratio because of optimism about the company's future.

Index
A list of stocks created as a proxy for a particular market as a whole. For example, the TSE 300 includes 300 stocks trading on the Toronto Stock Exchange that represent about 85% of the value of all Canadian stocks. An index gives investors and other market observers a snapshot of the daily performance of the market. So if the TSE 300 is down on a given day, that would be considered a bad day on the market even though some stocks might have risen in value on the same day.

Index fund
One that contains all the stocks in a particular index.

Management expense ratio (MER)
Also called management fee. Includes commissions, trailer fees, salaries or fees to fund managers, and other operating expenses (excluding the costs of trading stocks and taxes) paid by a fund, expressed as a percentage of the fund's average daily net assets.

Momentum investing
A momentum investor looks for companies with accelerating earnings, better-than-expected earnings, and stocks whose prices are outperforming the market or those of similar companies.

Money market fund
A fund designed to provide income with no risk of capital loss. It invests in short-term government and corporate debt.

No-load fund
A fund sold with no sales commission charged to the investor.

Open-end fund
A mutual fund that offers new units for sale at all times and buys them back at all times at the net asset value per share. Almost all mutual funds available today are open-end funds.

Passive manager
One who buys and keeps all the stocks in a particular index.

Price-earnings (P/E) ratio
The price of a stock divided by its earnings per share. The P/E ratio can be used to compare the relative prices of different stocks. For example, a stock with a P/E ratio under 20 would be considered cheap, while a stock with a P/E ratio over 100 would be considered expensive.

Sector rotation investing
A sector rotator makes investments according to which sectors of the economy are expected to do well.

Securities
Stocks, bonds, and treasury bills.

Small caps
See capitalization.

Trailer fee
Sometimes called a trailing commission. A fee paid by a fund company to a salesperson, usually quarterly, for as long as the salesperson's client remains invested in the company's fund. The fee is supposed to compensate the salesperson for ongoing service provided to the client. The money used to pay trailer fees is extracted from the client's investment as part of the management expense ratio (MER).

Value investing
A value investor seeks good companies that are "on sale." These stocks tend to have low price-earnings ratios because the market does not fully appreciate their value.

INDEX

The text of this book was set in Minion, designed by Robert Slimbach for Adobe Systems in 1989. Minion exhibits the graceful letter forms of classical Renaissance type and sets clearly even at small sizes.

Book design by Ingrid Paulson